Anonymous

The Queen of the Colonies

Queensland as I Knew it

Anonymous

The Queen of the Colonies
Queensland as I Knew it

ISBN/EAN: 9783337154912

Printed in Europe, USA, Canada, Australia, Japan

Cover: Foto ©Andreas Hilbeck / pixelio.de

More available books at **www.hansebooks.com**

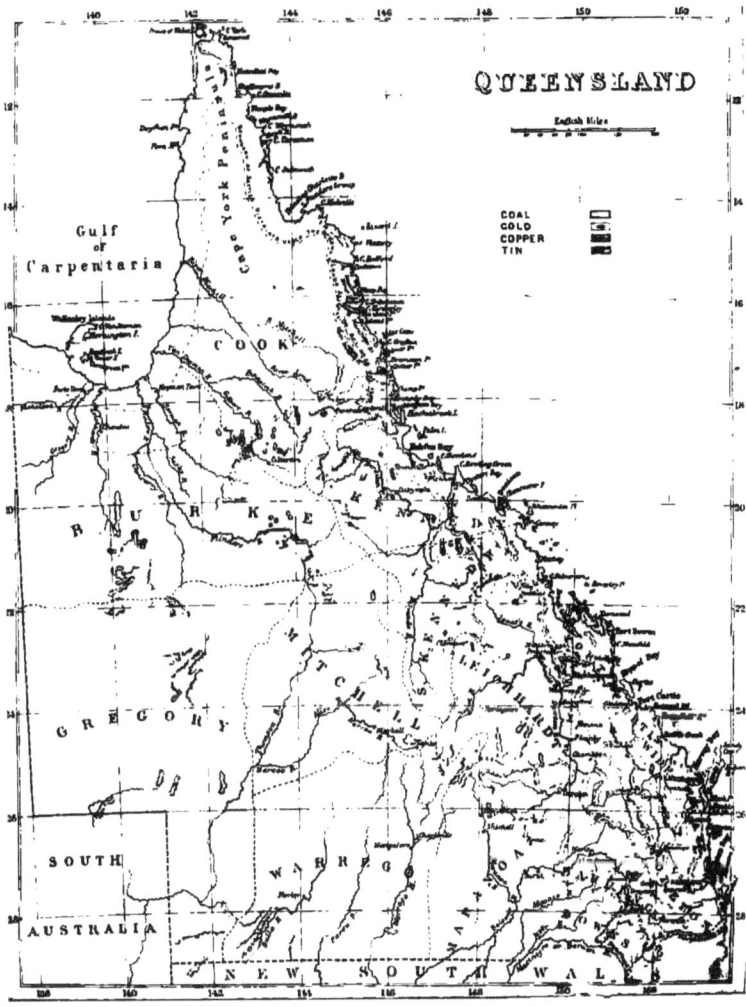

THE

QUEEN OF THE COLONIES;

OR,

QUEENSLAND AS I KNEW IT.

BY

AN EIGHT YEARS' RESIDENT.

London :

SAMPSON LOW, MARSTON, SEARLE, & RIVINGTON,

CROWN BUILDINGS, 188, FLEET STREET.

1876.

TO

THE RIGHT HON. THE EARL OF CARNARVON,

SECRETARY OF STATE FOR THE COLONIES,

This Book

IS, BY PERMISSION, RESPECTFULLY DEDICATED

BY THE AUTHOR.

CONTENTS.

THE QUEEN OF THE COLONIES.

INTRODUCTION.

PERHAPS in placing a new work before the public treating of one of the most valuable of the British colonies, it may be thought that no apology is needed. It is true there have been at various times books of more or less pretension published descriptive of the vast colony of Queensland. Of these the most comprehensive is the work of Dr. Lang. But the author wrote just when the colony was formed, and when, judging from the description given by him, the greater part of it was *terra incognita*, which considerably lessens the value of his work to intending emigrants especially. Another clergyman, the Rev. G. Wight, published a less pretentious volume than that of Dr. Lang, soon after the former appeared. But this too was evidently written when the author had a very superficial knowledge of the subject on which he wrote, and before he had gathered the extensive experience of which he can now boast. More recently Mr. E. B. Kennedy has published a very readable and accurate volume entitled " Four Years in Queensland," which may be read with pleasure and profit; Mr. Kennedy has, however, confined himself to a small portion of the colony, and his work can scarcely be looked on as furnishing sufficient information on all subjects, to preclude the necessity of any

B

2

further publications. Had he but extended his plan, he would doubtless have produced a work of a very valuable character, his easy style and evident conscientiousness having enabled him to produce a very interesting volume.

The writer of the following pages having spent over eight years in the colony, during which time he has mixed up in a variety of scenes, and mingled in almost all phases of society, brings to the task he has marked out for himself that first essential of authorship, a thorough acquaintance with his subject. Probably few men in the period referred to have passed through more adventures or seen more of the ups and downs of colonial life. Having also at various times been connected with the press in different parts of the colony, he has had special means of acquiring information, and looking behind the scenes. His reasons for troubling the public with another book are various. The many misapprehensions as to the colony, existing in England, call for a plain statement of facts as they exist: the evils which have arisen from ignorance as to the class of persons necessary for and suitable to the colony; the great interest felt in the Polynesian question; and the temptation felt by every man to keep a diary or write a book on a voyage, have all conduced to the publication of the following work. He has only to add the wish that it may please the reader in its perusal half as much as it did him in the production, in which case there will, he is certain, be a feeling of mutual satisfaction. With this hope he launches his little craft upon the sea of literature.

The foregoing, as well as the larger part of the following pages, was written in the months of October, November, and December, 1871, during a voyage home from Queensland. Various causes—among others the author's diffidence as to the value of his work, which is not by any means exhaustive—have conduced to delay its publication. Material changes, all of them of a favourable character, have transpired in Queensland, which has in the space of four years taken immense strides in material prosperity; these, as well as a long-hoped for and most desirable change in political affairs, have greatly improved the condition of the colony. Many of the evils in connexion with the land have been remedied; the astounding discoveries of mineral wealth in gold, copper, and tin ; the success in meat-preserving, and consequent rise in the value of sheep and cattle ; the wonderful prosperity of the sugar-growing and other agricultural pursuits; the discovery of vast tracts of the most fertile soil, watered by fine rivers and rendered accessible by safe harbours; the great growth of population and wealth ; the increase of the revenue enabling large and valuable public improvements to be inaugurated—these and other most important matters, of the first interest to the emigrant, which have transpired since these pages were written, appeared almost to forbid their publication. But the recollection of the fact that scenes described by an eye-witness are usually the most interesting, and that most of his descriptions are of that nature, and also that the general conditions of emigration are always the same, of which intending emigrants are glad to have some plain accounts, as well as the advice of friends who have perused his manuscript, have determined the writer in issuing his book.

Concluding chapters and notes have been added with a view of presenting to the reader the present state of the colony, which was never so prosperous as at the present moment.

Although it would be improper to exclude all description of the geography of the colony in a work of this nature, it is not purposed to enter into a long and dry account of the

country such as would be suited to an elementary school
book. The author proposes, however, to give such a
description of the various portions of the colony as may
enable an intending settler to come to his own conclusions
as to which he may think most suitable to his tastes and
proposed pursuits; he will dwell most fully on those
districts in which he has resided, and of which he will be
able to give his own actual experience and observation.
As to the other portions, he will be careful to draw his
remarks from the most authentic and latest sources.
Although in a country extending from Point Danger in the
south to Cape York in the north—a distance of 1550 miles
in a straight line, and from the sea-board to the 138th
meridian of longitude, there must naturally be found a
great disparity in many respects, yet on the other hand the
broad features of the country are to a great extent the
same everywhere, while of course the habits and customs of
the people and the laws by which they are governed are
the same in every part. The reader who follows the author
through the following pages, will, it is hoped, be able to
arrive at a very fair idea of the character of the country,
and to form a tolerably accurate opinion of his chances of
success in emigrating to the young colony of Queensland.

CHAPTER I.

QUEENSLAND is divided into two great divisions by the range of mountains known as the Dividing Range, which runs parallel with the coast at a distance of from fifty to seventy miles from the sea. As a rule, the country on the east of this range is of a much more tropical character than that to the west, which is at a greater altitude, and consequently enjoys a cooler climate. This Dividing Range is one of the principal physical features of the colony, and in many places presents an almost insuperable obstacle to the opening of roads into the interior from ports that otherwise are well fitted to become important centres of trade. This is particularly true of the port of Gladstone, which although long opened, and possessing one of the finest harbours on the Australian coast, can never be of much importance in consequence of the absence of any good road over the range into the interior. Between this range and the sea lies that tract of country where the cultivation of such crops as sugar, cotton, indigo, coffee, arrowroot, and other tropical productions, is being or may expected in future to be carried on. On the more elevated country beyond the range the crops familiar to the British farmer can be grown, as also maize, tobacco, and similar products. Nature has so blessed the coast country, however, that while able to produce the crops of tropical

countries, it also yields to the cultivator nearly all the
crops and fruits which can be grown beyond the range.
Devoted as the author is to the promotion of settlement,
and believing that by the creation of an agricultural population the future wellbeing of Queensland can alone be placed
on a permanent basis, he cannot fail at the same time to
point out the fact that up to the present time the squatting
interest has been far and away the most important in the
colony, both in regard to the number of people to whom it
gives employment and the amount of capital invested in
the pursuit. The amount of land in the hands of agriculturists is but a mere bagatelle as compared to the enormous
territory held by the squatters. Hence in speaking of the
agricultural capabilities of any given locality, it should
always be borne in mind that the larger part of every
district is still in the hands of the crown lessees, for whose
purposes only is the major portion of the land of the colony
suitable. As a rule, it is only on the scrubs and rich flats
on the banks of the various rivers that land will be found
suitable for agriculture. The great bulk of the back
country, consisting of forest land, as distinguished from
scrubs, will probably for many generations be used for
grazing purposes alone. The lands on the Darling Downs
and a few other places are a marked exception to this rule.
It must not, however, be supposed that on this account
good land is scarce in Queensland; in the more settled
portions of East and West Moreton it is certainly the fact
that a large proportion of the best lands have been taken
up, but so numerous are the rivers and creeks on the coast
that it will be long before even in these older districts
there will be no good land to be had. In the districts to
the northward millions of acres of the finest land in the
colony await the share of the cultivator.

From circumstances connected with the administration of the land laws in the early years of the colony, mentioned elsewhere, it has only been since the passing of the Land Act of 1868 that the best lands began to be generally taken up, even in the Moreton districts.

Queensland is divided into the following districts, the relative position of each of which may be easily found by a reference to the map:—East and West Moreton, Darling Downs, Wide Bay, Burnett, Port Curtis, Kennedy, Leichardt, Maranoa, Mitchell, Warrego, Gregory, Burke and Cook. Of these the districts of East and West Moreton, Darling Downs, Wide Bay, Port Curtis and Kennedy, as including all the agricultural and mining population as well as every town of importance, will be principally referred to in the following pages. Having never visited any of the others, which are purely squatting districts, the author will content himself with a very brief description of their resources and present position, choosing as far as possible to speak of those portions of the colony with which he has a more intimate acquaintance.

CHAPTER II.

THE East Moreton district for many reasons demands priority in any description of the colony of Queensland. It is the oldest settlement, has the densest population, and in it the port and city of Brisbane, the capital, is situated; there the major portion of immigrants first land, and there the author spent the first two years and a half of his residence in the colony. In the official descriptions the district of Moreton is treated as a whole, but as there are many material differences in the districts of East and West Moreton, it is thought more convenient to treat of them separately in the present instance.

The district of East Moreton commences at the southern boundary of the colony, at its junction with the mother-colony of New South Wales, running westerly by this boundary until it joins West Moreton. On the east it is bounded by the sea, on the north by the river Mooroochy, and on the west by the Dividing Range and West Moreton. The distance from Point Danger on the south to the Mooroochy River on the north is about 200 miles; so that this district alone, supposing it to have an average depth of fifty miles, is by no means an insignificant principality, including as it does the various islands along its coast.

To the stranger arriving in the colony the first great

feature of attraction is the beautiful and extensive bay which gives its name to this district. Moreton Bay was first discovered and named by Captain Cook in the year 1770. It is formed by two long sandy islands running north and south, named respectively Stradbroke and Moreton Islands, and which enclose between themselves and the mainland a splendid sheet of water sixty miles long by thirty broad, dotted here and there with other smaller islands, some of which, as St. Helena, now used as a penal settlement, are very productive. Like most of the Queensland bays, this has a large portion of shallow water. But there is a sufficient amount of deep water for all the requirements of a very extended commerce, greater indeed than is ever likely to be requisite for the trade of Queensland. Many writers, whose ideas are gathered sitting by their drawing-room fires, have expressed great wonder that Captain Cook did not discover the Brisbane or any other of the rivers running into this splendid bay. But had they had practical experience in the navigation of the shallows of the Queensland coast, they would have known that nothing is easier than to overlook a fact of this character. As a rule the coast-line within Moreton Bay—and the same remark is true of other bays to the north—is a low line of country bordered by mangrove swamps. The Brisbane, like most colonial rivers, has a bar at its entrance, which would render it still more difficult to discover. Hence it arose that not only Captain Cook, but also Lieutenant Flinders, another noted navigator, visited Moreton Bay without discovering that a large river embouched into it. It was not until the year 1823 that Mr. Oxley, the Surveyor-General of New South Wales, on a voyage of discovery made in these northern parts, ascertained the existence of the Brisbane River by falling in with a couple of white

men who with another companion had been blown out to
sea in a boat on a trip from Sydney to the Five Islands,
about fifty miles south of Sydney, and had landed on either
Moreton or Stradbroke Island, where they had been well
treated by the blacks. Crossing over to the mainland
somewhere at the north end of the bay, they had started to
walk overland to Sydney. In carrying out this intention
they had been taken across the Brisbane by the blacks in
their canoes. Losing heart, two of them returned to their
original camp, while the third persevered in his determination to reach Sydney, a distance of 500 miles, and was
never more heard of. Some few weeks after this, Mr.
Oxley, on a return trip from Port Curtis, anchored in the
bay, and was visited by these men. Acting on the information received, he next day explored the river for some
distance in his whale-boat, and named it after the excellent
old Peninsular officer who was at that time governor of
New South Wales. Thus the discovery of this fine river,
one of the most important in Australia, was made by a pair
of timber-getters. To the same industrious and enterprising class of men we are indebted for many other discoveries
of importance, as well as the opening for settlement of
many places along the coast.

As we before said, a bar existed at the entrance of the
Brisbane River, which for a long time impeded its navigation by any but small craft. From a return made in the last
session of Parliament, we learn that up to that time the sum of
168,260l. had been expended in dredging on the bar and
the shallows of the river. At the present time vessels of a
draught of sixteen feet can pass the bar through Francis's
Channel and anchor off the township of Lytton, and craft
of twelve feet draught can pass over the Eagle Farm Flats,
farther up the river, and reach the wharves at Brisbane.

As the process of dredging is still being carried on, it is probable before long that much larger results than this will be obtained. At present emigrant vessels either anchor in the bay or at Lytton, according to their draught of water, and the passengers reach town by a steam-boat.[1]

The first sign of civilization noticed on arriving in the bay from seaward is the lighthouse on Cape Moreton, the northern extremity of Moreton Island. About here the pilot comes on board. After passing into the bay, the pilot-station is seen on the inner side of the island, on a low strip of land nestled under a high hill. All this and the southernly island of Stradbroke are vast masses of white sand, with only a few stunted trees and a very poor description of grass. The pilot-station consists of some eight or nine buildings, used as a boat-house, church, and school-house, and the dwellings of the pilots and a school-master. Here is a telegraph-station communicating with the lighthouse at the Cape and the head office at Brisbane. Lying at the anchorage, a fine view is had of the bay and surrounding country. On the east is Moreton Island, to the south of which is the South Passage, through which all the paddle-wheel steamers of the Australian Steam Navigation Company pass, as well as some other vessels. Many years ago a steamer called the " Sovereign " was wrecked in this passage, and with her were lost many prominent colonists of New South Wales, in which Brisbane was then included. This caused this passage to be avoided for many years, but of late it has come generally into use for the class of vessels referred to above. In this passage also capital schnapper fishing can be had. A few days before leaving the colony a party of gentlemen went

[1] Emigrant and other vessels are now able to proceed up the river to Brisbane, and unload at the wharves.

down to this place in a little steamer from Brisbane, and
in a few hours caught many hundred schnapper with the
hook and line. To the south of the passage is Stradbroke
Island, which runs away to the south end of the bay,
where it forms the Boat Passage, a narrow and somewhat
dangerous channel in consequence of the heavy tides.
Many years ago an enterprising speculator took a number
of cattle on to this island for the purpose of forming a
station. The station has long been abandoned; but a
number of wild cattle still roam at their own sweet wills
among its sandy hills and hollows in a perfect state of
nature. Some three or four years since an establishment
was started here for the manufacture of salt, which has,
we believe, been attended with success, the salt being
obtained by boiling the sea-water in shallow pans. It is
of a good quality, and commands a fair price in Brisbane.
Away to the south the view is shut in by the island of
St. Helena, Mud Island, and a few others. Among these
isles the small craft pass that ply to Cleveland (a township
on the mainland) and to the Logan, Albert, and Coomera
Rivers. Nearer at hand is the double row of lights and
beacons which both by day and night point out to passing
steamers and vessels the entrance to the river through
Francis's Channel. The prison hulk for refractory seamen is a prominent object in this part of the bay. Here
also is the light-ship, on which reside the men and their
wives who attend to the various lights. The mouth of the
Brisbane River is hidden by the low mangrove swamps
which run out on each side and skirt the coast for many a
mile. Inland, opposite these mangroves, the bay is too
shallow for any sort of navigation, the flats drying for a
long way out at low water. Farther on to the north-west
the coast rises and presents something like a cliff. Here

the Cabbage Tree Creek—a name to be met with in
all parts of the colony—runs into the bay, and on the
high bank is situated the pleasant little watering-place
of Sandgate. Boats from the shipping, which lies
about four miles off, can land at most times of the tide
opposite the creek, and a very pleasant day can be spent
on shore by the long pent-up seamen. There are two
good hotels here, and horses or a daily coach convey
passengers to Brisbane, a distance of twelve miles,
through the old-settled district of German Station. To
the north of Sandgate, some two or three miles, is the
mouth of the Pine River, an unimportant stream, navigable
for a very little distance by small steamers. Running out
from here is a bold point of land officially known as Red-
cliff, but popularly as Humpybong. Here, in 1824, the
first penal settlement was established in Moreton Bay, but
was very soon abandoned for the site of the present city
of Brisbane. As all the Government buildings were left
when the place was abandoned, the natives gave the spot
the name by which it is now known, which merely signifies
dead-house, " bong " being dead, and " humpy " a house,
in their language. For many years Humpybong was
only resorted to by lime-burners, who drove a good business by burning the enormous quantities of oyster-shells
found here into lime, which they sold in Brisbane. Of
late the land has been taken up by farmers, who carry on
dairying and other branches of agriculture. Our remi-
niscences of the neighbourhood are connected with huge
and savage wild boars, which haunted the mangrove
swamps, impervious almost to dogs, and where they
bade defiance to anything short of a bullet. Wherever
pigs are kept it is quite usual for a host of wild ones
soon to be found in the neighbouring swamps and

scrubs, as they are entirely independent of any artificial
food.

Northward of Humpybong is a low stretch of country,
just a little above tide-water, stretching away to the
Caboolture River. Beyond this again is Bribie Passage
and Island, running parallel with the coast for about thirty
miles. Opposite this island is the deep-sea entrance to
the bay. The only other feature worthy of notice is the
curious appearance of a group of hills many miles inland,
which spring so abruptly from the level country as to
have earned for themselves the designation of the " glass-
houses." There are several of these curious mountains,
and on a clear day they are by no means an unattractive
portion of the scenery. It will thus be seen that no less
than seven rivers, all navigable for a greater or less distance, empty their waters into Moreton Bay. One of the
chief points of difference between Queensland and the other
colonies of Australia consists in the large number of rivers
found in the latter, a sure indication of the greater rainfall in the former, which is one of its great advantages.
Queensland is in fact " a land of rivers and streams."

Leaving the ship's side in a steamer, the immigrant
passes between the lines of beacons and enters the mouth
of the Brisbane River. From here to the capital is fifteen
miles. At first each bank is a mere mangrove swamp,
but soon after passing Lytton the southern bank rises in
altitude. Here the Brisbane is of a noble breadth ; and
to the eye of the beholder, after a three months' voyage,
the bright green fringe of thick mangroves which line
each bank and cover the low mud islands in the river
presents a cheerful and pleasing sight. Soon after passing
Lytton, where is a small pier, a telegraph-station, and the
residences of the water-police, the mouth of Doughboy

Creek is passed on the south side. Here begin the evidences of cultivation. On the high point of land between the river and creek is a house commanding a fine view of the river and bay on the one side, and the farms and plantations on both banks of the creek on the other. From the verandah of this house may now be seen a charming prospect of smiling sugar-fields and waving groves of the graceful banana. Directly under the hill is the plantation of the owner, with the sugar-mill which turns the cane into a merchantable commodity. Dotted among the fields are the houses of the sturdy settlers, and the church and school-house for the district. Nothing of this truly rural scene can be noticed from the steamer's deck, but the emigrant may be told by some old resident, as an encouragement to himself and as indicative of the future of the colony, that for many years the farmer whose house he sees before him, and who brought with him to Queensland not only an experience gained among the fields of England, but also in those of Victoria, had hard work to eke out a decent subsistence by the growth of oaten hay, corn, potatoes, green-stuff, and such vegetable crops as were marketable in Brisbane, and how, when all these failed to give an adequate return, what through lowness of prices, floods, droughts, &c., he finally, some four years since, planted a few acres of sugar-cane. First crushing his crop on shares at the neighbouring mill of Captain Hope, of Cleveland, he next essayed a small mill for himself. The writer happened to meet him a few days before sailing from Brisbane, and learnt the sequel of the story of the sugar speculation. Last season a young Queenslander, who had had a little experience at another mill, undertook to boil the sugar. Unfortunately he had only succeeded in making molasses which had to be sold at 4d. per gallon to make rum, and as he had not only dealt with the farmer's own cane but that of some neighbours, a heavy loss of money and reputation had followed. This season other measures had been adopted, and already something like fifty tons of sugar, worth from 35*l.* to 38*l.* per ton, had been manufactured and sold. We have made this digression to give one instance in many scores of the present position and future prospects of the Queensland agriculturists. This farmer's position is that of a majority of his brethren, who by the assistance of sugar-cane are just drawing their heads above the difficulties which have so long enveloped them.

From Doughboy Creek the south bank of the river is bold and soon becomes picturesque. Farm after farm is passed, all the homesteads being more or less buried in groves of bananas. On the north bank the powder magazine is seen, and after passing Eagle Farm Flats the houses become thick on that side also. Now we pass the home-like mansion of Bulimba, erected by one of the oldest of our colonists; but which has lately changed hands for a second time. It is now embowered in the all-pervading sugar-cane, and has an air of homeliness quite refreshing. On the other side the low lands have given place to high hills, dotted here and there with the residences of well-to-do citizens. A " linen-draper bold" has ensconced himself on one of the highest hills, in a beautiful house which is said to have cost a very large sum, from which the outlook must be splendid.[2] Here is " Lowden's Folly," a high

---

[2] This gentleman has, since the above was written, been elected to Parliament, and become a member of the Cabinet, has in fact passed from behind the counter to hold the purse-strings of the colony, although still retaining his position in business : a not at all uncommon event in Australia, where, like the ancient Roman, men may often be found busily and successfully attending to their private concerns one day, and directing the public counsels of the nation another.

hill which was once cleared *in mistake* by a colonist of
that name, who spent a very considerable sum in stumping
and clearing a piece of land, which he subsequently discovered belonged to some one else,—a practical lesson
that all young colonists should take to heart. The scenery
from here to Brisbane is very lovely, and calculated to
raise the spirits of the beholder. Breakfast Creek and
the residence of the Hon. G. Harris, M.L.C., of the
firm of J. and G. Harris, are passed, and here it is
likely a salute of small guns will be fired and a flag
run up in honour of the new arrivals, Mr. Harris's
firm being the agents of the London line of vessels.
Residence after residence is passed, Kangaroo Point is
reached, and the lovely suburb of Bowen Terrace has
hardly been admired before the steamer sweeps around
the Point, and Brisbane, looking very lovely, is suddenly
reached.

Whatever may be the destination and future calling of
the immigrant, he cannot do wrong by passing a week or
two in Brisbane. He will find hotel accommodation at
from 1*l.* to 3*l.* per week, and each very good at its price;
or if he be a man of family, and anxious to save every
penny of his money, he can leave his family for a day at
the Immigration Barracks, and look out a cottage for their
reception in the town. He will be able to obtain a three
or four room cottage at from 5*s.* to 10*s.* per week. In
1863 cottages of every description commanded at least
1*l.* per week, and every article of domestic use, except
butcher's meat, which was 3*d.* and 4*d.* per pound, was high
in price. A very diminutive cabbage as big as one's
fist, was worth 6*d.*, while other vegetables were almost
unknown, and the two-pound loaf stood at 7*d.* and 8*d.*
Now for 6*d.* enough vegetables of all sorts can be had to

serve an ordinary family for a day or two, and the two-pound loaf costs 4*d*.[3]

There is much in Brisbane to interest the stranger who has an intention of settling in the colony. Probably one of the first thoughts which will occur to any one from home will be that he is in a town first founded by convict labour. He will, however, look in vain at this period for anything to remind him visibly of that fact. Almost all the old buildings raised by that species of labour have given way to other erections, and he would search a long time among his casual acquaintances for any one who could speak personally of the old times, much less before he would find an " old hand " himself. In another place we shall advert to the convict system, and its effects on the population : in this Chapter we desire to describe places rather than persons.

If he arrives in an immigrant vessel, that is, a ship bringing out immigrants under the auspices of the Colonial Government, the new arrival will be landed at the Government Wharf, contiguous to the Immigration Barracks, a fine brick structure, not by any means open to the objections urged against the old building in use eight years since, and where the fresh immigrants are all lodged and boarded until they obtain situations, at the public expense. Emerging from this, he finds himself in William Street, on the opposite side of which is situated the Government Printing Office, an extensive establishment, from which first-class work is turned out, and where a large staff of hands is always employed. Next comes the Telegraph Office, which has for its head a gentleman of eminent

---

[3] With the greatly increased prosperity of the last four years, we believe that rents have considerably advanced, house property having materially improved in value in Brisbane and all other places.

scientific attainments, and which is connected not only
with all the other colonies, but with every township in
Queensland of the least importance as far north as
Cardwell. From the Report of F. J. Cracknell, Esq.,
the Superintendent of Telegraphs, dated 1st of April,
1871, we learn that "on the 31st of December, 1870,
there were 2183 miles of line and forty stations, worked
by seventy-eight officers, in operation" in the colony; and
that on the completion of the line under contract to the
township of Norman, on the Gulf of Carpentaria, which
was to be completed in August last, there would be 2891
miles of line and fifty-four stations, with ninety-four
officers on the permanent staff of the department, the
terminal station at Carpentaria being 1450 miles from
the central office : certainly something for a young
colony like Queensland to have achieved in eleven years.
Here every day wind and weather reports, and meteoro-
logical observations from various parts of the colony, are
received and posted for general information, together with
shipping intelligence from all ports in the colony, as well
as from Sydney, Melbourne, and Adelaide. Some idea of
the gratuitous public business of this nature performed in
this office may be gathered from the fact that no less than
225 such messages are received here daily. Public expec-
tation is raised by the hope that a few months more will
see Brisbane and the other Australian capitals in daily
communication with England. At present a deal has been
done to annihilate space, and the last mail news before
the writer left the colony was only nineteen days in
reaching Brisbane from London. Nothing tends more to
cement the ties existing between Great Britain and her
colonies than the quick transmission of intelligence, and
we hope before long to see two or three different lines of

telegraph wire connecting Queensland with the mother
country.[4]

Passing onward, the stranger sees a low, one-storyed
building, known as the Colonial Secretary's Office. Here
is the office of the present Premier, a burly squatter, to
whom we may probably refer again. Then comes the
Church of St. John, the oldest edifice belonging to the
Church of England in the colony. Of late years this
church, which is built of dressed stone, has been very
greatly enlarged. It is now a very fine edifice. Contiguous to it is the parsonage. Farther on is the office of
the Registrar-General, the Colonial Treasurer's Office, and
other public buildings, and then, turning the corner, Queen
Street, the principal street of the town, is reached. At
this point a fine view of the river is had, and of the town
of South Brisbane beyond. Here is the approach to the
unfortunate bridge which, begun several years ago, has
never been brought to completion. At one time indeed
the contractor erected a wooden structure, which was
opened with great *éclat* by Sir George Bowen, the first
Governor of the colony. It was intended to work from
this temporary bridge to build the other, but after it had
been opened some time, and several of the tubular piers of
the iron bridge had been either partially or wholly put
down and bricked up, from various causes, prominent
among which were the local jealousies of the Ipswich
people, the mismanagement of the corporation, and the
failure of the Oriental Bank, followed by the winding-up
of the Bank of Queensland, the works came to a stand-
still. Then followed a flood which swept away a portion

---

[4] The submarine communication with England has been some time
in operation, and English news of the previous day is now published
regularly in the colonial papers.

of the temporary bridge, and there being no funds at disposal even to secure the remainder of the tottering structure, nor secure the castings of the iron bridge, the whole affair remained for years one of the most melancholy exhibitions of colonial failures it is possible to conceive. Little by little the wooden bridge dropped to pieces, or was carried away by succeeding storms, until hardly a vestige of it remained. Latterly the financial difficulties which stood in the way of its completion have been smoothed away, and while we write the work of erecting the permanent bridge is being proceeded with, and the remainder of the castings are on their way from England. The original cost of this bridge was to have been 60,000*l.*, but it is now understood that it will very much exceed that amount. When it is finished it will be a very fine structure indeed, and from the great traffic it will carry is expected to be a paying speculation. At present the trade is carried on by three different ferries; two others plying between the city and Kangaroo Point.[5]

The city of Brisbane is built in what is colonially known as a " pocket " of the Brisbane River. A " pocket " is that portion of land contained in a sharp curve of a river. In this instance Queen Street may be supposed to cut the city in two parts, running as it does from the river on one side to the river on the other side of this pocket. On the one side is the city proper and on the other rises at a little distance the hill known as Spring Hill, which is more like a suburb than a portion of the city itself. The extreme point of this pocket is occupied on the one side by the Government House and grounds, and on the other by the

[5] This bridge was completed and formally opened by his Excellency the Marquis of Normanby on the 15th of June, 1874, the day being one of the grandest ever seen in Brisbane.

Botanical Gardens. Confining our attention for the nonce
to Queen Street, we will suppose a " new chum " to take
his first walk down it after having duly enjoyed the lovely
prospect presented to him by the appearance of the river
and South Brisbane beyond. Like all the other streets of
this and all the older towns in Queensland, Queen Street
is very narrow, being only one chain wide. It is recorded
by Dr. Lang that when Governor Sir George Gipps visited
this part of the colony of New South Wales, he was aghast
to find that the surveyors, with unpardonable excess had
marked each street a chain and a half wide ! The worthy
governor, who does not appear to have had a mind suitable
to the management of anything more extensive than a
cabbage garden, at once ordered that all the streets of
townships in Moreton Bay should be reduced to one chain,
chiding the surveyors for their reckless wastefulness in
dealing with the Queen's bush. Thus, through this
paltry policy, are Queenslanders compelled to walk
through narrow streets entirely unsuited to the climate,
while millions on millions of acres of land lie waste and
unoccupied.

But narrow though it be, Queen Street is by no means
a mean or insignificant street. There are in it many shops
which would do credit to any capital in the world, both as
to their architecture and extent and the style of their
interior fitting up and furnishings. To an Englishman a
peculiar feature of this street will be the verandahs which
on one side almost run from end to end without any
intermission as far as the retail shops extend. These
verandahs reach right across the side walk; and afford a
protection alike to the goods in the shops and the
pedestrians, from the heat and glare of the sun. On the
left-hand side of the street going towards the Kangaroo

Point Ferry, the visitor passes the Post Office, a low and mean building, totally unsuited to the requirements of so large a town, and which is soon to give place to a fine Post Office now being built farther down the street.[6] The business done in this establishment is very large, and, to meet its growing requirements, building after building has had to be added at the rear, until now, every inch of space back to the next street has been occupied. Here too is the Savings' Bank, an institution deserving of some notice. Following Mr. Gladstone's lead, the Queensland Government some years since associated the Savings' Bank with the Post Office with the happiest result. From the last report of this establishment laid before Parliament we learn that in 1870, 206,931l. 4s. 1d. was deposited, and 189,350l. 8s. 9d. withdrawn last year by 5821 depositors, and that on the 31st of December, 1870, the sum of 332,843l. 0s. 7d. was standing to the credit of these depositors; showing very plainly that a very satisfactory state of things exists among the working classes, when we remember that the population of the colony was calculated to be about 110,000. For the benefit of immigrants it may not be amiss to state that last year a regulation was made empowering the Agent-General for the colony in England to receive deposits up to 100l. from intending emigrants from the United Kingdom, which they can draw at any Post Office Savings' Bank in Queensland with five per cent. interest, which rate of interest is allowed on all sums not exceeding 200l. This provision has been found to work so well that it is at once to be extended to Germany.

The next building to the Post Office is of far higher

---

[6] The new post office, a very fine building, we believe, is now finished and occupied by the department.

pretensions. It is the Town Hall and Exchange, and is a
very noble structure of three stories. In its front is a
row of shops, only the entrance of the Hall and the
Exchange in the rear of the shops being on the ground
floor. Above are the Council Chamber and other municipal
offices, together with the Chamber of Commerce, a very neat
hall. The third floor is devoted to the Town Hall, which
is a very fine room indeed, with stained glass windows,
and capable of containing from 2000 to 3000 persons. This
hall was built in the "good times" prior to the failure of
the Queensland Bank, before referred to, and entangled the
corporation in many difficulties. To make things worse, it
was given out that the hall was unsafe, and that the first
time a large audience gathered there the roof would tumble
in on them. This rumour was so far believed that for a
length of time no meetings were held there, and the
architect and all concerned in the erection of the building
were looked on with much disfavour. An investigation
was ultimately made, which showed that the building was
sufficiently strong, public confidence was restored, and
meetings were held there regularly. A few days after the
arrival of the present Governor, the Marquis of Normanby,[7]
the writer was present at a lunch given there by the
Mayor and Corporation, when the hall was crowded by an
enthusiastic audience, and probably not one for a moment
allowed his mind to revert to the idle stories which for so
great a length of time prevented this fine hall being used
by the public.

Farther down the street on the same side is a public
building of a very different appearance and history. This
is the Court House, in which the sittings of the Supreme

---

[7] The Marquis of Normanby left the colony in the latter part of
1874. Mr. Cairns, a brother of the Lord Chancellor, is now Governor.

and Insolvent Courts are held. Here also are the Judges' Chambers, the Sheriffs' Office, those of the Crown Solicitor and the Official Assignees. Years since the Legislative Council and Assembly sat in this building, but these are now removed to larger and more suitable premises. This Court House is a low, solid, two-story building of stone, and is one of the few remaining mementoes of the convict system. It was formerly the female penitentiary and workshop, and as only the worst class of female convicts were sent to Moreton Bay, we may suppose that these walls formerly contained as much vice and infamy as could easily be found in any like space on the earth's surface. Both sides of the street are occupied by shops, hotels, and other business places for some distance below, then the site of the new Post Office, which is on the other side of the way, is reached. To make room for this, a portion of the old police court had to be taken down, and notably the archway, underneath which used to stand the triangles on which every morning many a poor fellow was stretched, and had his two dozen or twelve, as the case might be. The police court is the old one extant in these good old times, and is a mean, low room, worthy of the men and the period.

Standing in front of the new Post Office one sees the School of Arts beyond, with a fine row of shops in front. The entrance to the reading-rooms and library, which is in fact the principal entrance, is in Creek Street round the corner. This institution was long heavily in debt for the construction of its new building, but we believe by coming to some understanding with the mortgagees, the institution has been relieved of its debt, and is now able to devote more funds to purely literary purposes. There is a fine library and very commodious reading-rooms here, which can be availed of by strangers on very reasonable terms. There is also an excellent hall in connection with the institution, fitted up in a superior manner, and often used by theatrical companies and for other public purposes.

Among the other public buildings in this street are the banks, all of some pretensions to architectural excellence. Farther on is the Kangaroo Point ferry and the gas works. The street continues to Fortitude Valley—a large and important suburb, sending its own member to parliament—passing on the way the Roman Catholic nunnery.

The Servants' Home, the Lady Bowen Lying-in Hospital, the Free Library and Reading-room are all excellent institutions standing in the streets behind Queen Street, as also are the Masonic Hall and the Normal and National Schools. The new Grammar School, a little farther removed from the town, is a neat building, a part of the plan of which has only as yet been carried out. The foundation was laid by H.R.H. the Duke of Edinburgh, on his late visit. There is no lack of churches in Brisbane or its suburbs. A great improvement has taken place in this as in every other respect since 1863, when the writer first saw the city. The Church of England, Roman Catholics, Presbyterians, Wesleyans, Congregationalists, Baptists, Free Methodists, Primitives, Bible Christians, and Jews are all represented, and in most cases have excellent and spacious places of worship. The principal ecclesiastical buildings are St. John's and Wickham Terrace churches, belonging to the Church of England, the Wickham Terrace Presbyterian church, the Baptist church, and the Wesleyan churches in Albert Street and the Valley. A very pretentious cathedral has been in course of erection by the Romanists for nearly eight years. After languishing for many years, principally we believe through the difficulties encountered by Bishop Quinn in his land speculations, this undertaking has of late been carried on with more vigour, and the edifice has now reached a stage which gives promise that when completed it will be one of the finest buildings in the city.[8]

The visitor to Brisbane can by no means afford to overlook the Botanical Gardens. Situate with Government House in the very point of the pocket on which Brisbane is built, these gardens have a very pleasant situation, and are a very favourite lounge for the citizens. Under the care of Mr. Hill, the Curator, and assisted by an annual legislative grant, a little paradise has been here created. Few men so well fitted for his position as Mr. Hill could probably have been found in the colonies : it is certain that not only has he brought these gardens to a pitch of perfection which makes them the pride of Brisbane, but that by his constant and elaborate exhibits in the various exhibitions in the colonies as well as in Europe, he has done more than any other person in bringing the resources and productions of the colony before the world at large. Here will be found gathered not only most of the plants and shrubs indigenous to the colony, but the most important and useful of every other country whose climate approximates to that of Queensland. The most striking feature in the gardens is the splendid row of bunya-bunya trees which lines the walk skirting the river bank. These trees, which bear the bunya nut, are a species of pine, and as they grow in a sugar-loaf shape, throwing their branches out from the ground to the top, are of a highly ornamental character, especially when young. No expenditure was ever made by the colonial legislature which has returned

[8] This cathedral, known as St. Stephen's, was finally opened on May 17th, 1874.

better interest than the very modest grants which have been made for the maintenance of these gardens. As showing the practical advantages which are accruing to the colony from the Botanic Gardens we extract some passages from the Report of the Curator laid before Parliament in its last session, dated March, 1871.

"In the Experimental Department the plants of commercial value, which have been enumerated in former Reports, continue to thrive as well as ever. Of these, particular mention may be made of the *Indigofera Tinctora* (Indigo), the *Rubia Tinctora* (Madder), the *Coffea Arabica* (Coffee), the *Thea Bohœa* (Tea), the *Zingiber Officinalis* (Ginger), the *Curcuma Longa* (Cardamom), the *Amomum Melgueta* (Grain of Paradise), the *Manihot Utilissima* (Cassava); the fibrous plants, viz.:—the Jute (*Corchorus Capsularis*), the Sun Hemp (*Crotolaria Juncea*), the Queensland Hemp (*Sida Retusa*), the China Grass Cloth Plant (*Bohmeria nivea*), &c., &c. I have been careful in cherishing the development of these and kindred plants, in order that they may be kept before the eye of the public; and it is matter of satisfaction to know that beneficial results will likely follow from the increased interest evinced in their cultivation, as is shown from the numerous applications for seeds and plants which have been made during the past year.

"With respect to the valuable practical results that have followed the introduction of several of this order of commercial and food plants, it is a source of gratification to be able to state that in many instances private enterprise has proved successful, the first experiment having been made from seeds or plants procured from the gardens. This especially applies to the articles cotton and sugar, which, as generally known, are becoming year by year more important as staple exports of this colony. It is to be hoped and trusted that other plants of commercial value and importance, such as coffee, tea, tobacco, &c., &c., may claim the attention of the settler, as they are no less a source of profit, nor less easily cultivated, than the sugar and cotton plant. In some of the districts—particularly on the sea-coast —some thousands of plants of the coffee have been distributed in response to applications; and without doubt we shall hear ere long of the plant being extensively, if not generally, cultivated.

"The demand for cuttings and young plants of the silkworms' tree, *Morus alba* and *Morus multicaulis*, is greatly on the increase, more especially from East and West Moreton and the Darling Downs districts.

" We have received during the past year hundreds of cuttings of the various valuable grape vines from the vineyards of Mr. David Randell, Seacombe, and Mr. Bickers, of Port Adelaide, South Australia; and nearly all these, with several American varieties already on hand, have been distributed to persons embarking in the cultivation of the vine. They are mostly wine-producing sorts, and consist of Verdelho, Reisling, Tokay, Temprana, Doradilla, Pedro-Ximines, Shiraz, Carbenet Sauvignon, Mataro, Grenache, Molar Nigro, Quick's seedling, White Madeira, Muscat, Gordo Bianco, &c., &c.

" In the department of sugar-canes, of which there are thirty-six varieties, there has been an immense demand for cuttings during the past year. From all the sugar-growing districts, the applications have far exceeded any previous demand, all of which have been duly supplied.

" The applications for various products of the gardens are largely on the increase, so much so, that it takes most of one man's time to pack and despatch the several consignments. The grand total of receipts of plants and seeds from the gardens number 530 persons, irrespective of societies or private individuals, where no such associations exist, who have from time to time been supplied with seeds, &c., for purposes of distribution. Among this number of persons 60,980 of plants, cuttings, and packages of seeds of various kinds have been supplied, thereby showing the valuable influence and assistance exerted by this department in the general propagation and distribution of the indigenous and foreign vegetable products of the colony. In this matter I am careful not to clash with the interests of our nurserymen, and for this reason distribute nothing which may be procured in their collection, except for our own public reserves and experimental purposes."

We fully endorse the following very pertinent and practical remarks with which Mr. Hill concludes his Report :—

" The very important good which must necessarily result from Intercolonial Exhibitions cannot be over-estimated. It can hardly be doubted that the tangible products of a new colony, when exposed to the view of other colonists, would exercise a far more practical and beneficial influence in attracting skilled labour and capital to our shores than could be effected by any other means. The best exertions otherwise employed are, to a great extent, paralyzed by want of faith, and

not being able to realize that which is not seen, as also by the contra-
dictory testimony of disappointed immigrants or others writing home
to the press, or their own personal friends, and quoting the experience
of their own failure as a general rule whereby to judge the colony."

That many such reports of a highly-coloured and un-
truthful character have been sent home there can be no
question.

Contiguous to the gardens, and forming one of the most
prominent features in the landscape, is the new Parliamentary building. This is by far the largest structure in
the city. In fact, it has been built on such a large scale
that it has up to the present been found impossible to
finish it, the plans having comprised another wing and
verandahs and balconies. It is of cut stone from a local
quarry, and presents an imposing though rather *outré*
appearance from the absence of the balconies and the
consequent lack of any ornamentation in the stone work.
The interior has, however, been finished, so far as built, and
is of ample extent for the public business to be carried on
there. The chambers of the Legislative Council and
Assembly are splendid rooms, much superior to those the
writer has seen in the British American colonies. Indeed
great feeling was created in the colony by the outlay
incurred in erecting this building, which was felt to be far
too large and expensive for its requirements and revenue.
But it was urged that the plan had been adopted at a time
when the colony was in a highly prosperous state, and when
every one was anticipating a continuance of its then rapid
growth, a growth almost unparalleled in the history of
colonization. Queenslanders have the satisfaction of knowing that however much their colony may increase in population and importance, they have now a parliament building
adequate to their wants and grand enough for their dignity.

On the outskirts of the town, beyond Fortitude Valley, is another very imposing building—the Hospital. This also is built of dressed stone, and is pleasantly situated on a slight eminence. It is, like all other Queensland hospitals—and they are to be found in every township of any importance—maintained by local subscriptions, and a legislative grant to double the amount of such local funds. Queenslanders are justly proud of their hospitals, which offer a refuge to that large portion of the sick public who have no friends or home in the colony, as well as to those whose circumstances compel them to seek there the attention they cannot command at their own residences. Scores of young men, who leave home because they can do nothing for themselves and are a burden to their friends, and who after " knocking down " the few scores or hundreds of pounds given them to make a start in the colony, when without friends or shelter, and suffering from diseases brought on by their excess, here obtain skilful medical treatment and careful nursing, in many cases leading to their restoration, and in others soothing the last days of a wasted life. Could the records of this and other hospitals be written, they would show many a ghastly picture of this sort. People in England little know how often a young scapegrace, thus banished for family reasons to " the colonies," closes his earthly career in one of the hospitals so nobly supported by the benevolence of the colonists. There is a lock hospital in connection with this establishment, and we may add a Contagious Diseases Act in force, with excellent results, in Brisbane and one or two other towns of the colony.

Nearly opposite the hospital is the Bowen Park, the property of the Acclimatization Society. This Society is supported by subscriptions and a legislative grant, and is

rather pretentious in its character. Besides introducing
rabbits in a few localities, a few deer and other animals
which graze in their grounds, and placing a few Murray cod
in one or two ponds, we do not remember any very great
benefit the Society has conferred on the colony, if we
except the creation of their park itself and its maintenance
as a pleasure-ground, to which admission can be had on
application; but the funds of the Society have usually
been at low-water mark, and perhaps it has done something in the way of attracting notice to Queensland, as
well as by introducing a few useful plants and fruit-trees.

The manufactures of Brisbane are not very extensive;
but it is pleasing to record that they have very materially
increased since 1863, at which time it might truly be said
that the only manufacture was that of streets and houses.
Then every one appeared possessed of the idea that the
laying out of streets and erection of houses was the quickest
and surest means of making a fortune, and for some time
it really looked as if this idea was correct; but a collapse
came. For various reasons, prominent among which was
the undue interference of Parliament with the land order
system, together with that other cause, the bad quality
of the lands open for selection, immigration fell off,
house-building ceased, and the city, having lived on its
own growth, was soon thrown into a state of panic, and
hundreds and thousands had to leave the town, some to
follow those agricultural pursuits which they had before
sneered at, some to take situations in the bush or stations,
while many more left the colony.

But a gradual but most advantageous change has been
wrought in this respect. Doubtless the evils suffered in
the panic partially account for the change, but the growth
of the sugar industry and the wonderful development of

the gold-fields has also had much to do with the increased attention which has of late been paid to manufactures. There are now in Brisbane two saw-mills, in connection with one of which is a mill for drying and grinding maize. Singular as it may appear, although maize is one of the surest crops which the farmer can plant, there was until recently a strong prejudice against the use of maize-meal as food. While in all parts of Canada and the States maize or corn-meal enters largely into the domestic *cuisine* of all classes of society, in the latter colony it was considered as only food for cattle. This arose, no doubt, in a great measure from the fact that in the penal times the convicts were fed on this sort of food; and thus having a natural aversion from an article which reminded them of old times, they had in this, as in many other matters, given a tone to the general sentiment of the community. To a Canadian or American it will sound singular to be told that Queenslanders, who could grow their own maize but had to import and pay cash for all their flour, had to be educated to the practice of eating the former most wholesome and palatable cereal. Yet such is the fact, and to Mr. Pettigrew, of the Brisbane saw-mills, belongs in a great measure the praise of having first erected a mill for producing maize-meal, and then inducing his fellow colonists to avail themselves of it. Even at the present time there is not one quarter as much maize consumed for culinary purposes as there is in a like population in America; and as wheaten flour has yet to be largely imported, the colony is impoverished in proportion. Procuring the timber for the use of these two mills gives employment to a large number of timber-getters, bullock-drivers, punt and raftsmen, besides one or two steamers and occasional sailing-vessels, the timber being fetched

from as far south as the Coomera and Nerang Creek on
the border of New South Wales, and from the Mooroochy
and Mooloolah on the north. The timbers principally
sawn up are cedar, pine, beech, blue and red gum, iron-
bark and cypress-pine. None of the hard woods of Queensland will float in water, so that all timber but pine and
cedar has to be conveyed in punts from the banks of the
rivers, except when it can be lashed on to a raft of soft
wood, as is sometimes done with beech and cypress-pine.
As a large proportion of the timber sawn up is exported to
the southern colonies, the trade is exceedingly valuable.
It is in fact the only sort of manufacturing industry which
swells the exports, and thus introduces capital into the
country, besides employing a considerable number of sea-
going vessels.

Eight years ago it was almost impossible to get a
plough, or any other agricultural implement, manufactured
in Queensland; and the few people who needed such
implements had to be content with very inferior articles,
as the importation was very limited, of poor quality, and
very high in price. Now the case is far different; there
are two or three agricultural implement makers who turn
out an article well adapted to the peculiar requirements of
the soil, at a very moderate price. There is also a foundry
where very good sugar and quartz crushing machinery,
with the requisite steam power, is manufactured. Many
cheap horse-power sugar-mills have also been manufactured
here. A small brewery produces a very palatable beer,
much more suitable to the climate than the English ale,
which, as it has to be made very strong to stand the
voyage through the tropics, is too heady for a constant
beverage. A considerable amount of jewellery has lately
been manufactured from the produce of the neighbouring

gold-fields. Several cabinet-makers, coopers, carriage-builders, copper and tin smiths, supply the local want in their several lines. One or two extensive boot and shoe manufactories are in existence ; but the local supply is by no means equal to the demand. Of late years the demand for rum casks has suddenly sprung into considerable dimensions; but unfortunately there is a lack as yet of colonial timber suitable for this purpose, the strong gum or antiseptic or other properties rendering those woods already tried objectionable. It is hoped this difficulty will soon be overcome. A rapid fortune awaits the fortunate man who shall introduce some process of preparing some of the otherwise excellent Queensland timbers for use for rum casks and other like purposes, as the demand is fast becoming very extensive, and the supply of timber endless. At present casks have to be imported from England in staves.

A few miles from Brisbane is the only tannery in the Moreton districts and, with one exception, the only one in the colony. From some reason this undertaking, although over seven years in existence, has not been very successful. This must arise, however, from accidental circumstances, as the hides and bark are to be had in any quantity. We believe that in this as in many other manufactures a foolish and unreasoning prejudice against local productions has had to be contended with. Much too is to be accounted for on the score of insufficient capital to enable the speculator to overcome the preliminary expenses, which in every new enterprise in Queensland are generally from 50 to 100 per cent. more than is first calculated on. It would appear that for men practically acquainted with the trade and a fair amount of capital, Queensland offers a splendid field for starting in this business. Not only the

wattle-bark, which is exported to England in considerable
quantities, but the iron-bark and others, too heavy for
exportation, are made use of with good results. At
Breakfast Creek is an ice manufactory which in the
summer season affords the citizens a supply of this
delicious luxury at a very moderate rate.

One manufactory which formerly existed has happily
long been disused. Prominent on the boldest outlook in
the town stands a round building similar to a windmill,
and known to the present generation as the Observatory.
From here the flags which denote the arrival and character
of vessels in the bay are hoisted, and below is the Russian
gun which daily proclaims the hour of one to the citizens.
This building was erected in the convict period, as a windmill for grinding the maize meal which made the hominy
of the convicts, or, as they are usually called in the colonies,
lags. It was, however, often used as a tread-mill, and the
convicts had here literally to earn their bread by the sweat
of their brows. When the settlement became free the
tread-mill of course fell into disuse. Although now in one
of the most fashionable parts of the town, the windmill
was then quite in the bush. No use was made of its
machinery, and if we may credit an old man who had
often stepped out his four hours there, it was gradually
and quietly removed by a neighbouring blacksmith when
iron was dear, and worked up into horseshoes and other
articles of his trade. After standing unused for many
years, the building was soon after separation turned to its
present use.

Three miles out on the old northern road, at a place
called the Three-Mile Scrub, is a small establishment
deserving of notice. Here is manufactured the desiccated
meat prepared by Dr. Bancroft. The method on which

this description of meat-preserving is carried out is very simple, it being dried until all the watery parts are removed. The process is so inexpensive, and at the same time is said to be so effectual, that nothing but the proverbial want of capital has prevented a large trade from growing up. At present beef and mutton are principally treated; but two valuable denizens of the bay, turtle and dugong, are occasionally prepared with a view to testing the market.

A great many improvements have been effected in Brisbane since 1863. None, however, is of greater value to the citizens than the construction of the Ennoggerra Water Works, by means of which the water of this creek is brought into the city, a distance of about six miles. A large reservoir has been formed by throwing a dam across a narrow place in a deep gully and a sufficient supply of water is thus obtained to last for some years without any rainfall whatever. Before these works were carried out the water supply for the whole city had to be carted in barrels from a water-hole, dignified by the name of " reservoir," but which was usually of a rich yellow colour. This water was sold at from 1s. to 1s. 6d. per barrel, and even more in dry times. Unless a house was provided with a cistern, this was the only means of obtaining this precious fluid—doubly precious in a hot climate like Queensland. Now every one can have the water laid on to his own door, supplied without stint, and of an excellent quality. There can be no question that this adds much to the healthfulness of Brisbane; in a domestic point of view it is an unspeakable boon. A rate is levied to meet the expense connected with this improvement. It may be added here that in every other town in the colony the water supply is obtained from the water-carriers, as was formerly the case

in Brisbane, excepting of course where people have cisterns
equal to their requirements.   Gas works were established a
few years ago, and the principal streets are now lit by gas
on moonless nights.   When the moon shines with a splendour unknown in Great Britain, and a light nearly equal to
daylight here, gas would be a superfluity.

There is in Brisbane a market building, and market dues
are collected from every person offering any farm or garden
produce for sale in the streets : but the authorities have
never succeeded in inducing producers or consumers to visit
the market-house, which is entirely unoccupied, except a
portion let off as a produce-store.   There is nevertheless an
excellent supply of dairy and garden produce, the latter
principally supplied by the German settlers in the district.
A wonderful change has been wrought in this respect of
late years.   In 1863 the food of the citizens had perforce
to be made up of butcher's meat and bread, vegetables
being both scarce and dear, and often not attainable at any
price.   The same was true of poultry and dairy produce,
eggs, for instance, being from 2s. 6d. to 3s. per dozen.   All
this has undergone a change, and there are few places where
living is now cheaper than in Brisbane.

The soil in the neighbourhood of Brisbane is almost all
of a very inferior character.   The only exception is the
scrub land on the banks of the rivers, and this is very
limited in extent.   The site of the town having been
selected only with a view to its suitability for a penal
settlement is a sufficient reason for this.   In no other
district of the colony have we seen so large a proportion of
poor land as in the district around Brisbane, and the immigrant who proposes settling on the soil will do well to give
up that most absurd notion which most new chums possess,
of settling close to the capital.   No small portion of the

evils which have befallen the colony have arisen from the prevalence of this feeling and the failure to appreciate it which has been exhibited by the authorities. Hundreds of men in the early days after separation were ruined by taking up portions of land in this district which were entirely unfitted for cultivation, and by expending their capital and labour in fencing and clearing land, which even when fenced and cleared would have been unfit to give them more than a bare subsistence. It nearly always occurs that the most worthless land has the heaviest timber, and thus costs the most money to clear.

We will now notice the various farming settlements in the East Moreton district.

In the immediate neighbourhood of Brisbane, and within a distance of a dozen miles, will be found the settlements known as Eagle Farm, German Station, Nudgee, Sandgate, and Bald Hills on the north side of the river, and Boggo, Oxley Creek, Cooper's Plains, and Bulimba on the south. Most of the farms on the north, with some trifling exceptions, are on what is usually known as forest land, in contradistinction to scrub land.

As these terms scrub and forest land will often recur, it may be well to say that in Queensland the rich alluvial lands on the banks of the rivers and creeks are generally covered with a dense growth of trees, usually intermingled with which is a still denser growth of vines and creepers—one prickly cane in particular is known as the " lawyer " from the peculiar shape of its prickles—which in many places render these scrubs entirely unpassable without the assistance of a knife or tomahawk. These vines run to the tops of the highest trees, and, passing from one to the other, interlock and bind them in every direction, often assuming the appearance of vast ropes and cordage.

The appearance of a scrub is entirely tropical. The verdure is profuse and the colouring lovely. Near the bank of the creek or river, cabbage and other palms shoot up into the sky with only a few feathery-like leaves at the top. The huge fig-trees tower high over the lesser trees, and spread their vast limbs and dark green branches in every direction. The bunya and pine shoot upward far above the surrounding trees, and the huge red cedars with their vine-trellissed boles and branches are here and there encountered. Below the broad leaves of many a strange plant hides the view from the beholder, who slowly struggles through the mass of vines and creepers, bending here and twisting there to gain a passage. It requires no great stretch of the imagination to picture here and there the solemn arches of some vast cathedral. The whole scene is one full of interest, not altogether bereft of a sense of awe to him who sees it for the first time. If seen at early morning or about sunset, other sights and sounds attract the attention. The whole scrub seems full of life. Vast flocks of pigeons of a dozen varieties are busily eating the figs or berries, and cooing to each other the while. Cockatoos and parrots of lovely hues scream and chatter as they fly from limb to limb. Cat-birds, bell-birds, whip-birds, laughing jackasses, and a host of others, some with strange and discordant and others with merry and cheerful note, flash before the eye in every colour of the rainbow, and fill the air with their notes. On the ground, scrub turkeys, scrub wallabies, paddy-melons, and bandicoots cross one's path and bound out of sight; and here and there he catches a glimpse of a snake or iguana gliding quickly away. Such is a scrub at sunrise and sunset. But in the heat of the day all is still and quiet as a vast tomb, and he must be an unfeeling man who does not at such a time have a sense of the grand and sublime steal over him. The timber for the most part is of a different growth from that of the forest land. In short, no contrast could be drawn between two countries in different parts of the world which would be more striking than the characteristics of Queensland scrub and forest in those districts east of the main range. The blue gum and a few other forest trees may occasionally be met with in the scrub, grown to a gigantic size, but this is usually at the outskirts and near the forest land. Besides the valuable pines and the cedar, the beech, ash, and other merchantable timbers are found in the scrubs. But by far the larger number of trees are as yet considered of no value, although there can be no question but that many of them will yet be recognized as of use for the finer sorts of cabinet ware. Some of these woods are of very peculiar description. One known as the sassafras has a soft thick bark which emits a most pleasant odour. Another, the iron-wood, is, as its name indicates, so very hard as only to be cut when green, and then by the keenest axe; fortunately this tree never attains a large growth. Prominent in those scrubs where it grows is the bunya, which often attains a height of 200 feet. Many very beautiful scrub woods known only by the generic name of "scrub timber" are capable of receiving a high polish and are very beautiful. The myall grows in scrubs which take its name, more in the interior, and is not common on the coast; this wood is much used for stock-whip handles, and emits a pleasing fragrance when smartly rubbed with the hand. As a rule, the majority of scrub timbers quickly rot on being cut down, the stumps being easily got out after the third or fourth year; here also showing the difference between scrub and forest timber, the latter being of the most lasting description, and the stumps capable of resisting decay for a generation at least. Of course where vegetation is so profuse, no grass could be expected to grow; such in fact is the case, the only covering of the soil being the decayed leaves, where they have not been swept away by floods. Except for the thick growth of vines and creepers, and the profuse vegetation of all sorts, the wanderer might almost fancy himself stalking among the forest trees of Canada, and treading on the decaying leaves of the maple and the beech. There is also the same coolness in the air, for though it be the height of summer, so dense is the foliage overhead that the rays of the sun and the heat of the day are alike excluded. The writer recalls many a journey through these gorgeous though wearying Queensland scrubs, perchance on horseback, under the guidance of a faithful blackfellow, who with tomahawk in hand cuts away here and there the bushes and vines which stop up the almost undiscernible blackfellow's track, only to be distinguished by a slight notch in a tree or the twisted top of a bush. Following our conductor, sheath knife in hand, to cut any too attentive vines, sometimes on foot and sometimes on horseback, now descending into a creek of cool and clear water and anon climbing with difficulty the steep bank above, we travel on until by and by the dim light and cool atmosphere of the scrub is suddenly left behind and we emerge into the open forest with its bright green or brown burnt-looking grass and tall scraggy trees, the glare of a semi-tropical sun and the heat of a cloudless sky. But if it is hotter and less pleasant in the forest, the scene is more extensive and the road open, and the cautious progress of the scrub gives place to a swift canter.

Other denizens the scrub has more disagreeable than dangerous. We refer to the scrub leech and the tick. If

one has stopped for a few minutes in the scrub, he is almost
certain on arriving at the next camp to find a fine able-
bodied leech or two, bloated with blood, hanging on to some
part of his body, or perhaps he first discovers the presence
of these phlebotomists by finding his boot half full of blood.
They are perfectly harmless as a rule, most persons in
Queensland enjoying such robust health that they can
afford the loss of a little blood. Leeches are also very
plentiful in some water-holes in the forest, where sometimes
they attack the bather in such numbers as to become
really dangerous. Once, at a noontide camp, the writer in
company with his companions, bathed in a fine, clear, deep
water-hole, where they soon found their persons becoming
clotted with leeches; of course a retreat was at once
sounded and the blood-suckers wiped off before they had
attained much size. At first they are very small, some of
them almost as fine as hairs, but they will swell as large as
one's little finger. Speaking of the matter, one of our
party related an instance where two young men were
bathing on a run in the Moreton district subsequently to a
long ride after cattle. The day being hot, they remained
swimming a long time. Fortunately a friend riding up
noticed, what they had failed to observe, that their backs
were almost covered with leeches; they at once swam to
the bank, but it was only with assistance that they were
able to come out of the water, and on the leeches being
taken off them their bodies were covered in blood, one of
them fainting away before the blood was stopped. It is
always well to caution new arrivals of the danger to be
incurred from incautiously remaining too long in detached
water-holes without observing whether any leeches are in
the water, as, singular to say, one never feels their bite.
It is very amusing after bathing, or bogying, for that is

the colonial phrase borrowed from the blacks, in company with a "new chum," to see the look of horror and disgust that spreads over his face on emerging from the water to find three or four black, bloated leeches pendant from his person. But like many another thing, one soon becomes habituated to this, and looks with contempt on his former squeamishness.

The tick is a far more dangerous and painful parasite. There are two kinds of these in the scrub, the black and the bottle tick. The latter of these, as its name imports, is of some size, and can therefore be easily detected, being something like the tick found in sheep in England. But the black tick is so small as to be easily overlooked. It will probably be days after the latter has attacked one that it will be noticed, and by that time it will have eaten so deep into the skin as to make its removal a work of some difficulty. In this case great care must be taken not to sever the head from the body, for should that occur, a very painful inflammation will set in, not easily cured. A smart pull is always needed to remove them, and on this being effected considerable pain will be felt in the part, limited by the length of time during which the tick has been eating its way in. These pests are never fatal to mankind, but are frequently so to dogs and other animals. Singular to say, if a dog has once been bitten by ticks and had them picked off before their virus has had time for fatal consequences, it seems to become impervious to subsequent attacks; for, after recovering from the first effects, it is very unusual for it afterwards to succumb to them. Many a valuable dog has been lost in this way, and it is usual to search young ones daily for these vermin, when they have been anywhere likely to harbour them. Calves and colts often die from their attacks. The writer once saw a splendid "pocket" of fine grass which was entirely useless from the large number of ticks in the contiguous scrub, which made it a fatal pasture for any young cattle.

In an agricultural point of view the scrub land is nearly always to be preferred. Although costing much more than ordinary forest land to clear, yet it is so much richer, that very few would cultivate the latter when they could obtain the former. There are exceptions to this rule of course, but not in the East Moreton district to any extent. The Darling Downs and the rich flats on the Pioneer River are among the most prominent instances where forest or open land is preferred. But scrub land has this great drawback, it is nearly all subject to those floods which from time to time devastate the settled districts, not only of Queensland, but to a far greater extent those of the southern colonies. Every cloud has its silver lining, and we must not forget that these floods, coming as they do on an average every four or five years, fertilize the farms of the settlers, and, by leaving from one to three inches of alluvial deposit on the land, manure it in a way that could not otherwise be done without an enormous outlay. There are spots, however, where the current, instead of leaving a deposit of this nature, sweeps away the native soil, or perchance covers it with sand or gravel. But these places are but few, and with care can be avoided by the purchaser. Most parts of the world have more poor land than good, and even the Queensland scrubs are not all agricultural land. Some of them are sandy and others stony, and in all probability will remain under timber to the end of time.

We must not forget to mention that in the interior there are scrubs known as myall, brigalow, salt-bush, and other scrubs, according to the sort of wood of which they are for the most part composed. But these are beyond the reach of agriculture, and need no special notice. It is only the vine scrubs such as we have attempted to describe, growing near the coast, that will attract the attention of the settler.

The forest land, as being more common-place, needs less description than the scrub. As a rule, it is far less beautiful, being in fact usually monotonous and wearisome from its sameness and the prevailing greyish or brown tint of its foliage. In the East Moreton district the forest land is for the most part of very secondary quality and heavily timbered. Especially is this the case in the neighbourhood of Brisbane, where there is scarcely one good farm of forest land to be found. Great efforts have certainly been made to reclaim the forest in some of the settlements we have mentioned; but the only place where anything like a good farm of this sort is to be found is at the Bald Hills, and there the area of tolerable forest land is limited to a few farms. In fact, when speaking of forest land, it may be laid down as a rule that the heaviest-timbered land is the worst, and that the soil increases in value as the timber thins. Of course some swampy land will be found with few trees on it, but except in a very dry season few people would make the mistake of selecting that sort of country. Much of the country near the coast in East Moreton, and this remark will apply to the coast country to the North, is utterly worthless either for grazing or agriculture; being low, wet flats, either covered with a thin growth of a sort of rush, or with a shrub known as wallum. Other districts abound with low ridges and swampy gullies, on which grows a poor description of grass suitable only for cattle and horses, the timber being too thick and there being too much brushwood to fit it for sheep pastures. In the various settlements around Brisbane the larger portion of the forest lands have been purchased from Government, and much of it enclosed in paddocks. But as a rule this country is so very heavily timbered with the different gums, iron-bark, blood-wood, Moreton Bay ash, she-oak, &c., as to make the work of clearing far too heavy for the benefits to be expected from such soil. Hundreds of persons of limited capital ruined themselves in the earlier years of the colony in endeavouring to cultivate this sort of country, and their failure has had a very deleterious effect upon the growth of the colony. Had there been the same knowledge as to the whereabouts of agricultural land and the actual capabilities of the soil ten years since as now exists, many men who lost their all would be living in affluence, the population of the colony would be something like a quarter of a million, and Queensland would enjoy that high character to which its vast natural resources entitle it. But great blunders were made alike by Government and people, and the effects of these will long be felt.

CHAPTER III.

THE district around Brisbane though, as before stated, for the most part consisting of rather poor soil, has by the perseverance and industry of the settlers come to be studded with smiling homesteads and flourishing farms, vineyards, orchards, and gardens. Situated so near the metropolis, many of the farmers have entered into the dairy business, which has always been lucrative, and by their proximity to town have been enabled to enrich the naturally poor soil with manure from Brisbane. These poor soils are also excellently adapted for the growth of vines and fruit-trees, and this fact has been in every direction taken advantage of. The farmers on the Brisbane River, Oxley and Bulimba Creeks have grown maize and oats, English and sweet potatoes until lately, and are now almost to a man growing sugar-cane; several mills having been erected to crush their crops, while a floating mill and distillery has been built, which visits the outlying farms and receives their crops from the bank, thus saving the trouble and expense of punting. Owing to floods and frosts since this new state of things was inaugurated, the returns in this district have not been very high. The Inspector of Distilleries in his last Report gives the average return of sugar per acre in the Oxley district, which includes the Brisbane River, at 15 cwt., and in the Cleveland District, which includes the Bulimba plantations, at a little over 27½ cwt. In the Eagle Farm, German Station, Sandgate, and Bald Hill Districts, on the other hand, corn, oaten hay, and potatoes, are still the principal crops, while great attention is paid to dairying and the growth of fruit.

A ride from Brisbane to any of the last-named places cannot fail to be highly interesting. The neat houses of the settlers are almost always embowered in vineyards and orchards, and large plantations of pine-apples everywhere abound. Prominent among these horticultural decorations will be seen the gorgeous passion-fruit which here fruits prolifically, producing a very pleasant, tart fruit, creeping over fence, verandah, and roof, making the house a veritable bower, and forming a cool shield from the sun's rays. In the garden will be seen all the vegetables of an English garden growing beside melons of various sorts, sweet-potatoes, ginger, arrow-root, pine-apples, and various other tropical productions. The fruit-trees mingle in tropical redundancy of growth, showing among others the banana, loquat, grape-vine, custard-apple, granadilla, mulberry, peach, orange, lemon, citron, pomegranate, and guava—all yielding their fruit with the greatest readiness in this lovely climate. Nowhere probably can so many descriptions of fruits and plants be found growing in the same garden as are to be found in Queensland, the incomparable climate appearing to suit equally the productions of the temperate and the torrid zones. Under a judicious system of irrigation a garden in this favoured colony can be made to produce almost everything edible which grows in any part of the world. In consequence of the numerous gardens in its vicinity, Brisbane has now a most plentiful supply of fruit at extremely low prices.

E

A large quantity of pines and bananas are exported to
Sydney and Melbourne, besides much fruit sent to the
North where the settlements are not yet old enough to
supply themselves, and also to the Downs where the
climate is too cool to produce many tropical fruits, but
where the gooseberry, currant, apple, and pear, &c., can
be grown to advantage.

It has often been observed that Queensland is peculiarly
blessed among the Australian colonies, in the possession of
so large a number of navigable rivers. Of these four lie to
the south of Brisbane—the Logan, the Albert, the Pimpama, and the Coomera. All these are now lined with
thriving sugar plantations. A good many of these plantations have already mills erected, and from the excellent
returns from some of them—and these only horse-mills put
up at an expense of a few hundred pounds—there is every
reason to expect that this southern portion of East Moreton, usually known as the Logan District, will continue to
advance in importance and wealth. The average return of
186 acres of sugar, the whole crushed on the Logan in the
season of 1870 was 23¾ cwt. per acre. On the Albert
221 acres were crushed, with an average return of 27½ cwt.
On the Pimpama and Coomera the return was much less,
but only a very small acreage was crushed. As showing
the rapidity with which this industry is increasing in the
district, we may say that, while in 1869, 243 tons of sugar
were made, and 3345 gallons of rum distilled, in 1870,
602 tons of sugar and 14,224 gallons of rum were produced.
The land under sugar in this district is principally scrub,
except on the Albert, where fine alluvial flats, nearly clear
of timber, existed. Mr. Henry Jordan, for so long the able
agent of the colony in England, has a large plantation on
the Logan, where he had last season 45 acres under crop.

It certainly speaks well for the colony and Mr. Jordan's *bona fides* that, after retiring from the influential position he held in England, and after being instrumental in inducing so many people to settle in Queensland, he too should settle down as a sugar-planter, and invest his all in the colony. There is still a considerable quantity of good land open for selection in this district. But there, as elsewhere in East Moreton, the land most available for water carriage, including the frontage to the river, has already been alienated.

Lying to the east of the Logan Road is the township of Cleveland, situate on the shore of Moreton Bay, at a distance of twenty-two miles from Brisbane. This township, though having only a small population, was at one time intended as a rival to the capital as a shipping-port. A jetty was built at a considerable expense, but it was found the depth of water was too small at some considerable distance from the wharf to admit of these ideas being realized. Cleveland is now known principally as the place where sugar-growing was first practically tested in the colony. The Hon. Captain Hope, of Kilcoy station, purchased land and spent a very large sum in the growth and manufacture of sugar. From various reasons, principally, it was understood, through the incompetency of the person employed as sugar-boiler, the speculation was not at first successful, and for a season or two the plantation lay dormant. But the plucky investment of so much capital had directed public attention to the growth of cane, which it was proved at Cleveland could be brought to perfection in the colony. Of late years the plantation has been in full work, and in March, 1871, 165 acres were under cane on this plantation. Besides crushing his own cane Captain Hope crushes largely for the farmers of the neighbouring settlements: he has

also a distillery in connexion with the sugar-mill, which
last year turned out 6447 gals. of rum.   There are a few
other considerable sugar estates in this part of Moreton
Bay.   As a rule, the farms and plantations of this district
are cultivated in a style that does great credit to their
proprietors.

The Oxley Creek district is mostly rich scrub land, and
is occupied by men who having carved their farms out of
the dense primeval forest, are now mostly living in a state
of independence on lovely estates, where they have all the
necessaries, and many of the luxuries of life in abundance.

Passing now through Brisbane, the tourist wishing to
visit other portions of the district would pass the Bald
Hills, close to which is the South Pine River, spanned by
an excellent wooden bridge, and after a ride of four miles
over level country reach the North Pine River, a broad but
shallow stream, easily fordable except at high-water spring-
tides. These two rivers unite lower down, but even then the
stream can barely be said to be navigable, only the smallest
steamers being able to ascend for a few miles at high tide.
The country here begins to be more open, and consequently
more valuable.   On the upper part of the North Pine some
very excellent forest land, almost clear of timber, has,
since the passing of the Land Act of 1868, been thrown
open for selection. Large breadths of this are being put
under cane, which is likely to do well here, although, unlike
most other sugar districts, this is far above navigation.
Mills will probably soon be erected, and if so the district
around Samford will doubtless become an important sugar-
producing one.   At present, however, the principal returns
made by the settlers are from their cows and dairies, more
especially the latter.

Following the main Gympie Road the traveller reaches

the Caboolture River, at a distance of twenty miles from
the North Pine, through an undulating, heavily timbered
country, entirely unfitted for cultivation.   Six miles before
reaching the Caboolture, Stoney, or Burpengary Creek is
crossed.   On the tidal part of this creek are two or three
thriving sugar estates with mills on each.   One of these
comprises a portion of land formerly known as " The
German's Mistake," from the fact of its having been
settled on by those Moravian missionaries who came to
the colony in 1838, under the auspices of Dr. Lang.   These
zealous men proposed to form a cattle station here at one
time ; but after the settlement had been made it was
abandoned, we believe, in consequence of a scarcity of
water for the cattle.   Another station was formed some
miles further up the creek, which is yet held by some of
these missionaries and their descendants.

On the Caboolture are the plantations of Captain Whish,
Whish and Trevelyan, and Raff and Co.   These plantations are of considerable extent, and to Captain Whish is
due the honour of being the first person who practically
demonstrated that the growth and manufacture of sugar
could be made a financial success in Queensland.   It is
true that the Hon. Captain Hope was the pioneer in the
formation of a plantation, and Parliament has so recognized
him by passing an Act granting him 2000 acres of land
for the service thus rendered to the colony.   But as we
have before said, his attempts at manufacture were dead
failures, and many wiseacres were to be found who promul-
gated the idea through the press, that although Queensland would produce sugar-cane, yet from some peculiarity
of the climate the cane contained no sugar.   We may say
en passant that probably no new country has produced more
of that excellent and valuable class of people, vulgarly known

as " croakers," than has Queensland, and any progress she
has made has always been in the teeth of these people and their
prognostications. But the failure of the Cleveland plantation, and the heavy outlay there made, would have most likely
deterred any one else from embarking in the new enterprise
in the face of all these assertions, had not Captain Whish
just at the nick of time, when all was in doubt, proved the
falseness of these evil predictions by producing a fair crop of
sugar, which sold readily at 28*l.* to 32*l.* per ton. His outlay had been comparatively small on his plantation, everything having been effected with that economy and practical
knowledge of details, so requisite to success in a new enterprise; the crushing machinery was said to have been erected
for about 600*l.* Although not able to produce a high class
of sugars, something like two tons per acre of a very saleable
quality was produced, besides sufficient rum to cover working expenses. This very successful effort on so modest a
scale drew public attention more than ever to sugar-growing, and from that time dated the permanent establishment
of this lucrative industry in Queensland, which now bids
fair to become equal in extent, and far more remunerative
than squatting itself. We gladly pay this well-merited
tribute to Captain Whish as the real pioneer of successful
sugar-growing, the more readily from the fact, that his
leaning to Polynesian labour prevented him from becoming
popular among the farmers of East Moreton, who, when he
offered himself as a candidate for legislative honours some
time since, rejected him unanimously, he not receiving but
four or five votes in a constituency of more than as many
hundreds. The writer felt compelled at that time to oppose
his candidature, as believing Queensland to be fitted for a
white population, and desirous to see it settled by the teeming
masses of his own countrymen, rather than the coloured

races of the South Seas. Captain Whish has since been nominated to the Upper House, and the same measure which was meted to him has been given to his neighbour, Mr. G. Raff, another employer of and advocate for black labour. The people of East Moreton have thus twice shown their utter abhorrence of the Polynesian traffic, and their determination to do all in their power to put it down. Besides the plantations of these gentlemen there are two others of considerable extent in this neighbourhood, and many smaller ones are being brought into cultivation. As in many other places the good land here is a mere margin on the banks of the river and creeks, the outside land being of that description known as "coast-land," some of which is fairish grassland for cattle or horses, while more is utterly worthless for any purpose.

Some distance above the plantation referred to, at about the head of tidal water on the Caboolture, which is also sometimes spoken of as the Deception River, is a pleasantly situated pocket of very good forest land, buried amid the scrub, and known as Deadman's Pocket. As the story exhibits some characteristic incidents of white and black alike, it may be interesting to relate how this piece of land came by such a melancholy name; and if the reader will kindly fancy the story to be told while the low, swampy piece of country bordering the Gympie Road is being passed on the way to the next northern settlement, it will serve to relieve the tedium of the journey through this monotonous country.

Many years since, when this part of the country was almost uninhabited, and the scrub bordering the river was visited only by a few timber-getters for the sake of the pine and cedar with which it abounded, a party of four or five men were camped for this purpose on the north side

of the river.   Two of them, Peter Glynn and another,
crossed over to the south side for the purpose of looking
for timber to suit their purpose.   They were accompanied
by two blacks, one of whom was called Barlow.   On their
return towards their camp their road lay through this
pocket.   According to Glynn's account, they were marching in the following order:—Glynn was ahead, the blackfellows next, and his mate behind.   The latter was armed
with a gun, while Glynn had a pistol.   Contrary to his
advice and wish, his mate constantly amused himself by
pointing his gun at the blacks and pretending to fire at
them.   This conduct and some expressions he made use of
at length exasperated them so much that they determined
on revenge.   Glynn appears to have had some dread of
this, for he cautioned his mate to cry out if the blacks
made any aggressive, movement.   This caution was un-
heeded, for suddenly both blacks sprang on Glynn and
struck him on the head and hands with their nullah-
nullahs—short, small clubs of very heavy wood.   So sudden
was this attack, that from the blows he received, Glynn
was unable to draw his pistol, and called on his mate to
fire.   Had he done so, he could easily have wounded or
killed one of the blackfellows; but, although the cause of
the outbreak, this man was too frightened to make any
movement, but actually stood agape with his gun in his
hands during the whole fray.   Glynn ultimately managed
to draw his pistol and fired at Barlow, inflicting a terrible
wound in his side.   The savage leapt, according to Glynn's
account, at least ten feet into the air, and when Glynn
was hoping to see him fall dead, he again rushed at him,
and, with his companion, dealt him such blows as brought
him to the ground.   In endeavouring to wrench the pistol
from his grasp, they struck him so severely over his hands

as to break them both, and, thinking him to be dead, left
him to attack his cowardly mate. This man actually
allowed the blacks to walk up to him and seize his gun
before he made the least sign. Then waking as from a
trance, he turned and fled for the scrub. A dead gum-tree
lay in his path, which still lies in the same place; in
jumping over this he fell, and the blacks, who were close
at his heels, brained him with the butt of his own gun.
They then disappeared with haste into the scrub. Glynn,
after lying as still as possible for some time in deadly fear
of the return of the blacks, finding they did not again
appear, essayed to beat a retreat from the fatal scene.
Although his companions were camped within a mile and
almost within cooey, his terror was too great to permit
him to go towards them, as it was in the same direction
in which he had seen the blacks enter the scrub. Twelve
miles from where he lay was the cattle-station of the
German missionaries already alluded to, called Flagstone,
and to this place the poor wounded wretch determined in
his desperation to proceed. He was in a pitiable plight
for travelling. Both his hands were broken and useless;
he had many severe cuts on his head, besides other wounds;
and, worse than all, in the fray his moleskin trousers had
come down about his feet, and become so entangled that
he was unable to walk, while the condition of his hands
precluded his remedying this accident. He was, therefore,
obliged to crawl on his elbows and knees, and thus he
actually made his way through scrubs and bush, over
swamp and hill to Flagstone. It took him no less than
seven days to accomplish this, which, incredible as it may
sound, he did without a morsel to eat, but fortunately
without any lack of water. When he reached the station,
which was only a very small one, the lad who first saw him

was horrified at the apparition of a creature bearing little resemblance to a human being, covered with blood and dirt and haggard beyond description. From having travelled over a deal of gravel and quartz-ridges, his legs and arms were quite raw, and his track could be traced for miles by his blood. Careful treatment gradually brought him round, and he was ultimately restored to health.

On these facts being reported in Brisbane, the native troopers were sent out to punish the blacks. Reaching the neighbourhood, they carefully concealed their presence until they had discovered the camp of the blacks in a pocket near the river. This was some time after the murder had been committed, and apparently the blacks had forgotten all about it. They were met from all the district round to hold a corrobboree. Various tribes were represented, and among others was a black-boy (the blacks who work on a station or farm are always, like the blacks in the Southern States, called boys) from Flagstone itself, who had received liberty for a few days to attend the corrobboree. While the glee was at its highest, suddenly a deadly volley was poured into their midst from all sides. A rush was made for the scrub by those unharmed or only slightly wounded, and the black troopers rushed in, despatching the wounded and then massacring the babes or piccaninnies, and burning and destroying all the mi-mis or huts, together with dilly-bags, spears, boomerangs, nullahs, and yellamans or shields. Twenty-two blacks of all ages and both sexes were killed, but unfortunately the murderers, one if not both of them, were unhurt. Among those who escaped was poor Larry, who had gone to the corrobboree in all the splendour of new crimson shirt and white moleskin trowsers, but who presented himself next day at Flagstone minus clothes, and covered with

scratches and wounds obtained in his hasty flight at night
through the scrub. Barlow lived to recount his prowess
and show his wound for many years, and was often hired
by the settlers about Breakfast Creek in after-days to do
odd jobs of wood-cutting, &c. Like all his race, he had
no objection to give the history of the whole transaction to
any one with whom he was on intimate terms. He was
gathered to his fathers at length; but Larry yet survives
to depict the horrors of that midnight onslaught. Peter
Glynn, as if to exemplify the fact that a man may survive
danger and hardship almost miraculously to meet his death
afterwards in the simplest way, was drowned by the up-
setting of a boat in Moreton Bay some years after these
events transpired.

It may not be inappropriate to state here, that under no
circumstances should white men, when travelling on foot
with blacks, walk in front. Why, we cannot say, but it is
certain that if this caution is not observed, the blackfellow
has an almost irresistible impulse to slay the person who
thus offers his back to the blow. When engaged in hand-
to-hand conflict blackfellows always wound each other in
the back and never in front, and perhaps some association
of ideas induces them to practise on the white man. We
remember on one occasion a blackfellow in our own
employ, and who possessed finer intellectual qualities than
the majority of whites, when travelling in the scrub with
a white man, suddenly in great agitation desiring the
stranger to go behind him, for said he, " Supposing you
go on first time, directly me killum you along a road."
His whole manner when making this curious statement
was hurried and excited, and from an intimate knowledge
of his character we have no doubt that it had required the
exercise of an amount of self-command quite foreign to the

ordinary black to enable him to spare the life of this white
man.   Being asked at the house afterwards, what induced
him to act so, he was unable to give any definite reason,
but strongly advised that no white man should ever " walk
before blackfellow." I have journeyed often with this
man, eating and sleeping at the same fire, alone sometimes
for days together, and believe him to be more trustworthy
than the average run of white servants.

   Leaving the Caboolture by the Northern or Gympie
Road, the road, as already indicated, lies through a poor
and monotonous country for a distance of over thirty miles.
On the way are passed those singular mountains known
as the Glass-houses, which suddenly rise from the level
country in some cases, and in others from ridges of greater
or lesser height.   Their bold, bluff appearance is very striking when suddenly approached from the thick forest, probably the first sight being caught of one through the
branches of the trees towering on high in the blue heavens,
like some huge castle.   Some of these mountains rise
precipitously on all sides and others gradually taper to a
peak from their base.   The ascent of such of them as can
be scaled well repays the traveller, who sees stretched
before him the heaving forest for many a mile, the bright
waters of the bay to the east, and the blue mountains of the
range to his left.   Away to the north the eye surveys the
various bays and indentations of the coast, with other
ranges all clothed in the sombre-coloured forest foliage.
Close by him he will be almost startled by the presence of
many others of these huge mountains, closing in the view
here and there.   It requires no great stretch of the imagination to fancy these frowning and silent sentinels of antiquity
to be the impersonations of the gods and giants of past
ages, looking down in silent grandeur on the white intruder

on their everlasting repose. Perhaps from few places in the world are more extensive views to be obtained uniting more of the sublime and beautiful than from the top of one of these Glass-houses. In future years, when the country is more populous and its beauties come to be better appreciated, we doubt not that troops of excursionists will climb these hills and drink in, as we often have, the glories of their grand and lovely prospects. As might be supposed these mountains are not without their traditions, and the blackfellows of the neighbourhood tell many a quaint legend of love and battle connected with them. Close to the Glass-houses is a little settlement with two or three houses for the accommodation of travellers.

The next settlement reached is on the Mooloolah, and owes its existence almost entirely to the growth of the sugar interest. Many considerable plantations have been started here on the borders of the creek on some excellent open country, which however has the disadvantage of being occasionally flooded. Two or three plantations have also been started on the Mooroochy, a river a few miles further to the north, the watershed of which forms the northern boundary of the Moreton District. All these settlements are too young to allow us to speak of any returns, but from the character of the soil it may be anticipated that very satisfactory results will crown the labours of the settlers. There is on the Mooloolah a plain of about nine miles in extent, of excellent land nearly free from timber, it being possible to plough many acres in one piece without any preparatory clearing. This occurs also on the Albert and to some extent on the North Pine, and is more common further north. But why we draw particular attention to this piece of land is to refer to a peculiarity in the surface of the land here and in many other parts of the country.

This is known as "melon-hole" country, and presents a surface as if eaten out by some terrestrial small-pox. Nothing is seen like a smooth solid surface, but the whole is broken into little mounds of all sizes and shapes, while the intervening hollows are of greater or less depth and breadth, but all alike covered with grass. On some of these melon-hole flats it is possible to ride a horse accustomed to that sort of country without much danger at a good pace. In other places the holes are too deep and wide to admit of any but the most painstaking progress being made; and again, in other places, like some of the plain in question, they are too deep and rugged to enable any sort of riding but a series of jumps from hill to hill. Of course in wet weather these holes are full of water, which being retained for a much longer time than it would be on a plain surface renders this country wet and unfit for pasture, except in a dry season. Nothing satisfactory is known as to the formation of this melon-hole country, which is greatly disliked by all colonists. It is only found on flats, and was most likely originated by the action of water on those places. But why if some damp flat lands have become melon-holey, others have not, it would probably puzzle a philosopher to decide. Graziers and farmers have alike execrated this honey-combed country, and it was left for the sugar grower to think of utilizing any of it. Many a poor new chum, careering wildly after a mob of cattle, a kangaroo, or dingo, has been brought to grief by his horse turning a somersault among the melon-holes over which he has incautiously allowed him to gallop. On the Mooloolah plain many of these holes were three and four feet deep and strong bullock ploughs were needed to break down the hills and bring the land to a level surface. If this process was to some extent slow and costly, yet the comparative

absence of trees to be grubbed out still left the advantage
with the owner of this land over scrub or forest, while it is
considered to be eminently adapted to the growth of the
cane.

The country about Mooloolah and Mooroochy was first
opened by timber-getters when this part of the country
was a *terra incognita* and strange tales were told of the
bloodthirstiness of the natives. Many years since, in the
penal times, a convict accompanied some officials from
Sydney to the district on a botanizing tour. He noticed
the enormous cedar-trees growing in the scrubs, and wisely
thinking the possession of this knowledge would be of
importance some time, kept his own counsel on his return
to the settlement, as Brisbane was then called. In due
course of time came freedom and the end of the penal
period. After some time, having saved sufficient means
to provide an outfit for himself and a mate, he started off
with his wife, also a convict, for the cedar scrubs, which
were to him a veritable mine of wealth. Schooner after
schooner visited the Mooloolah, and loaded the rafts of
cedar he and his party floated down to the river's mouth,
and had he not been addicted to the vice of intoxication,
so common among his class, he might have become a
wealthy man. But every schooner in coming to load
cedar, was sure to bring, besides the requisite rations and
stores, many cases of brandy and kegs of rum, so that the
loading of each vessel was the signal for a prolonged
saturnalia, in which whites and blacks alike mingled; so
that what should have been a mine of wealth only furnished
means for repeated debauches. To such an extent was
this carried, that we have heard it asserted that now and
then a cargo of cedar, worth many hundred pounds, would
be entirely forgotten in the reckoning kept by the wife

who, like her husband, was no scholar, but had a large
capacity for drinking. In course of time other persons of
a different character settled down at Mooloolah in the
same trade and a settlement sprung up, giving occupation
to a small steamer which ran regularly between Brisbane
and this place every week.

This man and his wife were specimens of the "old
hand" of a very common type. We shall never forget
first seeing this woman in a state of intoxication with a
bottle of rum in her hand, treating indiscriminately
bullock-drivers and blacks. Her mouth full of obscenity
and blasphemy, with scarcely any attribute of the female
sex remaining, she struck us as being one of the most
loathsome and repulsive sights we had ever seen. The
female convict of Moreton Bay was at best the lowest and
most debased of the worst strata of society, and this
woman fully bore out the idea of intense degradation and
utter abandonment conveyed in the term, female convict.
It is hardly possible to over-estimate the moral contami-
nation arising from constant intercourse with people of
this class. The calm observer cannot but detect the moral
virus which has impregnated colonial manners from the
presence of these people. Some year or two after we saw
her, this woman shot dead with a gun, in cold blood, a
young man, a bullock-driver at Mooloolah, with whom she
had been on improper terms of intimacy, from a feeling of
jealousy. She stood her trial in Brisbane, but there having
been no witness of the tragedy, by some legal quibble she
got off. Soon after this the Gympie diggings broke out,
and both husband and wife joined in the rush. He had a
good claim, out of which he might easily have saved a few
hundreds, but the same habit overpowered them; while
the poor wretch, his wife, was glad to seek in the rum

bottle that insensibility denied her in sleep, when, as she averred, the ghost of the murdered man always stood before her, making her life a constant horror, so that she wished she had been hung.

A couple of miles from the mouth of the Mooroochy, in the open sea, is a small rocky island, called by the blacks Manumbah, connected with which they have a very pretty superstition. They tell you that this island is sacred to two lovely females, "young-fellow gins," who reside here all the day in a cave, of which only they know the entrance. For their food they come across every night to the main land in a canoe, and no blackfellow is permitted to see, much less molest them. They live in a state of perpetual youth, and as no black-fellow would think of landing on their island even if in danger of his life, they live for ever in a state of seclusion and privacy. We were never able to learn why or for what purpose those vestal virgins are supposed to lead this romantic existence.

East Moreton, which terminates at the Mooroochy River, ninety miles north of Brisbane, is by far the most important district of the colony, and must for many years, if not always, remain so. It returns seven members to parliament distributed as follows: East Moreton two, Brisbane three, South Brisbane one, and Fortitude Valley one. There has for years past been an agitation to amend the representation, it being felt that this important district should be more fully represented, and both parties have pledged themselves to carry a measure of this sort. A Bill for this purpose was actually introduced last year, which proposed to divide this large constituency into three divisions, bounded northerly by the Logan, Caboolture and Mooroochy Rivers respectively, and giving to the two Southern divisions two members, and one to the

r

Northern. Some measure of this nature must doubtless soon be passed.[1]

There is little gold-digging in this district. Five or six years since a small "rush" took place to a place at the head of Ennogerra Creek, some twenty miles from Brisbane, and a little gold was got, principally in small nuggets. Lately a reef said to contain gold has been discovered by some men in the employ of a Brisbane solicitor, who proposed forming a company to work it. Gold has frequently been found in minute quantities about Spring Hill in the city of Brisbane. We remember that more than eight years ago considerable excitement was created in Brisbane by the discovery of a few "colours" of gold in the gizzard of a duck reared on Spring Hill. Shafts have been sunk in many places there without finding gold, or more than the mere colour.

[1] In 1872 an Electoral Act was passed, dividing the colony into forty-two electorates, each returning one member to the Assembly. Of these, nine are from East Moreton.

CHAPTER IV.

WEST MORETON is divided from East Moreton by the Woogaroo Creek and Brisbane River and runs westerly to the Dividing Range. Its southern boundary, like that of East Moreton, is the range bounding the colony of New South Wales; on the north it is bounded by another range known as D'Agular's Range. As in East Moreton, the most densely populated portion is the central, lying about its chief town Ipswich.

This prettily situated town has rather suffered a decadence since the completion of the Southern and Western Railway, and has lost much of its prestige and importance. At one time it was a worthy rival of Brisbane, and it still has an equal weight in the politics of the colony, having together with West Moreton, six members in the House, who have, up to the present, invariably been Ipswich men, who, by their united action, have earned the titles of the Ipswich Phalanx, or the Ipswich Clique, according as they are spoken of by friends or opponents.[1] Ipswich is situated twenty-five miles inland, from Brisbane, on the road to the Darling Downs, and fifty miles by the Brisbane River and Bremer Creek, the latter being the stream on which the town is situated, up which boats have to ascend at high tide about sixteen or eighteen miles. The road is an

---

[1] The influence of Ipswich has been lessened by the new Electoral Law.

excellent one for Queensland, and fast coaches travel each
way every day except Sunday. But the visitor who wishes
to see the most for his money will go to Ipswich by water,
a steamer plying each way once a day, as the tides suit.
Leaving Brisbane pretty views are had of the Parliamentary
Buildings, barracks, gaol, and other public buildings, and
many suburban residences, half hidden by foliage, meet the
view.   As reach after reach of the river is passed, flourishing farms, banana groves, cotton fields, orange groves,
sugar plantations, and sugar mills are passed in rapid succession.   By-and-by the confines of West Moreton are
reached, and a very fine view is had of the Lunatic Asylum
at Woogaroo. This establishment is on a considerable
scale and does great credit to the humanity of the colony.
Sorry we are to have to add that in no part of the world,
except among the Spiritualists and Spirit Rappers of the
United States, is there greater need of an establishment of
this sort than in Queensland, where the drinking habits of
the people and the isolation of the shepherd's life united
prove fruitful of insanity.

Passing Woogaroo, known also as Goodna, which is a
pretty little village on the Brisbane and Ipswich Road,
with two churches and a school, the steamer soon reaches
Redbank.   By this time the character of the country is
changed.   Instead of the deep rich scrubs and fruitful
farms of Boggo, Oxley, Indooripilly, and the Seventeen-
mile Rocks, open forest lands are seen, and the curious
stranger will notice that the banks of the river are deeply
fringed with a thick growth of the castor-oil plant, which
has probably been propagated by a few seeds left at some
season of flood.   Redbank is noted for its coal-mines, the
property of Campbell and Co., which for years supplied the
coals for the steam-vessels which visited the port of Bris-

bane. Other coal-pits are now worked in this district, which compete with these mines. The method of obtaining the coals is very inexpensive, as they are run out in trucks from the side of a hill on a tramway and emptied into shoots, from which they are easily passed to the holds of the lighters and steamers. West Moreton is rich in coal-mines, and is looked on by many as likely yet to become a great manufacturing district. In fact some years since it was proposed to start a cotton factory in Ipswich, and as the staple is grown in the neighbourhood, and during the cotton famine in England thousands of cotton operatives settled in Queensland, there was every reason to anticipate a reasonable amount of success. But, as in nearly every other new undertaking, capital was wanting. It was proposed to raise the requisite funds by the formation of a company with 1l. shares; but the opposition of some influential persons threw cold water on the affair. There can be little doubt, however, that with the advantages offered by a heavy tariff, and the natural facilities of the district, both cotton and woollen mills will yet be started. At this time there is neither cotton, woollen, or paper mill in the colony although the raw material for each abounds, as well as a ready and certain market.[2]

There is at Redbank one of those manufactories that bid fair to add very largely to the wealth of this great pastoral country. Towns and Co. have here a meat-preserving establishment, at which in 1870 over 35,000 sheep were preserved. This is not by any means so large a quantity as some other places have preserved. The rapid growth of this business in nearly all parts of southern and central Queensland promises to reanimate the pastoral interest ere

[2] Another, and we believe, a more successful attempt has recently been made at establishing a cotton factory at Ipswich.

long, and to prove as great a boon as was the introduction of boiling-down establishments.[3]

After passing Redbank the junction of the Brisbane and Bremer is soon reached. Before this, several shallow places in the river have to be crossed which require all the skill of the steersman safely to pass. The Bremer is very narrow, being more of the nature of a canal than a river, just admitting of the passage of the class of steamers built expressly for this navigation. So narrow is the creek at Ipswich, that the steamers have actually to be turned before reaching the wharf in a wider part than ordinary, hence called the Basin. On reaching the wharf the first sight which attracts the attention of the stranger is the fine iron railway bridge, on piers, which crosses the river just beyond at a considerable height.

Ipswich, which delights in being characterized as " the head of navigation," was before the construction of the railway a very busy thriving town. In those days it was no unusual thing to see from a dozen to a score bullock drays standing in the street at once, either unloading the ponderous bales of wool—the clip, perhaps, of some station 400 to 500 miles in the interior—or loading stores for the next year's supply of some far-off station or country store. It by no means followed that these bullock-teams were owned by the person whose property they transported. As a rule this was not the case. By far the greater number were owned by the drivers themselves, or some one by whom

---

[3] This prediction is now more than realized. Cattle have at least doubled in value, and a tide of prosperity has set in for graziers that apparently has no limit. Since meat preserving has become fully established as a regular manufacture, cattle stations have become a most desirable and lucrative property. Cattle that ten years ago sold for 25s. to 30s. are now worth 90s. to 100s.

they were employed, who made "carrying" his business, and more likely than not resided, when at home, in Ipswich itself. There were hundreds of these teamsters, or as they are always called bullock-drivers, who, if not resident as married men in Ipswich, spent the bulk of their money and procured all their varied and expensive requisites there. Hence the continuous arrival of these teams was a great source of wealth and prosperity to the town. Situated at the point where the land carriage terminated, not only did the town itself rapidly grow in importance and population, but its storekeepers amassed wealth and spread the ramifications of their business into every part of Southern Queensland. From 1861 to 1866 the population had more than doubled, while the enterprising and energetic character of its inhabitants—in this respect far superior to the more sleepy people of Brisbane, who have never been able entirely to shake off that stagnation peculiar to penal settlements—gave the town a commanding influence in political matters. But a great change has taken place now in every respect but that last mentioned.

The completion of the railway to Dalby and Warwick, which was to have done such great things for Ipswich, has operated in precisely the opposite way to that which was contemplated. The growth of the town has been retarded, business has fallen off; in consequence of the stopping of the carrying-trade by bullock-teams population has decreased, and in many of the streets the grass grows where once was bustle and activity. In older countries the introduction of railways, although annihilating some branches of industry, developes others which more than compensate for this first loss; but this has not been the case in Queensland. The dominant party has so managed affairs that the railway has lessened business and decreased

the population. Their interest is best served by the absence of population, or, what amounts to the same thing,
they think so, and the result is that the people of Ipswich
have to suffer under two evils—the cessation of business
and a largely increased taxation to meet the interest on
the railway debt. One great benefit this state of things
has produced, it has forced large numbers of people who
were settled in the town, and were consumers rather than
producers, to take up land and commence farming. That
this large increase in the agricultural population will
ultimately effect a most beneficial change on Ipswich
itself there is no doubt; but the benefits arising from the
spread of agriculture, though the most permanent, are of
far slower growth in a new country than those arising
from other industries. The land has to be cleared, fenced,
and brought into cultivation. In the case under consideration not only had those preliminaries to be gone
through, but experiments had to be made as to a suitable
and remunerative crop. Unfortunately there was, so lately
as 1866, an almost universal and insane objection to
agricultural pursuits, and the man who engaged in them
was looked on as a sort of lunatic, harmless to every one
but himself and family, if he chanced to have one. All
these obstacles had to be overcome before much farming
was done in West Moreton. Grim necessity bore down
prejudice, and the excellence of the soil and the in-
domitable perseverance of the Anglo-Saxon has done the
rest. In 1863 the value of cotton grown in Queensland
was 3056*l*., in 1872 it amounted to 59,774*l*., of which the
larger part was from West Moreton. Experiment has
shown that this crop, in favour of which one had only to
speak a few years since to be laughed at for his pains, is
well adapted to the soil and climate of this district, and it

is now universally grown. There are some large plantations, but the greater part is grown by farmers holding
from 40 to 320 acres of land, on which the work is principally done by the farmer and his family. As in every
other part of the colony, a large proportion of the settlers
in this district are Germans, whose descendants in the next
generation become entirely absorbed in the English population, in a great majority of cases not being able even to
speak their mother tongue.

Ipswich contains many good buildings. It has an
excellent grammar-school, which until lately was the
only one in the colony. It has several large and handsome churches, with a hospital, school of arts, &c. Being
built on a limestone formation, it is much dryer and
cleaner in the wet season than most Queensland towns,
but has the drawback of being very hot in the summer
season; there is, however, nearly always a fine breeze
blowing on the surrounding hills. The railway buildings
are handsome and roomy, while the business done in them
is ridiculously small. It is no very unusual thing for a
train to come in or depart with a solitary passenger, while
four or five is about the ordinary number in each train.
In the wool season a considerable freight comes down, but
the policy of the Government in keeping up a high rate of
charges does not tend to promote business. It sometimes
happens when grass and water are plentiful that the bullock-
drays bring their loading direct to Ipswich, being able
to compete with the enormous rates charged on the railway.[4] Perhaps our English readers will hardly believe

⁴ Since the above was penned a vast change for the better has taken
place. The discovery of the Queensland Tin Field, the great improvement in every department of business, and, last but not least, a change
of government and government policy has wrought a happy change

that in a country producing the most excellent and durable timber in the world, Government saw fit to order all the station-houses of the English ironfounders; yet such is the fact. The large and expensive stations on this line, preposterously large for the business to be transacted in them for many years to come, were all made in England and sent out to the colony to be put up. In fact, one large station is still lying in pieces, the Government having been apparently unwilling to outrage public opinion further by putting it up at the time when thousands who could have built it were almost starving in the colony. Thus has this magnificent colony been mercilessly overweighted by its rulers, and the people whom the railway threw out of work were heavily taxed to pay the interest on a debt contracted for an almost useless line. Had the money which this line cost been spent as far as possible in the colony, the mere circulation of so much capital—the life-blood of a young country with such vast resources as this—would have gone far to have enabled the people to endure the extra taxation necessary; but the engineers and others interested in the matter took care that not one penny should be spent in Queensland that could by any means be laid out with their English friends. Hence the fine iron station and bridge at Ipswich were constructed in England, while the soil teems with timber scarcely less durable than iron, and far more suitable to the climate; the only connection between the people of Queensland and the major part of the two or three millions their railway has cost being the 300,000*l.* they have yearly to pay in the shape of interest. Most of the loan reached

also in railway matters, and we believe the railway traffic now pays not only the working expenses, but also the interest on the railway debt.

Queensland, not in cash, but iron castings. Even the navvies employed on the line were brought with them by the English contractors as a portion of the plant to be removed on the completion of the work. As to their wages while in the colony, the understrappers of the contractors obliged the men to spend their money for the most part in their "shanties,"·and not with any outsiders. Thus a few railway men were enabled to enrich themselves at the public expense, and when the line was completed left the colony with large fortunes. The public, awaking to the fact that the railway loan had not been judiciously expended, visited their wrath upon the Minister of Works, who, although a very able man and entirely free from any imputations on his own character, was obliged to resign his office and retire for a time into private life.[5]

In looking at the Ipswich Railway Station one cannot but compare the policy of Queensland with that of the United States. There, the idea is strictly worked out of opening up intercommunication on the cheapest and most economic principle. While lines of rail are laid down with unparalleled rapidity, very little attention is paid to the beauty or elegance of the stations. Even in the older and wealthier cities this holds good. New York itself, when last visited by the writer, had not a more pretentious station than that at Ipswich. The Hudson River Railway Company, one of the best paying lines in the States, were content to carry on their large business in a building much inferior in appearance to this one, to be used for the accommodation of a dozen daily passengers and a few parcels of merchandize.

As the history of the colony is, in a great measure, con-

---

[5] This gentleman, the Hon. Arthur Macalister, has since returned again to Parliamentary life, and is now Premier of the colony.

nected with this railway, and the policy which has retarded
its growth gave rise to its construction, we have endeavoured
to lay before our readers a sketch of the whole transaction,
and the policy which originated, and for several years rendered it almost useless.

The gold-fields of West Moreton are not extensive or
rich as yet, but in many places several men have been able
for years past to obtain a subsistence, and sufficient inducement to cause them to cling to the various places in which
they are located. These small "rushes" would appear to
indicate that considerable gold deposits, most probably in
reefs rather than alluvial ground, will yet be found in
this portion of the colony.

In 1863 the Darling Downs squatters, a powerful and
compact aristocracy, induced the Ipswich party to join
them in urging the building of a railway from that town
to Toowoomba, the principal town on the Downs. Various
arguments were made use of to overcome the objections to
this measure of different parties. The squatters of the
Maranoa and Warrego were told that it would at once
cheapen the cost of carriage—always a matter of grave
importance to the outside settlers—and that ultimately the
line would be carried on to them. To the Ipswich and
West Moreton people it was pointed out that the making a
railway through the district, of which Ipswich would be
the terminus, would give employment to all classes of
labour, would increase the present business of the town,
and tend to consolidate it by drawing to it the trade of the
Dawson and Burnett, which now went to Rockhampton
and Maryborough.

On the townspeople of Toowoomba, Drayton, and Warwick it was urged, that the opening up of the splendid
agricultural country on the Downs by a railway, was

the proper and rational method of settling a thoroughly
agricultural population on these unrivalled lands, and that
by this means it might be expected that the same results
would follow there as had been witnessed in Illinois, and
other western states of America. The same picture, with
some slight additions, was held up to the gaze of the people
of Brisbane and East Moreton. To them it was said that
the ultimate destiny of the colony was undoubtedly to
become an agricultural one. That the numerous navigable rivers and creeks which everywhere open communication between the rich scrubs lining their banks and
the metropolis; the admirable character of much of the
soil east of the Main Range, as well as the unequalled
fertility of the Darling Downs, only awaiting the plough
of the settler to become the granary of Queensland, and
a source of untold wealth, all indicated that if only
means of travel were provided farmers would flock to the
colony by thousands; the facilities afforded by a cheap
railway would cause the lands now occupied by sheep to
pass into their hands; and that before many years a sufficient quantity of wheat and other cereals would be
grown in Queensland, not only for home use but for
export. It was further pointed out how greatly this would
enhance the wealth of the port and town of Brisbane,
while the addition of so large a number of settlers to the
population, would tend to increase the political power of
the agricultural party in Parliament, now feebly represented
by the two East Moreton members.

We may remark here that at this time the splendid
country in the north-west of the colony, was almost if not
entirely unknown. Even the Peak Downs were but little
known, while the splendid grazing country on the Barcoo
and Thompson, and other rivers in that direction, were

without a hoof of cattle or sheep. These districts are now known to be far superior even to the Darling Downs for grazing purposes; but in 1861 and 1862 many were in the habit of regarding the Darling Downs as the most valuable section of country in the whole Australias. Were these lands turned to the use which was contemplated when this railway was proposed, their contiguity to the seaboard would have indeed rendered them one of the most valuable districts not only in Australia, but in the whole empire or the wide world.

Prior to this railway agitation there had been a company formed for constructing a wooden tramway from Brisbane to the Downs. There can be little doubt but that this plan was much more suitable to the requirements and resources of the colony than the more ambitious and expensive railway. But various interests, in particular that of Ipswich, were opposed to it, and the idea of a tramway was abandoned, and the promoters made a heavy loss. The arguments which had been used in favour of the railway were sufficient to secure the votes of all the southern members, but those of Brisbane and East Moreton. In Queensland, from the first, it has been the custom to view every question in a mere parochial light. Perhaps, in this instance, it was a sufficient reason for the Brisbane members to oppose this measure because it was likely to benefit Ipswich, just as the latter town usually opposes any measure favourable to the former. The Brisbane men could scarcely have foreseen the underhand and deceptive means by which the building of this road would be made to retard instead of increase the settlement of population. Of course, the northern members, of whom unfortunately at that time there were three less than at present, opposed the bill, but by some means on a tie-vote the Speaker, who was member for Wide Bay—

a district entirely opposed to the railway—was induced to give it his support, and thus the initiative was taken in the matter. The following session, 1862-63, the southern members who had at first opposed the railway, now that it was commenced, gave their support to votes for a larger loan for its completion from Ipswich to Toowoomba.

It is not our intention, nor would it be interesting to our readers, to give a minute account of the legislative action that followed. Vote after vote was taken, and at first, through the preponderating influence of Mr. Herbert, the first Premier of the colony—now Under-Colonial Secretary —and subsequently through the exertions of Mr. Macalister, who afterwards rose to the same position, the line has been extended from Toowoomba westward to Dalby, a distance of 105 miles from Ipswich, and southerly to Warwick, near the New South Wales border, a distance of sixty-five miles further. To close the mouths of the northern members it was found necessary, also, to vote enough money for a short line from Rockhampton to Westwood, a distance of only thirty miles, with a promise of a further extension of this otherwise perfectly useless work at some future time. Besides this an expensive jetty was built at Bowen, which is nearly as great a waste of money as the Westwood Railway.[6]

As the whole history of the rapid decline of the colony of Queensland in public estimation is closely connected with its railway policy, we felt it necessary to point out how and why that policy originated. We will now proceed to show why the construction of a railway by a young and vigorous colony should have proved so detrimental to its

---

[6] The Southern Railway is now nearly completed between Brisbane and Ipswich, and the Northern is being carried farther into the interior. A line is also being surveyed from Maryborough to Gympie which must ultimately be carried through to Brisbane.

prosperity as this undoubtedly did for many years. At the first blush it would appear as if no measure could have been more advisable. Certainly the arguments adduced in favour of it were sound and judicious, and had the promises implied in them been fulfilled the result would have been satisfactory. But so far from this being the case, the policy of the then colonial government in reference to the land and emigration questions—of which this railway was to have been only a portion—was up to the year 1868 most unfortunate for the colony itself, and for that portion of the British public which was induced to emigrate, wholly and entirely unsatisfactory and misleading. It was a repetition on too large and tragic a scale of the live Rocky Mountain Buffalo humbug recounted by Barnum in his Autobiography. Just as in that case the people of New York were induced to visit Hoboken in thousands to see these animals, and after looking at a few half-starved yearlings returned home too ashamed to warn their neighbours of the nature of the swindle, so by the false promises put into the mouth of Mr. Jordan were tens of thousands of our countrymen and women enticed to leave their homes on the pretence of obtaining a free grant of thirty acres " of the best land in the colony." Let us not be misunderstood ; it was not Mr. Jordan who was to blame in this matter. It was well understood when he left the colony that the lands adjacent to the railway should be thrown open for selection ; that in fact the emigrant should be allowed with his land order in his pocket to travel over those lovely Downs and select his land from a large parcel which government was pledged to have surveyed in blocks of 10,000 acres ready for settlement. Not only Mr. Jordan, but the people in all the towns of the colony, and the very few settled on the land near these towns as gardeners—there was scarcely such a thing as a farm in the colony at this time—fully anticipated that the promises made in the House and apparently fulfilled in the provisions of the Land Act, would throw these lands open to the flood of settlers who were soon expected.

But that class to whom we have already alluded was strong enough to break all these promises and evade the provisions of the Land and Immigration Acts. The Darling Downs squatters, often spoken of in colonial parlance as the Black Soil men, had no intention of foregoing the privileges they enjoyed as occupiers of this fruitful district. It would appear that from the day of separation they had been casting about for some plan by which they could perpetuate their hold on these lands, and had struck out this one as likely to be successful. Whether that was the case, or whether the lack of statesmanship displayed by the Government and the strong spirit of rivalry between Brisbane and Ipswich first suggested the idea of using the opportunity thrown in their way, it is needless now to inquire. One fact is certain : from the day Mr. Jordan left the colony, authorized to grant land-order warrants for eighteen acres of land to be selected by the immigrant on arrival with a further land-order of twelve acres more to be obtained after two years' residence, the alteration of the laws referring to this matter began. The agent was instructed to inform the people at home of the value of Queensland lands both on the scrubs of the coast country and the open plains of the Darling Downs. He was further to tell them that the young colony of Queensland was so anxious to receive to her arms a portion of the overplus population of Great Britain and Ireland, that every person paying his own passage was to have the privilege of selecting his homestead by virtue of his land-order from the best lands of the colony[7]. To facilitate settlement, this railway was being built, which would not only give present employment to settlers, but open a market for those who chose to settle on the Downs.

Mr. Jordan did all that could have been expected of him. He pointed out the great natural advantages of the colony in the most eloquent language to vast assemblies in all parts of the three kingdoms. In some matters there is no question, either from too fervid an imagination or from misapprehension, he overdrew the picture and conveyed wrong impressions. In particular, in reference to cotton-growing and some other products he made this error. But at that time, as we have said, there were no farms in the colony; nothing of higher rank than market-gardens. In making his estimates we believe he had gone on the principle of learning from some person of this class, or from some amateur gardener, what results had followed the cultivation of a few yards of this or that article, multiplying these yards into acres and thus guessing at the probable results which could be attained on a large scale. It may be urged in his favour that he had no other means of learning the capabilities of the soil. But, on the other hand, it must be seen that such a computation would be vicious and incorrect, and no allowance would be made for all the many drawbacks which every enterprise experiences in a new country, when carried out on a large scale, which would not be felt by the mere amateur when experimenting. In particular would this be the case in reference to

---

[7] "The Government had assured him (Mr. Jordan), that the agricultural reserves would be situated in the best localities in the country, and they would do well not to hearken to those who would make them believe otherwise."—*Extract from Mr. Jordan's Speech published by himself.*

climate, droughts, floods, &c., the greatest difficulties attendant on Queensland agriculture.

But on the whole it must be admitted that Mr. Jordan was honest and energetic, and that his mis-statements arose from the lack of data from which to draw conclusions, and a very natural desire to make the best of his adopted country, of which he hesitated to say that the agricultural interest had yet to be established. But the case was very different in the colony. No sooner was Mr. Jordan fairly at work and it began to be seen that the colony was attracting the attention of emigrants, than a series of changes was initiated, all tending to weaken public faith in colonial laws and their administration. At first emigrants were very properly permitted to reach the colony by any vessel direct from home. For some reason they were denied the privilege of coming *viâ* Melbourne or Sydney from the first; but now it was announced that they must come from England in the ships of one company only, or forfeit their land-orders. We cannot follow the history of these land-orders through all the changes constantly being made in them. But never a year, scarcely six months, elapsed, but some change or other was made. These changes, as well as other obstructions to immigration, which we have yet to notice, usually emanated from the executive, in which the squatting party was paramount and which had unfortunately far too much power of issuing regulations.

It was in the administration of the Land Act, however, that the greatest proof was given of the determination of the Government and its supporters not to favour the settlement of a farming population on the lands. The Land Act of 1860 provided that in each of the districts of Moreton Bay, Wide Bay, Port Curtis, and Keppel Bay agricultural reserves of 100,000 acres should be set apart, and that within five miles of every town of 500 inhabitants an agricultural reserve of 10,000 acres should be proclaimed. These lands were to be open for selection at 1*l*. per acre or by land-orders at the same rate. It is true nothing was said in the Act itself as to these being good lands. But as before stated it was thoroughly understood in the House during the various debates, and Mr. Jordan was authorized to publish in England that these reserves were to be of the best agricultural lands in the colony. So far from this being the case, in nine cases out of ten these reserves were of a very inferior character. In some portions of the coast country good scrub land was attainable, while, as we have indicated in a former chapter, most of these lands were anything but "first class." But on the Darling Downs, to open up which a debt of over 2,000,000*l*. had already been incurred, the lessees were powerful enough to prevent any settlement whatever of a character consistent with the importance of the district, or the public funds being spent in connecting it with navigation. The small reserves around the towns of Toowoomba, Drayton, and Warwick were as a rule made on the poorest lands in the prescribed circuit of five miles; and as every care was taken by the neighbouring squatters to harass and annoy any person who was bold enough to settle on these lands, by impounding his cattle and the like, it may be supposed these reserves were not very popular with immigrants. One powerful species of annoyance in vogue in those days was to send, after the rain, and when the grass was springing, large flocks of thousands of sheep to graze over the reserves, and thus eat up every blade of grass close to the settler's fence, thus precluding the possibility of his horses or cows grazing on the reserves, while the poor settler's horse or cow would be at once impounded if found strayed off the bare reserve on to the neighbouring run of the squatter.

In many other instances large tracts of land were secured by what is known as "dummying," which means that various friends and servants were employed to select the maximum quantity of land allowed each individual under the Act, and then to hand them over to the squatter under a power of attorney prepared for that specific purpose.[s]

By many other devices, but chiefly by the utter lack of good land from which to select, the settlement of a considerable agricultural population on the Darling Downs was for many years almost entirely prevented. Thus when the "Jordan immigrants," as they are called, began to arrive thousand after thousand—one ship arriving in the Bay often before the last batch of several hundreds by another had cleared out from the depôts—they found, on obtaining their land-orders from the proper office that they were of little use for any purpose of actual settlement. The splendid lands on the Darling Downs which they had heard Mr. Jordan describe so glowingly, and of which the writers on Queensland spoke so highly, they found to be one vast sheep-walk, through which a railway was indeed being constructed, but for no good purpose so far as they were

[s] The present Administration has entered actions against many squatters on the Darling Downs, who hold between them enormous quantities of land thus obtained. It has, in each case that has so far been concluded, obtained verdicts of ejectment. An Appeal has in one case been taken to the Judicial Committee of the Privy Council, which it is understood will in its result govern the whole. So very extensive and valuable are the lands thus held, and the title to which the present Government contest, that in the recent elections the prosecution or otherwise of these actions was one of the questions on which the Government went to the country, and on which they obtained an overwhelming majority.

concerned. Some few hundreds of the more sanguine and adventurous selected land in the poor, thickly-wooded reserves in the neighbourhood of Brisbane or on the better lands about Ipswich, while some ventured as far as the Logan or Mary. Very few of all these have been able to go through the enormous outlay requisite on such farms and still retain their deeds. The far larger portion wisely abandoning all idea of agriculture, on seeing how they had been deceived, sold their 18*l.* land-orders for from 9*l.* to 15*l.* and left the colony for home, Sydney or Melbourne, or else settled down in some Queensland town. Thus was an astounding and gigantic act of deception practised on the British public and a bad name given to the colony which it by no means deserved, nor would have obtained had public faith been kept inviolate.

There are other causes which have conduced to the stagnation which for so many years hung over Queensland; but the main reasons for all the evils which have befallen it are the improper interference with the Land and Emigration Acts, induced by a desire on the part of the squatting party to hold their lands in perpetuity, to the exclusion of all agriculturists.

The locking-up of the good lands of the colony from the settler was not the only method adopted to retain these lands by the squatters. At first they had been very willing to join in a measure for the introduction of immigrants. At that time labour was scarce and dear. Wages for shepherds, even in the inside districts, was oftener 52*l.* than 40*l.* per annum, with rations. At lambing and shearing times large wages had to be given, as well as to bullock-drivers, sawyers, bush carpenters, and all artisans. The squatters had certainly nothing to lose by the introduction of immigrants. So a measure was passed in the same

session as gave birth to the Land Act, 1860, for the
encouragement of population. As we have seen, liberal
grants were to be made to those paying their own passages,
and assisted passages were to be given to males by payment
of 8*l.*, the females for half that sum. Besides this, certain
classes, especially domestic servants, were to be brought
out entirely free. Perhaps it did not materially increase
these latter classes, but it was at first provided that all
immigrants after two years' residence would receive the
12*l.* land-order, without reference to the means by which
they had come to the colony. The annulling this provision was the earliest alteration made after restricting
arrivals to one line of shipping. But from time to time
others were made. The labour market was soon well filled.
So many people who had proposed settling on the land were
driven to seek employment for the reasons already stated,
that wages rapidly fell. It is true the northern territory
was opened up and entered on, and towns arose with great
rapidity. But the influx of population was too great for
the restricted fields of labour, and soon the squatters saw
that the population was large enough for their peace and
safety. By this time the various contractors for the more
extended lines of railway had introduced many hundreds
of navvies on their own account, receiving the land-orders
representing their passages, so that even this means of
livelihood was in a measure shut up from the poor immigrant. As these lines drew near completion it became
evident to the squatters that they must either put a stop
to immigration or run the risk of being carried away by
the force of numbers, and lose the vast advantages which
had already accrued to them. Not only were wages now
reduced as low even as 20*l.* per annum in many instances,
and ranging from that to 35*l.*, but an unemployed floating

population began to show itself, which threatened to be
considerably increased on the cessation of the railway
works, which had now placed a heavy debt on the colony.
Practically shut out from the lands, these disappointed
people would perchance turn rusty, to the no small injury of
the present pleasant state of things.

It was not only by the increase of population and the
consequent lowering of wages that the Darling Downs
men had benefited.   The large holders there had now the
railway to their doors, or at least sidings constructed for
their convenience.   But another change had been effected
in their favour.   The land-orders which immigrants had
been unable to use to advantage had nearly all found their
way into the hands of the squatters at a great reduction on
their actual value, and had by them been made use of in
purchasing the best portions of their runs, or, in colonial
parlance, "picking the eyes out of the run," by using
their right of pre-emption, and thus giving them a double
security against intrusion.

Now followed one step after another, all tending to
impede the flow of immigration.   Of course it was necessary to get rid of Mr. Jordan.   The ground was gradually,
but carefully cut from under his feet; his promises were
rendered nugatory, until at last he sent in his resignation
as Agent General and returned to the colony.   Another
change was made which, although in some measure assuming to put a stop to dealing in land-orders, in fact, tended
to stop immigration without at all affecting that traffic.
The land-orders had been from the first a species of legal
currency which had assisted business to a very considerable
extent.   The intending emigrant finding he would be
presented with a species of promissory note which he could
always discount at a higher or lower percentage, was more

ready to turn his face to Queensland than would otherwise have been the case. In Brisbane and other towns of the colony much business was transacted on the basis of these land-orders, which often passed through several hands before being finally paid into a land office for land. But when one restriction after another was made with a view to stop this transfer, all this was changed. Emigration decreased, and trade fell off very considerably. Yet the Act had been so worded that it made it worth the while of the large purchaser to evade the law and purchase land-orders in an indirect way, by taking a power of attorney from the seller, who, of course, in consequence of the risk ran, had to be content with a less price than formerly. By degrees immigration decreased, until the crisis of 1866, the breaking of the Oriental Bank, the stoppage of the Bank of Queensland, and the consequent paralysis of the Queensland Government, may be said to have stopped it altogether for some time. During this period Queensland had no agent in London, all that was done being the occasional despatch of a vessel at long intervals by Mr. Wheeler, the chief clerk in the London Office. This was the position of affairs in the year 1868, shortly after the discovery of the Gympie Gold-fields, which may be considered to mark an epoch in the history of the colony.

CHAPTER V.

LEAVING an account of the gold-fields for a future chapter, we will now take a glance at the northern portions of the colony. In our description of the East Moreton District we have taken the reader as far north as the Mooroochy River, which forms the boundary between the East Moreton and Wide Bay Districts. Next after East Moreton, the district of Wide Bay is in many respects the most important in the colony. It has a considerable frontage to the sea, stretching from the Mooroochy at the south to the Kolan River at the north, a distance of nearly 300 miles. Its navigable rivers are the Newsa, Mary, Susan, Burrum, Gregory, Burnett, and Kolan, on all of which are large quantities of excellent soil suitable for the growth of almost every variety of product of the temperate or the tropical zones. This district being newer, presents more attractions for the immigrant than the older settled districts to the south. Settlement up to a very recent period was confined to the Mary River, the other rivers having been either unknown to the mass of the people, or entirely neglected up to the time when such a large increase was made to the population of the district in consequence of the discovery of the Gympie Gold-diggings in October, 1867.

This district is at present noted for its gold-mines, its sugar plantations, its large timber trade, as well as for another trade which, although as yet only in its infancy, promises before many years to become of equal importance to any of these—its dugong fisheries. The principal town of the district is Maryborough, situate on the navigable part of the river Mary, sixty miles from its mouth, and being accessible for vessels with a draft of seventeen feet, in which respect it is superior to both Brisbane and Rockhampton. The population of Maryborough is about 5000. Besides this there is the establishment known as Dundathu, nine miles below the town, which boasts of being the largest saw-mill in the Australian colonies, and which would not suffer in comparison, either as to its size or the excellence and completeness of its machinery, with the large saw-mills met with in various parts of the Dominion of Canada. The population here cannot fall far short of 200. An equal distance above the town is the Yengarie establishment, with a population of between 200 and 300 engaged in sugar crushing, boiling, and refining, boiling down sheep and cattle for tallow, and in the manufacture of Tooth's Extract of Meat prepared on Liebig's principle; there is also a distillery at the place. Besides these two large establishments, which constitute villages in themselves, there are two other saw-mills, five other sugar-mills on the Mary and its tributary Tanana Creek, all within a short ride of the town.

Maryborough is a flat, uninteresting town, having the Mary River on three sides. The soil being very rich in the neighbourhood, some compensation for the monotony of the town itself may be obtained by a walk through the small farms and market gardens near it. The luxuriance of the foliage and its tropical character cannot fail to interest and please. Or should the traveller prefer a ride, he can, after an hour's canter through the bush, visit any of the large sugar plantations and mills, where he will always find a hearty welcome, and probably have an opportunity of passing his opinion on the production of the distillery. There are few sights more refreshing than after a ride through the dull and monotonous bush to emerge suddenly on a broad expanse of green sugar-cane, with its narrow roads and the mill perched on the bank of the river and half hidden by the luxuriant foliage of the cane. Thinking it may be interesting to the English reader we append a description of one of those mills furnished by the author to a local paper.

MYRTLE GROVE SUGAR AND CONCRETE MILL.

"On Wednesday last we paid a visit to the sugar mill of Mr. Mackeand, at Myrtle Grove, on the Upper Mary. A pleasant ride of a couple of miles from Owanyilla, brought us to the bank of the river just opposite the factory, which is on the north or Maryborough side. Leaving our horse to browse among the young grass and thistles at the bottom of a garden, we were ferried across by one of the mill hands who speedily answered our cooey.

"Seen from the opposite side the mill has a very neat appearance, the sheds being covered with galvanized iron, with openings between the rows for ventilation. Two small iron chimneys, rising to a height of eighty feet, with dampers at the tops give a finish to the buildings and proclaim their use. At the wharf were lying three large punts, which have been built by Mr. Anderson, of Dundathu, for the purpose of bringing cane to the mill. Like all the other mills on the river, this is situated at the top of a high bank, and to reach it a tramway of a steep gradient has been constructed; by the side is an iron piping to convey water to the boilers, and the 'clang, clang' as we ascend tells us operations are going on.

"Reaching the level, the first room we see on the right is the bagging-room, where two men are busy bagging and weighing the sugar, and piling it up in tiers. Passing on, we enter on the same side, the large shed, where, on the ground floor, are the coolers, and elevated a few steps we see the steam arising from the boiling syrup. Away at the far end is a lot of machinery, with here and there a little engine; but the whole is scrupulously clean and nice, and you at once see that by some means things are done very differently here from the usual method in our large sugar-mills on the Mary.

" In order to give the reader a proper idea of this new-fashioned concern, we will begin at the beginning and follow the cane from the field to the bag, which at Myrtle Grove occupies but a very short space of time in doing.

" Directly opposite the entrance from the river, on the left side, is the arrangement for conveying the canes to the rollers. This consists principally of an endless carrier, sixty feet long, somewhat similar to those used in some thrashing-machines for carrying off the straw. The canes being unloaded from the cart which brought them from the adjoining field, they are placed on this band, which takes them on to the man who feeds the rollers, and who is thus enabled to perform the work of three or four persons under other circumstances. The rise of the ground brings us to the crushing department. The rollers are very heavy, very well finished, and are driven by very large cog-wheels. Just in front is the small smithy, and rising a step or two here on to a platform, we find we have gradually attained an elevation which enables us to overlook the whole of the works. Just over the rollers is fitted a winch for hauling canes from the wharf up the tramway. The motive power of this machinery is a twenty-horse power engine, just at our feet, the boiler of which, also on the same level, not only drives the engine, but supplies that heat which is so prominent a feature in this process. An exhaust-pipe carries all the steam directly under the rollers and the iron mill-bed, so that the juice is actually being heated from the moment it is expressed, and is thus preserved from any chemical deterioration through the action of the air. To the touch the juice is perceptibly warm by the time it runs into the first clarifier, of which there are three, from which the juice passes to two subsiders of 400 gallons each, and from these to a supply-tank of 600 gallons capacity. During this time the juice is being raised in temperature according to Mr. Fryar's system. At the time of our visit the juice was only showing a density of six degrees.

" We have now followed the juice to the supply-tank, which stands at the top end of the shed. So far the only peculiarity in the concrete process which we have noted, is the heating of the cylinders, the mill-bed, and the pipes, From this point the process is entirely distinct from all others. To thoroughly understand it, the reader must recollect that the mill is built on ground sloping both ways—the crushing being done at the highest point, thus allowing the juice to flow on continually from one place to another by gravitation. The

whole length of the building is occupied with ten trays, each fitted
with three ripples, having a passage at one end, reminding one of the
ripples of a quartz-crushing machine, only that as a rule the juice
flows from end to end of the tray, and round the end of the ripple
instead of over it, thus, in fact, increasing fourfold the distance to be
travelled by the juice before it reaches the bottom. The heat under
these trays is not uniform, the first being hotter than the second, and
so on to the end, less heat being requisite as the juice grows thicker.
It was curious to notice the change in colour as one tray after another
was passed, the juice becoming gradually darker and denser.

"There are two methods of supplying these trays. The first and
ordinary one is by means of a tap which passes the juice from the
supply tank into the first, and so on. But it may sometimes happen
that the juice is getting too hot at any particular tray or all over the
lot; the remedy for this is an inflow of fresh juice from the tank. It
is obtained in this way; a long iron pipe is connected with the supply
tank, and runs on the outer edge of the trays to the bottom, where it
is connected with a pump, which we shall directly refer to. At the
pump end and at the tank end are taps to fill the pipe, and over each
tray is another tap. Now, if fresh juice is required the tank tap is
turned on, and then, of course, juice can be turned on wherever
wanted. Again, suppose the juice to have gone the course of the trays
and meandered round all the ripples, and yet not have arrived at the
proper consistency, a pump is connected with the tank into which it
runs, and by means of this pump it can be again pumped back to the
top tray, or to all the trays, and re-boiled. By this means the boiling
can be regulated with the greatest nicety, if only the requisite skill is
brought to bear.

"The boiled juice passes, as we have seen, into a receiving tank,
from which it is passed into the cylinder. This cylinder is also a
peculiar feature of the concrete process. It is a large hollow tube
worked from the outside, on the interior diameter of which the juice
revolves, and through the centre of which a current of hot air is being
continuously driven, and so to say, pumped out by a fan which
revolves with great velocity at the farther end. This cylinder is
worked by a little engine of three-horse power. To supply the hot
air for the cylinder there is a brick furnace and chimney at the end of
the shed. The chimney is filled with a large number of small tubes
which heat the air, which then passes by means of a square connexion
into the cylinder. Thus a constant flow of hot air passes into and out
of the cylinder, as well as a stream of juice which comes out either as

sugar or concrete, according to the length to which the operation extends. At the time of our visit sugar was being made, nor is it likely that concrete will be manufactured while the market remains as at present.

"From the cylinder the sugar is carried by a shoot into the coolers, ten of which occupy, with the sugar-room, one half of the building. As showing the care which has been evinced in the smallest details, we may mention that these coolers have iron bottoms, and that a current of cold air is always passing under them, thus materially assisting the process.

"From the coolers the sugar, when granulated, is taken to the centrifugal machine, which stands in front of the cylinder, and which is driven by an engine of five-horse power, being the third engine employed in the factory.

"The boiler which drives all the machinery is well worth inspection. It is quite unique in our experience, and is, we believe, the first of the sort which has been introduced to this district. It is a Cornish boiler with Galloway tubes, and it is these tubes which are the peculiarity. They are tubes of the shape of a sugar-loaf, placed transversely across the hollow of the boiler, and being connected with it, and of course filled with water, the heating surface is thus very materially increased. We were informed by the proprietor that they can get up a head of steam in an astonishingly short time. As an evidence of the thoroughness with which the rollers do their work, we may mention that the megass [1] is wheeled direct to the furnace and used for fuel, for which purpose it answers admirably.

"It will be noticed that we have said nothing of molasses. We saw none, and were informed that none were made, a fact which in itself speaks volumes for this process. We were shown a small piece of concrete which reminded us forcibly of the lumps of maple sugar which it has been our good fortune to attack in times gone by.

"The sugar which was being made was a good yellow counter, which, taking into consideration the lowness of the density, was in our opinion all that could be desired.

"There are two or three considerations which strike a visitor to this mill. The absence of bustle, the general cleanliness, the small number of hands employed—there being only two men from the rollers to the coolers—and the excellent character and finish of the machinery, which does great credit to the inventor, the manufacturers, and the engineer."

There are in Maryborough five churches, belonging to the English Church, the Roman Catholics, the Wesleyan

---

[1] The residuum of the sugar-cane after the juice is extracted.

Methodists, the Presbyterians, and the Baptists. There is also an excellent hospital, and a very respectable post and telegraph office; also a School of Arts with a very good library attached. The people here pride themselves on their solvency, and certainly there is no town in the colony which has weathered the "bad times" better than did Maryborough, although this is to be accounted for in a great measure by the outbreak of the "Gympie Rush." This town has of late obtained a somewhat unenviable notoriety in connexion with the Polynesian trade, some of the people interested in sugar growing having used great exertions to replace the white labourers by Kanakas. They have to a certain extent been successful in this attempt; so much so that of a Saturday night more Polynesians will be met in the streets than white men. But the whole question of coloured labour is too large to be treated of here, and we shall therefore speak of it in a separate chapter. On the whole Maryborough is one of the most thriving towns in the colony, and no new arrival can afford to overlook its claims to his attention. It already possesses the largest foundry in the colony, from which sugar and quartz-crushing machinery is turned out in considerable quantities, while the constant arrival and departure of vessels engaged in removing the productions of its saw-mills to all portions of Australia and the adjacent French colony of New Caledonia imparts an air of business to the port. Coals have been for many years raised in considerable quantities on the Burrum River, a short distance to the northward, and a company has lately commenced operations in raising coals from the same bed at a distance of seven miles from the town, on the banks of the Mary. There is a small brewery at the village of Owanyilla, a few miles up the river, to which place, and the township of Tiaro, still further up, a small steamboat plies regularly, thus furnishing the farmers on both banks of the river with a cheap and easy communication with the town.

There are few more pleasant trips to be taken in the colony than is afforded by an excursion up the Mary River from Maryborough to the head of navigation at Tiaro. On both sides are seen farm after farm and plantation after plantation, in all of which sugar-cane is the prevailing crop. Some of the houses are large and well built, and are evidently the abodes of well-to-do people. Others are of a much more humble character, but about all the groves of bananas, the peach, orange, lemon, mulberry, fig, loquat, and other fruit-trees give an air of homely comfort and abundance that is highly suggestive. Not that many places possess all these fruits. It is unfortunately the exception as yet where that is the case. But most of them can boast of some of these, and nestling among them the humblest slab hut has a beauty which no amount of architectural adornment can bestow. Here and there dark patches of the primeval scrub intervene, but every year these patches grow less, and more and more of the soil is put under sugar. Now and then the tall stack of a sugar-mill rises to view, and if it be the crushing season, punts loaded with the cane from some of the adjacent farms will be lying below unloading into trucks, which are hauled up an inclined tramway by steam power. The stranger from England would have his ideas sadly shocked by noticing that at most of these mills nearly all the labour is performed by black, woolly-headed men in a state of partial or complete nudity. He would at once see from their woolly heads that they are not the natives of the country, whose hair, although often curly, is never woolly. These are the Kanakas or Polynesians, without whose labours, many sugar growers say it would be impossible to make sugar-growing pay, but with whose assistance they manage to make an annual return of forty or fifty per cent. on their capital. To his honour be it told that there is one mill-owner who has never employed Polynesians either on his plantation nor in his mill, and yet finds the business so remunerative as to induce him to greatly enlarge his operations.

This river takes precedence as the largest sugar-growing district in the colony. There were, in 1870, 1495 acres under this crop, of which 525¼ acres were crushed, producing 756 tons of sugar, 62,063 gallons of molasses, and 4257 gallons of 32 o.p. rum. The average per acre in 1870, of sugar alone, was 1 ton, 8 cwt., 3 qrs., and 4 lbs., being the highest of any district in the colony except Mackay. In that year three floods had to be contended with, which doubtless materially reduced the yield, although it is supposed by some that the ill effects of a flood are not felt so much in the cane ready for crushing as in the crop of the succeeding year. The industry being in its infancy, this, like many other questions, is hardly settled as yet. As we have shown that the crop of cane in the ground was so much larger than the acreage crushed, it may be necessary to state for the information of the reader, that cane on first being planted requires from fifteen to twenty-one months to come to maturity; the large quantity thus shown in the Maryborough district, 970 acres uncrushed, is the amount of new land put under this crop in that year:[2] a fact in itself sufficient to show

[2] There is a slight error here as to this particular locality. Many acres of cane on the Mary were ready for crushing in 1869, but in consequence of the lack of machinery on the river all the cane could not be crushed. This evil was not entirely remedied in 1870.

what gigantic strides this young colony is making in the
growth of this one staple. The soil on which this cane is
grown is the richest description of scrub land, large
quantities of which are yet in a state of nature. Of course
the first settlers took up land near the town, and settlement gradually spread up the stream. All the navigable
part of the river is now more or less covered with cane-
fields, and a mill has lately been erected by Messrs.
Upward and Co. at Tiaro, the highest point to which the
river is at present navigable. We say at present, for it
has been mooted, that by the formation of locks the whole
river frontage to Gympie, a distance of about 40 miles
in a straight line, and more than double that by the river,
might be rendered navigable. The amount of good such a
measure would confer on the district is almost incalculable.
Both banks of the river being skirted by excellent land,
all could then be brought under cane or other highly
remunerative crops, such as tobacco, for which the facilities
that would then be offered for irrigation would peculiarly fit
it. This is one of the many instances in which English capital
might be laid out to the greatest advantage both to the
colony and the money lender. Were this work accomplished, and the exigencies of politics seem to indicate that
it yet may, the Mary River would then become the most
extensive and valuable sugar-producing district in the
colony, if not in the world. No difficulty whatever would
be found in paying the interest, or even the principal of
the money expended, as the lands thus afforded a navigable
frontage would be enhanced in value 200 to 300 per cent.,
and might be either charged with a sufficient sum to pay
the whole cost, or with a small frontage-tax to meet the
interest and cost of maintenance. While money is a drug
in the London market, and the uncertainty of European

politics induces caution as to the ordinary means of investment, there are millions of acres of land in all parts of
Queensland that might be incalculably enhanced in value
by the formation of extensive water-works, from which a
perpetual return to the money-lender of eight to ten per
cent. might be obtained.   Patriotism and policy alike point
out those magnificent colonial investments to the imperial
capitalists as in every respect more suitable than the funds
of rival and oftimes hostile nations.

Most of the mills on this river are of large size and were
erected at considerable expense.   Of Yengarie, Messrs.
Tooth and Cran, to which we have already referred, the
Chief Inspector of Distilleries in his Annual Report of 1870,
says it is unrivalled in the colony.   Since that report was
written large additions have been made to the plant of this
establishment, a sugar refinery having been added, which
like all other parts of the machinery there, combines all the
latest improvements.   The Maryborough Sugar Company
on Tanana Creek have also a very large mill and distillery.
Mr. Eaton, Mr. Gibson, Ramsay Brothers, and Mr. Rankin
have also extensive mills, most of them with distilleries.
There are also some small mills used principally for the
crushing of the proprietors' own cane.   But as the number
is continually being increased, it is almost impossible to
state anything with accuracy on this point.

Some years since an attempt at the growth of cotton in
some of the lighter lands beyond the scrubs, was made in
this district.   The adventure was disastrous to all those
who engaged in it.   Various reasons contributed to this
result; lack of experience no doubt had much to do with
it, but it was also found that the heavy rains that are
experienced here in the picking season, more than in
almost any other part of the country, militated much

against the growth of this crop. For some time cotton has in consequence been entirely ignored. The rains, which operated against it are, however, of the greatest benefit for other crops, and do much to give this district its pre-eminence in an agricultural point of view.

There are in the neighbourhood of Maryborough some excellent gardens, the proprietors of which have for years past, done their utmost to give a practical illustration of the wonderful adaptability of this colony for the growth of almost all kinds of ornamental and fruit trees, and the horticultural productions of the wide world.

Up to the present time, the Mary River with Tanana Creek has been the only part of this district where agriculture has been carried to such a point as to produce sugar. In fact until lately no settlers were to be found in any other part of Wide Bay. But the gold diggings have here, as elsewhere, produced a vast change. On all the many rivers which water this district, settlers are now planted, and flourishing farms and extensive plantations are rising. As these rivers are all of them worthy the attention of immigrants, and offer a fine field for enterprise we shall refer to them in detail.

The Newsa River, which runs into Laguna Bay, an open and shallow roadstead some thirty-five miles to the south of Wide Bay Bar, has lately attracted the attention of settlers. It was first opened up about the year 1864 by lumberers, who penetrated its scrubs and those of the tributary creeks in search of cedar. The river itself, although averaging a breadth of half a mile for about four miles inside the bar, is very short. Eight miles from its mouth it opens into a small lake called Lake Coorybah, which has a bar across its centre nearly dry at low tides. Above this lake the river is deep and sufficiently broad

until another lake called Boreen is reached. This lake is
also very shallow, although not less than ten miles long by
seven or eight broad. It is divided from the ocean by a
ridge of sand hills. Here the river is lost. Beyond, on the
north side of the lake are two creeks and two smaller lakes.
These lakes are all salt in dry seasons, but in the rainy
weather Boreen and the upper lakes are fresh. The scenery
is very lovely, and there are many beautiful sites where
residences could be erected commanding the most charming
scenery of lake, mountain, and forest. In these lakes are
flocks of gneering, or black swans. The author has often
enjoyed the pleasure of chasing them in a boat in the
moulting season, when they are unable to fly. As they
can swim very fast, and by the use of both wings and legs
can go very rapidly over the water, the chase is by no
means an unfair one. If the swan be in good condition he
is often able to tire out a boat's crew, for the boats are always
whale boats or other heavy ones used for lumbering or
rafting purposes, requiring a crew of two or four men to
pull. With four men at the oars and a blackfellow at the
bow, ready to plunge on the unfortunate swan when tired
out, we have passed many an hour chasing these birds.
Getting as close as possible to a flock and then selecting a
young one, we would give chase. For a long time the
swan, now flying a little, now working both wings and
feet, and again swimming in his swift stately manner,
would keep far ahead of the boat. By degrees, by cutting
off corners, for they never go far in a straight line, the boat
will creep up on the prey. Soon his beautiful white and
black feathers become wet with his constant struggles to
escape; the boat closes on him and he is almost within
reach; then of a sudden he makes a double and passing
close to the oars, is a long way back in the wake before

the boat can be brought round. Then is the time for the oarsmen to show their muscle. If blacks, they become almost too excited to manage their oars; again the boat is on his track, and the steersman learning caution tries to keep the bird directly on his bow. The poor bird soon begins to show fatigue. He utters a plaintive cry, and tries again to double or to elude his adversaries by diving. When he does this he is lost; a stroke or two of the oars, the unerring eye of the blackfellow on the bow follows his prey under the water and with a plunge he is down on him. But the fun is not yet over. The swan is a powerful bird, and he yets retains sufficient vitality to show fight. A blow from his wing is not a joke and a great splashing takes place between the swan and black. Especially is this the case if you wish to secure the bird alive to tame. For a long time the fight between the swan, held perhaps by the neck, and the blackfellow with only one hand at liberty is sufficiently ridiculous; but soon he comes alongside, or some of his friends jump over to his assistance, and the game is safely landed in the boat. These birds are very good eating when young, and even an old one is not always to be despised. Besides swans, there are plenty of wood and other ducks, divers, and other aquatic birds in these lakes, sometimes so plentiful as to cover many acres with one mass of life. Here too sails in majesty the stately and dignified pelican, not usually lonely like " the pelican of the wilderness," but more frequently in flocks or at any rate in couples. These birds have bills so capacious as easily to admit of a man's head being placed in them when extended. Brilliantly white, moving among the flocks of swans, most of whose plumage is black, they have a very fine effect.

Lately a township has been surveyed at Tewanton, a

fine position between two little lakes four miles from the
river's mouth. The land here is far from being good. On
Lake Coorybah many selections have recently been made.
The most valuable land, however, is on Kin Kin Creek, one
of the tributaries of Lake Borcen, a beautiful stream which is
nearly always running. One firm of wealthy diggers from
Gympie have here selected 6000 acres of splendid land,
partly scrub and partly forest, with the view, we believe,
of forming a sugar plantation as well as general farming
establishment. They have also erected a small saw-mill
to cut up the magnificent pine timber which grows on
these scrubs. As there is considerable good land on the
waters of this river, although lying somewhat detached,
this will no doubt yet be a thriving as it must always be a
beautiful settlement.

It is a peculiarity of the country in many parts of this
district that patches of most excellent land will be found
here and there, usually on the banks of the streams, which
will abruptly terminate in that worst of all coast-land
" wallum country," as it is called, from the native name
of the shrub which principally grows on it. The soil in
this wallum country is of the vilest description, producing
scarcely any grass and only a few stunted honeysuckle and
gum-trees, besides the never-ending wallum. This country is
the *habitat* of the emu, besides which there is scarcely any
other living creatures, except small birds, to be seen. The
wallum produces a long yellow flower, set round with
stamens very like a flue brush in shape, from which exude
a sweet juice somewhat allied to honeydew. This causes
them to be plucked and sucked by the natives, who are
able to gather sufficient nutriment in this way to allay
hunger. As this wallum country is usually level or rolling
ground with occasional low ridges it is very difficult for

any but an experienced bushman to find his way through it, from its sameness and the absence of any landmarks.

This sort of country stretches from Kin Kin Creek to the mouth of the Mary River, and to the scrubs around Maryborough. It stretches away to the northward from the Mary to the Burrum, and from there to the Burnett, and so away through the Wide Bay into the Port Curtis District. Hence, in speaking of the various agricultural settlements on the Wide Bay rivers, it must be understood that this dreary and unproductive country bounds them and divides them from each other.

From the Newsa to the Mary no stream of any size exists. North of the Mary, and running into it close to its mouth, is the Susan, a very winding river, on the banks of which is some good scrub land and some of a worse character. A few settlers are to be found here, but the place is at present in its infancy.

To the north of the Mary the first independent river is the Burrum, a small stream on which is found some good agricultural land, and where a few settlers have been for some time engaged in growing Indian corn, potatoes, &c., which they easily send to Maryborough by small craft which ascend the river for that purpose, as well as for the coals which are here dug. Another small river beyond this is the Gregory, on which up to the present time very little settlement has been made other than by the lumberers who resort there for pine. As an instance of how land is frequently taken up in the colony, we may mention the case of a saddler who has selected a nice piece of land on the Burrum, and which he is gradually bringing into cultivation. His capital at first was very small, and the few necessaries requisite soon swallowed that up. In order to keep the pot boiling he is in the habit of resorting at intervals to Maryborough, where a few weeks' work at his trade, always a good one in Queensland, enables him to discharge his store bills and continue his farming operations. Many a farm has thus been brought into cultivation in the colony which would otherwise have had to be abandoned. An instance occurs to us of a gentleman on the Logan who has brought his farm up to the paying point, and has now a considerable crop of sugar-cane, by turning his musical attainments to account. After the outlay of a very handsome sum, in the early days when there was much more to contend against than at present, he found his capital expended and his farm not sufficiently advanced to maintain his family. It occurred to him to turn music master, and since then he has kept things square by periodical tours to Brisbane and the Downs, tuning pianos and giving lessons. Another friend of the writer did the same thing by posting the books of a large squatting company, and other cases might be cited of a similar kind, where the large outlay and perchance the bad seasons have made such a course requisite to the retaining of land that has already cost a large outlay.

North of the last-named river is the Burnett, which, like all the rivers in this district besides the Newsa, empties itself into Hervey's Bay. This river bids fair yet to rival the Mary in its production of sugar. It was first settled, like all these streams, by the lumberers, and there has been for some time a saw-mill at work here, while another is being erected. A township, called Bundaberg, has been laid out, sold, and partially built on, while so high is the opinion held of the character of the soil that it is already very difficult to obtain land with a frontage to the river. A considerable quantity of land is already under cane, and a sugar-mill was being erected by

Mansell and Co. at the time of the author's leaving the
colony. In consequence of the forest country in most
parts of the district already alluded to being of the inferior
character described, the other settlements have been
singularly free from the ill effects of the dominance of
the squatters in the government. But here it is different.
On the Burnett is some of the most splendid forest or open
land in the colony, one run alone having enough of this fine
land to maintain an agricultural population of many thousands, where at present only sheep and cattle are found.
The Land Act of 1868 provides for the equitable division
of all coast runs by the local officer. Unfortunately for
the public, in this case, the proprietors had a near relative
in the member for the district, and by means too well
known in the colony, they have managed to obtain possession of nearly all this valuable tract of country, and thus
put an entire stoppage on cultivation other than a limited
amount carried on by themselves. Thus a great portion
of the lands on the Burnett must remain uncultivated to
the incalculable injury of the whole district, or will have to
be purchased at a fancy price of the present proprietors.
It is the great evil of responsible government in a sparsely
populated colony like Queensland, that it affords opportunity for a practical overriding of the laws to parties who
are able to bring influence to bear on members of the
legislature or executive. Had the lands on the Burnett
which are thus locked up from the public been open for
selection, a wonderful impetus would have been given to
sugar-growing on this river, for these lands being very free
from timber could have been brought into cultivation at a
tithe of the outlay required for scrub land.[3]

[3] Since the above was written Bundaberg has grown into a town of
considerable importance, the Australian Steam Navigation Company's

The only other agricultural settlement in this district is in the neighbourhood of Gympie. On this portion of the Mary River, as well as on several of its tributary streams, there are not only large scrubs of excellent soil, but also many alluvial plains or flats of first-class land, which, like the lands just spoken of on the Burnett, are unusually free from timber. These flats, like the scrubs, are mostly subject to inundation, and it is to this fact they owe their great fertility. On these lands, for many miles both above and below Gympie, farms have been taken up for the purpose primarily of supplying the Gympie market with maize, green stuff, potatoes, &c. Most of these farmers have also some cows, the produce of their dairies being often their means of support while bringing their farms into cultivation. The land here is everything that the most sanguine could wish. A fine clear river, which, unlike most Queensland streams, never ceases to run, abounds with fish of various kinds. On its banks are the scrubs, where turkey, pigeons, wallaby, bandicoots, &c., may be shot. Here, too, may be found the pine necessary for building purposes, and perhaps a large quantity more. In some parts a cedar-tree may yet be found, but these have mostly been removed by the lumberers. Beyond the

steamers, usually spoken of as the " A. S. N. Co.," calling there weekly both going and coming between Brisbane and Rockhampton. Being the nearest port to the rich copper-mines at Mount Perry, all the trade for that now important town passes through Bundaberg. We may also mention here, once for all, that the present popular Government are taking legal action to restore to the Crown portions of the lands in this neighbourhood as well as elsewhere, particularly on the Darling Downs, that had been illegally obtained by the squatters, with a view to their being thrown open for selection by *bonâ fide* agriculturists. No more important act than this has been attempted in the history of the colony, if we except the passing of the Land Act of 1868.

scrub open the flats alluded to, studded here and there with huge gum-trees towering heavenward. Often there will be found, close to the ridges of forest land that rise gradually beyond, a fine water-hole or two, covered with water-lilies of the most gorgeous description. At morn and night these water-holes are the resort of wild ducks, teal, &c. These are the more striking features of the lands settled on by the farmers in the neighbourhood of Gympie. As a rule they have not stopped to clear the scrub, but, after pitching their tent or "knocking up" a slab humpie on the ridge beyond the water-hole and beyond the reach of floods, the ploughshare is at once put into the virgin soil. If the weather be at all favourable, a bountiful return of maize or oaten hay will soon be obtained. When once thoroughly broken with a strong bullock or horse plough, what the English wit said of American land is true of this —"If you tickle it with a hoe, it will laugh a harvest." But here, as everywhere else in Queensland, there must be thorough cultivation, and then all depends on having enough rain to moisten the ground without sufficient to send down a flood to wash all away. This occurred in 1870, when three floods came one after another, and in most cases swept away all the farmers had in the ground, in some instances taking their live stock too. One poor fellow wrote the author that he lost everything, house and all, with the exception of three ducks and three fowls. He himself had a narrow escape. Finding himself surrounded by the water, which was still rising, he set to work and made a ladder long enough to enable him to climb into the fork of a gum-tree. Here he remained without any food or shelter for two days and two nights. A neighbour then came to his rescue in a boat, when he was too exhausted to have roosted it out another night.

We cannot refrain from giving another case, which had
a fatal termination in the same flood, because some facts
connected with it will give an insight into the condition of
affairs better than anything else we can say.   In the same
flood, which will long be remembered as the big flood of
1870, there lived, eight or ten miles above the settler
alluded to, two others who were carrying on business in
partnership, although each owned his own land adjoining
that of his partner.   One of these was an old colonist,
who had sold a smaller farm on the Brisbane River to
commence more extensive operations here.   With him he
brought his wife and a large family of young children.   At
the time of the flood he was absent in Brisbane.   The
other was a young gentleman of good family, and who was
unmarried.   Singularly enough, both himself and the
farmer who took refuge by means of his impromptu ladder
in the gum-tree, were from the same locality, and here that
seething whirlpool, a gold rush, had thrown them out side
by side on the banks of the Mary.   Like many, if not most,
of the young men of good family who come to Queensland,
L—— was in the habit of occasionally drinking too much.
It may be premised here, as a reason why so many families
were on this occasion caught by the flood, that prior to the
gold rush in 1867 there had been no settlers in this country but those employed on the cattle-stations, usually two
or three hands only; that no flood had occurred since that
time, and that as a consequence no one was aware of the
great height to which the flood rose on these occasions.
When the town of Gympie was being built, the writer was
told by an acquaintance that the mailman, who carried
the fortnightly overland mail from Brisbane to Maryborough, had said that he had seen the flat covered with
water.   He hardly credited this; yet in 1870 not only the

houses on this flat, but those a considerable way up the hill, were submerged, and many washed away. But to return to young L——. On the night in question it was suddenly discovered that the water was coming into the house, a substantial one-story building. Preparations were instantly made for escaping to a neighbouring ridge on the other side of the road. In those floods the water often rises with marvellous rapidity. Although the husband was absent, there were two men and a woman-servant, besides the family of the proprietor and L—— present. Seizing such articles of clothing as could be readily found, they sallied forth in the pouring rain to reach a place of safety. L—— had been that evening drinking enough to make him foolhardy. On the opposite side of a little gully he had a house of his own considerably nearer the river. For some reason he determined to pay this a visit, and in the darkness and tempest set off, in opposition to all expostulation, to swim this gully. The rest had enough to do to save the women and children, and poor L—— was swept away on the stream running down this gully to the scrub. All the rest reached the ridge in safety, and had to camp as best they might under the shelter of the gum-trees. When the flood subsided the body of L—— was found suspended in a tree into which he had been washed.

The particular reason the author had for referring to this tragedy was this: about seven months before this flood, he happened to be riding on the road from Brisbane in company with L——. About nineteen miles from Gympie is a beautiful flat skirting the scrub. We had often gazed on this piece of country with delight. There are but few trees on it, as it stretches away for a long distance up the river. Clothed in the finest herbage, it

was always dotted with herds of cattle and horses, who
never tired of its sweet pasture.   Here the plough could
have been put in and turned up scores if not hundreds of
acres, without the share coming in contact with a single
root.   The road runs along the side of a ridge which skirts
the flat and enables the eye to take in all the scene.   We
had often thought what a splendid opening it offered for a
capitalist to enter on the growth of sugar.   L—— told us
that he had secured it, and his business in Brisbane had
been to complete his selection at the land office, by paying
his first yearly instalment.   We rode in company with
him over a portion of it and he explained his views
respecting it.

　　More than a year after his death, we became acquainted
with the following facts.   Soon after his death a miner
who had saved a little money re-selected this land.   His
selection was permitted and his money taken.   He went
at once to reside on the land, built a house, put up fencing
and made other improvements.   Something like a year
after this he received notice that he must quit the land, it
being a part of the reserved half of the neighbouring run.
So the poor man, after laying out his all on the land, had
to leave it in this manner, although he was the second
person who had selected it and had his selection approved
by Government; the cash for the first year's payment
having been also taken from each.   The valley of the
Mary runs through the run in question, which consists of
the fine alluvial lands on its banks and the steep mountainous ridges beyond.   It was discovered that the surveyor
when carrying out the survey prescribed under the Act to
divide the run in equal portions, one to be held by the
lessee and the other to be open for selection, had actually
run his dividing line along the base of these mountains,

giving the lessee all the lands on the river for his share, and securing the mountains for the public as agricultural lands !!! This is one instance of what happens in countries where there is an aristocracy not of family but of wealth, which has the power to become practically an oligarchy.

From what we have said respecting floods many might be led to suppose that Queensland was worse off in this respect than her neighbours. This, however, is not the case. In New South Wales especially, the settlers suffer far more frequently and in a much larger degree than in Queensland. In 1870 the loss of life and property in that colony was truly lamentable, whole districts being entirely depleted of their wealth, in some cases the very fences being swept away for miles together. In Queensland, lives are occasionally lost in floods, but that loss has never been on a large scale and only at long intervals. As a rule floods appear to recur in this colony about once in five or six years.

It may not be improper to mention here, that in most situations the greater part of the loss of property and all danger to human life in floods might be avoided, so far as the agricultural population is concerned, were more care taken in the selection of building sites. In each of the cases alluded to there were ridges at a short distance, in one case not fifty rods distant, that were entirely above all flood level. Such spots can nearly always be found by the settler, but a desire to be close to his clearing, which is always on the alluvial flats, and in too many cases an entire ignorance and carelessness, induce him to build on the first spot that presents itself, without any thought or care about the wet season or the floods. Not only is much loss and real danger thus incurred, but most beautiful building sites are neglected, which with a little display of taste and labour would make the homestead far more attractive.

We should not complete our sketch of the agriculture of the Wide Bay District, did we not refer to the Chinamen's gardens around Gympie. This race of people adapt themselves wonderfully to all sorts of colonial industries. They are to be found in large numbers on the diggings sinking their little round holes, in which it is a perfect mystery to a European how they can work. They will work poorer ground than others think it worth their while to engage in. They are excellent cooks and are everywhere found in this capacity. As shepherds they are quite equal to white men. We never heard of their being engaged as stockmen, or bullock-drivers, but they are often found driving a team of horses as pedlars. In every town there are more or less Chinese storekeepers, principally in the greengrocery or sweetmeat line. But as gardeners they are pre-eminent, and supply a want that without them would be much felt on every diggings in the colony. In most other pursuits they naturally have to copy the processes of the European colonist, but in this they can carry out their old plan brought with them from the home of their forefathers. That it is far superior to the English system for such a country as Queensland, no one who has seen them both will for a moment doubt. In these gardens they can not only carry out their own system of horticulture, but with it they unite all the habits and modes of life peculiar to their country. Here they revel in all the luxuries of the short tunic, wide-flowing pantaloons, quaint pointed shoes, enormous wooden, straw or pith hats, and flowing pig-tails reaching well down their back. Instead of the wheel-barrow or horse-dray, they revert to their own bamboo and baskets, which serve them for every sort of carrying and fetching. In fact a Chinaman's garden is a miniature China, and the stranger on entering it can easily fancy himself transported to the Flowery Empire.

Even in the selection of the sites for their gardens the Chinese are actuated by an altogether different idea from that of the Englishman. The latter would certainly look around for the richest piece of ground he could find. Not so the Chinaman. His one great object is to find what a Yankee would call a water privilege, a site where there already exists, or where the nature of the ground permits of the formation of a large water-hole. Give the Chinese gardener a full supply of water and his fortune is made. In nine cases out of ten he has to obtain this by artificial means. Across some gully, or shallow creek, too small to admit of its being flooded in the wet season, a dam is thrown; the neighbouring ground on one side is cleared of its timber, which serves to make a pig-proof bush fence. In one corner of this lot the house is erected, which is never an important part of the work of improvement. Next, what is known to diggers as a California pump is placed alongside the dam, by means of which the water can be raised to a sufficiently high level to reach all parts of the garden. Then a regular net-work of canals is laid down. There are usually three or four of these main water-courses from which radiate lesser ones, until every walk in the garden has its little canal alongside it. These smaller ones are not always full of water, but are divided from the main streams by little dams with a wooden sluice-head. Beside these water-courses there are a number of tanks either cut out of the clay subsoil, or formed by letting zinc-lined packing-cases into the ground. These too have their inlets and outlets, and vary in size from a few huge ones into which the bodies of several dead horses could

float, to those the size of an ordinary drapery case alongside the beds. As the small canals are all connected with
the large water-tank, so are all these lesser liquid manure
tanks with one or other of the larger ones.

When once the construction of this machinery for the
supply of water and liquid manure is complete, it is an easy
job for the garden to be made to assume a flourishing
appearance. The beds are dug, and all the soil from the
canals and tanks, as well as from all the paths, is heaped
upon them, thus raising them a foot or eighteen inches
above the paths, and securing surface-drainage, the only
kind requisite. From the day the seed is placed in the
ground it is constantly nourished with liquid manure, and
moistened many times a day with water. Not content with
this, a large compost heap or tank is formed, and the young
plants of every description, as soon as large enough to
admit of that treatment, will have a handful of finely pul-
verized manure placed around their roots. Thus, from the
very first, the plants are forced, and as a consequence their
growth is very rapid. Highly concentrated dry manure,
liquid manure, and water, cannot fail to produce wonderful
effects in a climate like that of Queensland. The rapidity
with which these quiet, unassuming men will turn the dry
and arid forest into a smiling garden is almost miraculous.

The first time we had an opportunity of seeing the effect
of their system was at Gympie, in the early part of 1868.
On a visit to some friends who lived on the outskirts of the
diggings, we saw just in front of their hut, peeping through
the trees, the green beds of the gardens. A very few weeks
before, we had ridden over that very spot, and knew the land
to be a white, unproductive loam, of a hot, sandy nature,
about the most unpromising soil possible for a good garden.
Now a dam had been put up, the land cleared and culti-

vated, and a house built. Already, at early morning, the
dapper owners might be seen emerging from their garden,
with their well-filled baskets of vegetables of all sorts, which
found a ready sale among the diggers and at the eating-
houses and restaurants. On visiting the garden we were
courteously received by one of the owners, who, after eagerly
inquiring what we wished to buy, and learning our desire
to look around, at once granted permission. Already there
were splendid beds of cabbage, brocoli, turnips, Chinese
turnips—a white cuneiform root, softer and juicier than the
common white turnip, with a peculiar flavour, but not at all
unpalatable—and almost every vegetable to be found in
the colony, with cucumbers, English and American pumpkins, and several varieties of melons. We learnt that there
were fifteen men working here, proprietors in common. All
were busily employed. Some were breaking up new ground;
some working at the pump; some transplanting young
chalots and other vegetables; some with baskets of dry
manure were carefully placing it near the roots of the
various plants; others were ladling out the liquid manure
from the little tanks on to the beds; one was engaged in
making baskets from the split canes of the "lawyer" vine.
While some were away selling the vegetables, others were
visiting the neighbouring killing and milking-yards,
gathering the blood, offal, and manure, for the compost
and liquid-manure tanks. All this they carry with the help
of the indispensable bamboo in two large, strong baskets.
With these a little Chinaman will carry a weight which
would make a stout Englishman stagger; such is the force
of habit. It is curious enough to see them carrying these
loads. Accommodating their bodies to the swing of the
baskets, they trot along with a swaying motion and at a
good rate of speed, carrying either liquids or solids with

equal safety. In this painstaking manner is all the manure obtained which fructifies their gardens.

To men who have been for months living on dry rations, beef and mutton and flour being the staples, the fresh, crisp vegetables supplied by the Chinese are a great boon, and these gardens must be to their owners a veritable mine of wealth for some months after starting. Afterwards their plenty makes vegetables very cheap. On Gympie, at first, large prices were paid for them, a mere handful of anything costing a shilling. Soon, however, many such gardens were in growth, and vegetables became as cheap or cheaper than in Brisbane. Some foolish people, with an entire ignorance of the laws of chemistry, object to the Chinaman's vegetables, because they are raised with the assistance of so much manure. But as a rule they find a ready market, and the wiser portion of the digging community—which is happily much the largest—look on these gardens as supplying those requisites to their diet without which sickness and disease would be far more prevalent. They nearly always have fair play shown them. Occasionally, some blackguard, trusting to the greater whiteness of his skin, takes his vegetables without payment, and knocks down or maltreats his victim, or else makes the matter subject of jest; but happily these are very exceptional cases, and it is a matter of congratulation that on the diggings, where so much is left to individual action and public opinion, so few instances of this or any other species of lawlessness are witnessed. Nor are the Chinamen at all disposed to submit quietly to this or any other insult or injustice. They will show fight courageously if there is anything like an equality of forces. What they lack in size they make up in a dexterous and determined use of their bamboos, tough sticks about eight feet long, and sufficiently heavy to give a very respectable blow. They often do good execution with these in the fights between themselves and the other diggers. When, however, a Chinaman finds himself unable to cope with his oppressor in this way, he resorts to his tongue, which is for "John" an equally effective weapon as for a woman.

One feature of the Chinese character comes out in the working of these gardens, which places them in a fine light as compared to Europeans. Although a considerable number usually work in partnership, we never heard of a case in which any difficulty arose among them either as to the working of their gardens or the division of money. Old diggers, to whom we have spoken on the subject, have informed us they never heard of a case of this sort. They appear to have no quarrels among themselves when working in partnerships, or as the digging phrase is, "going mates." No actual partnership exists, and when they see fit, from the breaking out of other rushes, or other causes, some will leave the concern. We judge from this that a degree of honesty and fair play characterizes their dealings with each other, far superior to that found among Christians. The same remark holds good of mates in gold claims. Although they may have a commissioner's case with neighbouring compatriots, as to ground, &c., we never knew of a case in which the mates in one claim had any legal proceedings.

While on this subject we cannot refrain from remarking that, in our opinion, the English are apt to form too low an opinion of these remarkable people. Of their superior skill in gardening we have spoken. All the world knows their characteristic patient and industrious attention to every minute detail of their manufactures, and the ingenuity they display. If it comes to a question of swindling they

can hold their own with our most accomplished professors
of that art. The excellence with which they can manufacture spurious gold is known to most digging storekeepers. But they have higher claims than this on our
admiration. Every one in the colonies can testify to the
open-handed hospitality of the Chinese. Be it the shepherd in the bush, who hoards up a portion of his weekly
ration of flour to sell, and gives you of his tea, mutton,
and damper, or the wealthy storekeeper in the town, all
are alike in this respect. In the bush no one passes a
Chinaman's hut hungry, although he may often have
that of so-called Christians. The hospitality of a wealthy
Chinese merchant is on such a scale as to form an epoch
in one's life, a dinner for an invited guest often lasting
three or four hours, and the number of dishes and liquors
exceeding computation.

In married life " John " is likewise unexceptional. He
always marries, we believe, when he gets a chance, that is,
meets with a woman who will have him, who must of course
be a white woman, there being no Chinese women in the
colony. As might be supposed he only finds a wife, as a
rule, in the lowest class. But we never heard of an instance
of a Chinaman ill-treating his wife ; they are noted for the
opposite virtue. Nothing is too good or expensive for their
wives; and as they have a facility for making money,
Chinamen's wives are usually as well dressed as any portion
of the female world. With that arrogance which characterizes our countrymen, when in contact with those we
disdainfully call the inferior races, it is the custom to look
with contempt on Chinamen's wives. But as they are
always well cared for, and kindly treated, and as their hus-
bands are never drunkards, we have often thought they are
in a superior position to many other women. Their hus-

hands are, indeed, "heathen Chinee," but in a country
where there is so very little religion among any class as
Queensland, that is not such a cause of difference as it
might be.

We have often marvelled that no attempt has been made
by the Christian churches of Queensland to evangelize this
important portion of the community. Perhaps, no fact is
more suggestive of the low ebb of the real Christian faith in
the colony than this. There are in Queensland many thousand
Chinese, and not the least effort has ever been made to
enlighten their minds on this subject, although it would
seem that they are here found in conditions the most likely
to give efficacy to such an attempt. We had always thought
they followed the example of too many English, and left
their religion at home, until the following little incident
came to our knowledge in Maryborough. We copy the
paragraph containing it in full from a local paper :—

"It is singular not only to notice the many colours and races of
men that mingle in our streets on equal terms, but to reflect how
little we know, or even care, of each other's thoughts and feelings and
inner life. There move about among the population of Queensland
many thousand Chinamen, for instance, whom we all know to be
industrious and frugal, and who in many places supply vegetables at a
cheap rate, or work over deserted gold-claims to their own satisfaction ;
but of whose religious views we are entirely ignorant and profoundly
careless. We were reminded of the wide distance between the views of
these people and ourselves, by a little incident which happened to us
the other day. Happening to be in the shop of an acquaintance, we
noticed in his window one of those little sitting figures in brass, with
which we were all made familiar in youth as one of the impersonations
of the god Budda, and which enterprising Christians in Birmingham
send to China and India by the bushel. We inquired the meaning of
such a sight in a Queensland shop, and received the following explanation :—The little god in question came with other sundries into
the possession of our friend, and was soon spied by a neighbour of his,
a Chinaman, who told him that any one fortunate enough to possess

this image and carry it about him continually, would always be aware of any machinations or plots being hatched against him, as well as any slander spoken of him. He offered five, ten, fifteen shillings, and, finally, all the money in his pocket for the image, in his anxiety to possess it. Our friend being a conscientious man, and considering that taking money for such a thing would be tantamount to swindling, refused to sell it, to John's great sorrow. Finding, however, that his mind was set upon it, he subsequently made him a present of it, to his intense delight. Now comes the part of the story which reflects the most credit on the part of the poor idolator. Some months afterwards he received a visit from his celestial friend, who placed the little Birmingham god before him, with the following explanation. He was about to sell off by auction a quantity of his goods, and his wife—a European— was determined to include the little image. This touched the Chinaman's honour, and rather than make a gain by the gift of our informant, he brought him back the god again. When will anything be done in Queensland to introduce a purer and higher faith among a race who have so many noble traits as are to be found among our Chinese fellow-colonists?"

The children that spring from these marriages are of a peculiarly interesting character. The man referred to above had a fine family of little girls with delicate olive complexions—or perhaps it would be more correct to say with a light delicate straw tint, peculiarly soft eyes, somewhat like those of their Mongolian father, and very nice, oval features. We confess to having watched with great interest this new species of the human race. He must be blind that does not see that in future years there will be a large admixture of the Mongolian blood in the people of Queensland, more perhaps than of the southern colonies of Australia. The effect this will have on the future of the colony is a question of some importance. From what we have seen and heard of the Chinese in Queensland, we look on this union of races without the least alarm. The Chinaman has many practical virtues and very few vices. He smokes opium and gambles. He has also other vices which arise entirely from his isolated position. But truth compels us to add, that he is not alone in these, nor one jot worse than his white fellow-colonist. Were the Chinaman only christianized, there would be nothing to be desired in him as a colonist. At the present time, nine out of ten of the people of Queensland would prefer to see a large importation of Chinese, rather than of Germans, although we by no means agree with that feeling. This arises from their greater reluctance to accept a low rate of wages, a Chinaman never holding himself at a cheaper rate than a white man. The German, on the contrary, coming from a country where twenty pounds is a large sum, is nearly always ready to hire at first for whatever he can get. This which we look upon as a virtue on his part, of course gives umbrage to the working class. They forget, however, the great fact, that, however small his wages, the German always manages to save enough to enable him very soon to enter on land of his own, and become in his turn an employer of labour, thus doubly relieving the labour market. This the Chinaman never does other than as a gardener. He may remain in the colony in trade, never as a farmer. By far the greater part of them return home as soon as they have saved from 200*l.* to 500*l.* Their inability to obtain wives sufficiently accounts for this fact.

The wonderful influx of Chinese into the new settlements of the Anglo-Saxon race on both sides of the Pacific Ocean is in our opinion the greatest ethnological fact of this generation. Less than twenty years ago, we remember seeing from day to day a Chinaman sitting near the entrance of the City Hall in New York selling cigars. This man was one of a crew that some Yankee skipper had engaged in China on the understanding that they were to be taken back to their port of departure. The unscrupulous man deceived them and sent them adrift in New York. At that time Chinese were a sufficient curiosity to admit of this man and others making a living by sitting still to be looked at. Kind people purchased his cigars and paid him well, or threw him a dime or quarter dollar from charity. How vast the change now! In many places they are so plentiful as to make their introduction or otherwise a legislative question. Perhaps it would be a good policy on the part of the imperial and colonial governments to unite in a scheme of sending out as wives for them a few thousands of the " unfortunate " class of women from our large towns and cities. Whether John could be persuaded to marry by Act of Parliament we know not. We do not think he would make any objections on the score of morals, and if the colonial legislature would dower each bride with a fifty-acre country or a two-acre suburban land-order, we have an idea the whole lot would be eagerly snapped up.

It is not always, however, that John Chinaman contents himself with the lowest grade of our countrywomen. We have known instances in which they have married very respectable wives. One poor fellow, well known to the writer, was an actor in a little romance which we will give, if only to show that John's heart is in about the same place as that of a white man.

A friend of ours in Maryborough, a gentleman holding a prominent position in the Civil Service, had a fine-looking, buxom servant-girl, but recently arrived in the colony. Her charms soon brought two lovers to her feet. One was a rising young tradesman and the other our friend John. Whether as Cupid is proverbially blind, the vows and tears of the Chinaman had made some impression on the young lady, or whether like many of her sex in higher ranks she liked to have two strings to her bow, though one were a yellow one, we know not. Certain it is that she bestowed sufficient smiles on both to retain the pair as her admirers. One evening, when sitting on a log outside the fence talking to her white lover, the yellow one turned up. A quarrel ensued, which ended in John using his knife on his rival, who was just sufficiently injured to cause him to hurry home to have his wound dressed. John in a frantic state rushed into the house knife in hand, and informed the startled lady of the house, that the young man in question "want to take away his girl, his wife close up," at the same time breathing out threatenings and slaughter against him. After some time and much trouble he was pacified and sent home. The white man, fearing to be laughed at, kept the matter quiet, and nothing further came of it. Which of the two would have been the successful candidate after this display of valour on John's side, it is impossible to say. Unfortunately the young woman, while one day boiling the clothes on washing day, at a fire in the open air, as is the fashion of the country, set fire to her dress, and having on a crinoline, was so injured that death ensued. Now was the time when John showed the depth of his affection. He was almost heart-broken, and would not, if he could help it, be parted from the lost object of his affections. Although the young woman died possessed of more than sufficient money to defray the funeral expenses, he would not allow a penny of her money to be used for that purpose, making the outlay himself on a respectable scale and acting as chief mourner. He it was that must dig her grave, and erect the fence around it after the funeral. After the manner of his countrymen, he used afterwards to carry rice and other articles to the grave of his beloved one. In the early morning he was frequently

seen lying at full length on the grave in the utter abandon
of grief, as if he had lain there all the night.

This man afterwards married and is a drayman in very
comfortable circumstances, having a few houses of his own
at rent.   At one time a shopkeeper announced himself as a
candidate for aldermanic honours.   To express their opinion
of him in the most decided manner his townsmen elected
John as alderman in opposition to him.   John took very
kindly to the office and attended regularly to his duties at
the Council Board.   Among his brother aldermen was a
butcher, who having made a little money assumed some
superiority.   On one occasion Alderman Chiam, for such
was our Chinaman's name, saw fit to oppose the opinions of
this man, who thereupon took occasion to ridicule him on
the difficulty with which he read writing.   Our old friend at
once seized a pen, quickly wrote a few words in Chinese,
and pushing it across the table to his opponent said,
" Mr. B——, you say me no lead English, suppose you lead
that."   This of course he was unable to do.   "Ah," says
John, " you say me no belly good lead English, you no lead
Chinee at all."   The retort was both just and witty, and
turned the laugh against the bumptious butcher.

This story reminds us of another remark made by a very
clever blackfellow.   We were once endeavouring to enforce
on him the superiority of the white race by giving him
some account of our various inventions, &c.   We may say
that often in the bush the vast superiority of the white-
man is not so very apparent.   In fact, we have often
thought if our civilization had no greater evidences of
excellence than are to be found there, the black might be
pardoned for looking down on us with as much contempt
as some of them actually do.   On this occasion we were
vanquished with the following argument :—" Me think

whitefellow —— fool. You see blackfellow, that learn
talk whitefellow langwige right off; baal whitefellow
learn talk blackfellow langwige, that too much fool, I
believe." Thus it will be seen that if we look down on
other races with whom we are brought in daily intercourse
they often return the compliment, and that too with some
show of reason.

Up to within a very few years past Wide Bay was
entirely a pastoral district. Although agriculture and
mining have now thrown this interest in the shade, it is
still a very important one. The grass-lands are by no
means first class, although some of the rivers contain very
fair country. As most of this land is too poor to repay
cultivation, sheep and cattle will continue to hold their own
in this district, however greatly the other interests may be
enlarged.

As we have before indicated, the lumbering business is
of considerable extent. There are three saw-mills at Maryborough, one at Brundaberg, one at Gympie, and another
is being erected at Brundaberg, and one on the Newsa
Lake. To keep these mills in raw material, principally
pine, numerous parties of lumberers, or as they are more
frequently called timber-getters, find remunerative occupation. For many years the vast scrubs on the Mary River
and the Tanana Creek yielded all the timber used. As
these scrubs have been purchased they have gradually
become less available. For the timber-getter has no need
of purchasing the land he denudes of its pine or cedar. He
obtains a licence, which costs 2l. for soft wood and 10s. for
hard per annum, and armed with this he can enter any
crown lands, unless they are leased by the mile by others
in his own line.

At present the principal rafts which are cut up at Mary-

borough are obtained in the neighbourhood of Mount
Boppell, six or seven miles back of Tiaro, on the Susan and
Gregory, in Tin Can Bay, or on Fraser Island. This latter
is a sandy island, ninety miles in length, opposite the
mouth of the Mary and other rivers, and forming Wide
and Hervey's Bays. It is, like the land about Tin Can
Bay, an inlet to the south of Wide Bay, one mass of fine
white sand. On this grows a thin crop of grass, with here
and there scrubs well stocked with a splendid growth of
kaurie pine. Singular to say, although producing this fine
timber, the soil will not produce any sort of crop whatever,
so that when their timber has been removed these lands
will again revert to the solitude of nature. In other
places, as we have already observed, the timber-getter
is usually the pioneer of civilization and turns by a natural
transition into a farmer.

Rafting timber on the Mary and other streams in this
district is a peculiar and arduous occupation. The pine
timber for the most part is obtained in such places that it
can be drawn to navigable water. But it is different in
the cedar trade. This is usually obtained far above salt
water and has to be rafted or "freshed down" when the
river is swollen from recent rains. A large flood is not so
suitable for this business as a smaller rising, usually known
as "a fresh." Then with sufficient water to carry the logs
over all obstructions in the bed of the creek or river, the
work is commenced. The logs which have accumulated on
the bank are rolled in, and by means of a small boat are
followed down the swollen and rapid stream. Here and
there a log will be stopped by some tree growing out of
the bed of the stream, or perchance carried by an eddy into
the thicket of the scrub. Then the rafters have to plunge
into the water and push the log again into the current.

Again and again this operation has to be repeated until all the logs are brought down to a broad part of the stream, where they can all be united into a raft.

The pine timber in these scrubs and all over the Wide Bay District is of a superior quality, and has a high character in the Sydney and Melbourne markets. Some of the trees are of vast proportions. We have measured them in the scrubs on Kin Kin Creek as much as thirty-six feet in circumference; but as a rule trees of this enormous size would be hollow. It is not unusual to find them sufficiently large to square from four to five feet perfectly solid, and without a knot for seventy or eighty feet from the ground. For many years this business must continue to be of great importance and very lucrative. It offers many openings to men with moderate capital to erect mills, and to those in more modest circumstances to purchase a team of bullocks or horses, a timber-dray, and a boat to procure timber for the mills. An industrious man with such an outfit, will earn not less than 1l. per day, and he may often do twice as well as this. The men who fell and bark the timber and cut the tracks through the scrubs are also able to earn very large wages, usually getting a shilling per 100 superficial feet for this work. When the timber stands thick and is of good size, their wages will often approximate to that of the bullock-driver. More frequently a party of men will "go shares" in finding the bullocks, &c., a good team of which is worth 100l., and share equally in the returns from the pine. Up to the finding of gold at Gympie the timber trade was the main support of Maryborough, as it still remains one of its chief sources of wealth.

Another industry carried on in Wide Bay is the dugong fishery. This wonderful denizen of the Queensland waters

K

is sufficiently curious and unknown to furnish materials
for a separate chapter. These waters, being the southern-
most in which they are found in large quantities, here are
the principal fishing-stations for their capture. As the
great healing properties and other excellencies of their fat
or oil becomes more known, the demand for it largely
increases. There are at present three fishing-stations on
the shores of Wide and Hervey's Bays, where the animals
when caught are brought ashore and boiled down. Other
fishing is carried on to some extent in these bays. Oysters
abound of a very fair quality, and a considerable export
trade with the northern ports is carried on. Mullet are
also dried for the Gympie and other markets. It is a
matter of surprise that the wealth of the Queensland
waters has not before now tempted some persons with the
requisite capital to enter on the fishing business on a scale
of some magnitude. Mullet, whiting, schnapper, jew-fish,
a peculiarly delicate and well-flavoured fish called by the
natives dially, a species of herring, bream, and many other
sorts abound, to say nothing of hosts of turtle and crabs.
An attempt, which was tolerably successful, was made some
time since to procure shark-oil. The various ports have a
good supply of fresh fish, but no one has ever yet attempted
to cure fish on a large scale. From the plentiful supply of
fish and the market that can be made in the colonies alone,
there can be no question that the first parties who speculate
in this direction will have no cause to complain of the
results. It is a remark often made by those conversant
with the subject, that the waters of Queensland contain as
great wealth as its soil. All that is needed is some enterprising speculator to show how money can be made in this
way, and its bays would soon be white with fleets of
fishing-vessels. When that occurs, instead of sending

hard cash to Chili and Peru for their bread-stuffs, salt fish, always a saleable commodity in these countries, would be sent instead, and thus a constant drain of money be put a stop to.

CHAPTER VI.

THE GOLD-FIELDS.

THE most attractive industry in the Wide Bay District to the intending emigrant, as well as to most others, is its gold-mining. The wonderful richness of the early alluvial workings at Gympie, and the splendid results still being obtained from its quartz-reefs, have spread the fame of Queensland Gold-diggings all over the empire. The author visited Gympie within a fortnight of its discovery professionally, as correspondent for a Brisbane paper. He resided on Gympie, Kilkivan, and Jimna for two years, and had thus a tolerable insight into that curious and interesting phase of colonial experience—life on the diggings. The *auri sacri fames* is strong in the breast of most Englishmen, and it will probably be interesting to the reader to have some account of this kind of life.

In the month of September, 1867, Queensland was suffering from what was emphatically known as the " hard times." The various causes to which we have alluded in our account of the railway policy, had brought the whole colony to the verge of bankruptcy. A long drought had nearly ruined the few farmers, who in those days had only maize, potatoes, and oaten hay to depend on for a return. These they had to sell to storekeepers too poor to pay cash, and often too roguishly inclined not to take every advantage of the farmer that his exigent circumstances permitted; but this season even these crops were a failure. The towns of Brisbane and Ipswich were in a state of utter stagnation; large parties of labourers were working in "relief-camps," getting their rations and 6s. per week of Government, to work on the roads until times took a turn with them. Every one was wondering what would happen next, as no one believed times could be worse without starvation ensuing; this, in fact, appeared to be the pleasant outlook for many. Nearly all who could manage to do so had left the colony. As an instance of the pressure of the times, the author had for some time been engaged at the very modest salary of 3l. per week as agricultural editor of a Brisbane paper; he had to make room for an actor, who agreed to fill his position for 1l. per week, and also carry on his engagement at the theatre. His knowledge of agriculture or editorial duties was *nil*, but then 2l. per week would be saved, and that was an object to the company those hard times. Many farmers had given up their farms and gone into situations in the bush in order to find bread for their families, and eight out of ten of the rest would soon have had to follow their example. To such a pitch had this fine colony been reduced by the maladministration of its government. Poverty was become the lot of most.

Such was the condition of affairs when a wandering miner one day in September, 1871, presented himself at the camp of a cedar-getter on the upper waters of the Mary. He had come across from the little diggings at Nanango, where a few scores of men had eked out a living for two or three years. Since then he had prospected his way thus far and announced his intention of prospecting down the western side of the Mary. If he met with no luck until he reached Maryborough, he would be obliged

to take a job at shearing or otherwise, as his funds were
very low, almost at low water. This man was James
Nash, the prospector. He belonged to a class of men who
even in the colonies are *sui generis*. With a pick, shovel,
tin dish, and bag as tools, a blanket, billy, and quart-pot
as equipment, they swarm over the country "trying" it.
Wherever they come across a "likely-looking spot" they
dig or "bottom" a hole, take out a dishful of the "wash-
dirt," if any is found, and try it by washing at the nearest
water-hole. If no water is near, they put a quantity of the
wash-dirt in their bag and carry it, sometimes a mile or two,
until they come to water. It is by these men that almost
all diggings are discovered. They are a silent, prudent,
painstaking, industrious and frugal class who deserve well
of their country. They occasionally come across a squatter
who is public-spirited enough to assist them by supplying
rations free while they are on his run. More frequently,
however, they are treated as the natural enemies of the
squatter. This is by that large portion of the class who
never wish to see a human being on their runs besides
their own people, and who look on the outbreak of a rich
gold-diggings, with its teeming and busy population, as
the greatest possible calamity. There is something in
the secluded and semi-barbarous life of the bush which
engenders an extreme selfishness in men who, in any other
position, would perhaps be characterized by the opposite
quality.

Nash was advised by the cedar-getter to vary his
course and cross the river to the neighbouring station
of Traveston and prospect down the east side of the river.
This man, whose name was Denman, had formerly been on
some of the Victorian diggings, and stated to Nash that on
one occasion when he and his men were "freshing" down

some cedar, he had been struck with the remarkably
auriferous appearance of a certain creek or gully which he
had passed. If we mistake not, he had seen gold in it.
He stated that it was only the imperative nature of his
work which admitted of no delays, that had prevented him
from "trying a prospect" himself, but he had always
intended to do so when he next passed that way. Nash
left Denman's camp, with a promise if successful to secure
a claim for the latter. It is but just to Nash to say that
he denies having received such plain directions. According
to his account Denman merely advised him to visit that
district, stating that he thought the locality a likely one
for gold.

Be that as it may, Nash, about noon of the day after he
left Denman's camp, came to a gully crossing the track to
Maryborough. We say track, for the road from Brisbane
to Maryborough on which he was now travelling, was in
fact only a mere bush track. A water-hole was near and
Nash, after lighting a fire to boil his quart of tea for
dinner, took his pick and shovel and tin dish to "try a
prospect." How must he have been gratified when, after
merely taking up a dishful of the stuff which lay on the
surface of the bottom of the gully, he obtained two or three
grains of gold on washing it. His interest was awakened,
and he tried another dishful obtained a little further up
the gully, and selected with more care from the face of the
bed rock. When this was washed, a nice little nugget or
two and some coarse gold-dust lay in the dish before his
delighted eyes. Before his dinner was eaten Nash had
washed out a few pounds' worth of gold from the dust thus
easily obtained, and had satisfied himself that he had at
last found what for many long years he had been in quest
of—a payable piece of ground.

As may be supposed, he did not allow the grass to grow under his feet. With that caution characteristic of his class, he removed his " swag" up a bend of the gully where he would be unnoticed by any traveller who might perchance pass that way,—a very rare occurrence,—and fell to work with might and main. Before night fell he was a richer man than he had ever been before. A day or two longer he worked on until he had some 200*l.* or 300*l.* worth of gold, and then he set off for Brisbane to send word to his brother in Sydney and bring up a mate from Fortitude Valley. It may be a matter of surprise to many how Nash could so soon obtain such a considerable sum. But in this place, since known as Nash's Gully, the digging was of the shallowest sort. In the bed of the gully the wash-dirt actually lay on the surface, and the dream of many a sanguine would-be gold-digger from home could here be realized, and big lumps of the precious metal were to be picked out of little " pockets" in the rock with the bare hand or a sheath knife. The nuggets lay about like pebbles or small potatoes only barely covered with the dirt or gravel. In the history of gold-digging there have been few gullies so short where such an amount of wealth has been so easily obtainable. There were deeper works further down this gully, as much as twelve to sixteen feet sinking, but in this part, above the road, four or five feet was the average depth, and this only when the works were carried into the sides of the hills. Up the gully for many hundred yards in its bed, for it is a water-course in rainy weather, the gold dirt was found on the surface.

Obliterating all signs of his work, Nash departed. In Brisbane his natural anxiety to secure himself before making his discovery public induced him to say, when selling his gold, that he had found it on the Morinish diggings, near Rockhampton. There are all over the Australias a number of miners who are always keenly on the watch for any news of the finding of new diggings. To such men, information which to the general public appears of little interest, is fraught with the weightiest import. To men of this class the news when published, that a man had sold seventy or eighty ounces of coarse, heavy gold—which means of large-sized pieces—of water-worn appearance, was sufficient to assure them from their great experience, that where this came from much more of the same sort was to be had. The consequence was that scores, if not hundreds, from all parts of Queensland and New South Wales, rushed off to the Morinish, to find themselves on the wrong scent. They had not long to wait, however, for the correct news. After sending for his brother, Nash with his friend returned *viâ* Maryborough to his diggings, from which town they are situate about fifty-five miles. They took back a horse and dray and a stock of provisions. For some days they worked away undisturbed. When the stockman from the neighbouring run would pass, they remained quiet; but he found them out, and they allayed his suspicion by giving a poor account—they were only prospecting and hardly able to "make tucker,"—earn their rations. But one day a stranger passed and their dog barking, he stopped and looked around. The dog was silenced, but fears of being discovered induced Nash to leave for Maryborough to make his discovery public. His reason for this was, that according to the mining regulations, any digger finding payable gold and making his discovery known was entitled to a prospector's claim, varying in size according to its contiguity to other diggings. At such a distance as this the prospector would be entitled to twenty ordinary

claims. He also became entitled to the reward in cash
offered by Government to the finder of any new gold-field,
which varies in amount from 1000*l.* downwards according
to the number of people the rush would maintain for the
first twelve-months. Should he, however, fail to report his
discovery, and it became known by any other means, he
not only lost all claim to extended ground, but also to the
money reward. Taking with him the result of his labours
up to that time, said by the telegraphic report to be 1000
ounces, but which we believe was less, Nash waited on the
Land Commissioner, laid his gold before him and claimed
his reward.

In a few hours the telegraph had flashed the news over
all the colonies. The people of Queensland were everywhere excited and forgot for a time their poor circumstances. But the news was too good to be true, there
must be some mistake, and they would wait further
information. The people of Maryborough, however, could
see the big nuggets for themselves; Nash showed them
his deposit receipt at the bank or the gold itself, and the
whole town was electrified. The sergeant of police was
sent back with Nash, in default of any other officer, to
mark off his claims and those of other diggers. A run
was made for miner's rights, and half the people of
Maryborough set off pell-mell for the new El Dorado.
On our way to the rush we were told at a neighbouring
station that only one storekeeper, who was too stout for
such work, and women and children were left in the town.
This was an exaggeration, but so many people left, that
work came to a stand-still. At the principal mills and the
sugar plantation, just then commencing crushing, making
a virtue of necessity, a fortnight's leave was given to the
employés.

On arrival at the rush Nash, as is the custom, had to wash out a few pans of dirt in presence of the officer and the crowd, with a view to proving whether or no the ground was payable and he entitled to a prospector's claim. Every dish washed showed the delighted on-lookers a goodly quantity of gold, amongst which was a fair proportion of the welcome nuggets. Twenty-one claims were marked out for Nash in a part of the gully selected by himself and where he had as yet done little or no work. His mate and brother had pegged off ground, and then the new comers were busy in securing each his own ground. There is no scene more exciting or curious than this pegging off. Here, as elsewhere, possession is nine points of the law. Every man holding a miner's right, which in Queensland costs 10s. per annum, is entitled on any diggings to mark off a claim of a certain number of feet, usually 40 × 30 as his "claim." Where it is wet sinking, that is, where it is necessary to bale water in working the ground, the claims are larger. Quartz-reef claims are forty feet on the line of the reef and of an indefinite width. Usually on the news being brought into any diggings that payable gold has been found elsewhere, the Commissioner at once sets off with the prospectors to the place. Such news flies like wild-fire over the diggings and although secrecy is practised in these affairs, to prevent the disappointment which too frequently follows from the rush turning out a "duffer," there will be hundreds ready to proceed with the Commissioner and his party. Every man carries his swag and rations, besides his tools. Usually a party of mates go together and carry with them tent, cooking utensils, and all their kit. Their destination is a secret to all but the prospectors, who have perhaps "laid on" a few intimate friends, who have started over-night

and will be on the ground and select their claims hours
before the others arrive. It is of no use to hurry ; so all go
on leisurely enough until the spot is in sight up the creek
or gully. Then comes a scene ; every man hastens forward
at the top of his speed to peg out his claim. The neophyte
now knows why it is called a " rush." The name is most .
appropriate. Those on horseback gallop ahead, one friend
after another bawling out, " Peg out for me alongside you,
old fellow !" or some such request. Arrived at the ground,
the experienced eye of the digger sees how the land lies at
a glance ; springing from their horses every man, without
troubling himself for the time what becomes of his steed,
quickly paces off two or four men's ground, and drives in
his pegs. The old stagers have cautiously cut four pegs
with their tomahawk some distance back, and have them
all ready to drive into the hard ground. Others seize any
dead branch that can be made to do duty for the present
and, making a hole with their pick, drive it in as best
they may. When the four pegs are in, there is time to
breathe. The kit is placed on the ground, and the miner,
conscious of possessing a stake in the country, can look
around him. On every side is confusion, hallooing,
swearing, quarrelling, and generally one or two fights will
take place. It is best not to leave your claim until things
are a little settled. With his pick, the old digger will
at the corners of his ground indicate his boundaries by
digging little trenches at right angles, and at once mark
off his shaft or hole and turn out the sods so as to bring it
into shape. When he has thus turned out a few spadesful
of earth he feels pretty secure. Old stagers, when mates,
will generally each peg out ground enough for all in
various localities, and by " shepherding " each claim, that
is, working or sitting on it daily for an hour, from ten to

eleven a.m., find out from the efforts of their neighbours
which way the run of the gold is; when, as is nearly always
the case, some of their ground is worthless, this will
be given up and the best, or, in digger's parlance, "the
likeliest ground," be retained. Here, as elsewhere, the
weakest sometimes go to the wall, and a little weakly man
will be overpowered by some big ruffian. As a rule,
however, the diggers act with the greatest justice; we
have seen rushes at which scarcely a hard word was spoken,
and where good fellowship prevailed on all sides.

The major part of the claims on deep sinking are not
worked until a few have been proved. Day after day you
see men sitting on their ground from eleven to twelve, chaff-
ing each other, or listening to a "blower" spinning a yarn.
Here you will see a crowd regularly sitting around the
shafts that are being put down, waiting to see the result,
which will entirely influence their conduct. If two or
three duffers are bottomed where only "the colour," that
is, a speck or two of gold, or nothing whatever is got, the
men begin to thin off daily. In fact on the best diggings
this is always the case to a great extent. Many holes
will certainly be bottomed on poor or unpayable ground,
and the desponding portion of the community clear out,
while the sanguine stop on and thoroughly prove the
ground, often to their thorough satisfaction. When the
author was approaching Gympie, about ten days after the
first rush, he found the road lined with people returning.
Their story was all the same. There were a few immensely
rich claims in Nash's Gully, but they were all taken up,
and the ground around had all been tried, and there was
no gold anywhere else: it was a mere patch. At that
time some of the richest gullies and creeks were open.

After the men have pegged out the ground, they have

time to wait on the Commissioner, who goes to the prospector's claim, sees a prospect washed and declares the
ground payable or otherwise. In the former case he marks
off their ground and hears any disputes which may have
arisen in marking out the other ground. When the miners
are finished with, he has other duties to perform. By and
by the drays and pack-horses of the storekeepers come up,
and there is now a second rush for business sites. Every
person holding a business right, which costs only 2l.
yearly, in addition to his miner's right, may peg off for
himself a business frontage on the street that is laid out.
This is a lot with 40 feet frontage by 120 feet deep. If
a rush has given a good prospect there will be a keen
competition for these sites; pegging out here as in the
claims is evidence of title, but the owner is obliged to
reside. If his lot is unoccupied for twenty-four hours it
may be "jumped," which is done by some one throwing
out his pegs and replacing them with his own. The
jumper, either of a business site or a miner's claim, will be
pretty certain to fall to work at once, so as to show some
practical right to his holding. Much money is often made
by selling these sites. A shrewd fellow will peg out two
or three, and pay miners to erect their tents on the extra
ones. If the diggings succeed, in a week or two a
wealthier class of storekeepers come in than those who
usually " follow the rushes," and finding all the good
sites occupied, are forced to give round sums to their
proprietors. On Gympie as much as from 60l. to 80l.
were given for a frontage within two months of the
first rush.

The scene on a new rush, if the weather be fine, which it
usually is, is of the most active and pleasing character.
Team after team arrives, and whole strings of packhorses,

with every variety of goods. As if by magic a street is formed of big tents or tarpaulins raised on a frame-work. Here a blacksmith has already got his forge at work, and there two or three men are busy in fitting up a stone or iron oven. Here is a carpenter just arrived with a load of new cradles, and pine boards, from which he has already begun to make others. Grog-stores and public-houses are in full blast, and are doing a thriving trade before an ounce of gold has been raised by any but the prospectors. The bar-room is easily adjusted; a large tent, a few forked sticks driven in the ground, one sheet of bark on the top and others at the side for a counter, a few bottles and glasses on a case or two behind, and the affair is complete, while a cotton sign, brought ready painted, gives you the name of the proprietor. At the next door is a general store fitted up in much the same way. Here is a man sitting under the shade of a big tree or an umbrella, with all his goods at his feet like a merchant of Cairo. This, perhaps, consists of a keg of rum, a square block of tobacco, a few boxes of matches, two or three tumblers, and a billy of water. Beyond is a butcher's shop, with plenty of beef and mutton, which he nearly always sells at about 3d. or 4d. per lb. His establishment consists of his tent or bark hut, and a green arbour of boughs with a bark roof for the shop. All these, and many others, will have sprung into full activity by the second or third day, thanks to the genial climate and the neighbouring tribe of blacks, who bring in the bark at a shilling per sheet, and spend their money between the baker, the butcher, and the publican, especially the latter. It is always the same on every new rush : drunken blackfellows are among the most common sights one sees. No licence is taken out for some months on a new rush, there being no establishment that can comply with the requirements of the Act. There is free trade in liquor as in everything else, and nearly every storekeeper has it for sale. On most of the rushes we have seen in Queensland the price of the nobbler of spirits or glass of ale is one shilling; that is also the price of a pound of flour and sugar. These are packhorse prices; in a few days, when a road has been found for the bullock-drays, with the large stocks they bring, prices fall, the nobbler to 6*d*. and the pound of flour from 4*d*. to 8*d*. This is where there is only from 50 to 150 miles' carriage: on the northern diggings prices are never so low as this, we believe. To make amends, butchers' meat, which can always be had close at hand, is never dear; for some years it has been as low as 1½*d*. to 2*d*. on Gympie.

On reaching Gympie the author found that, although less than a fortnight old, there was already a population of nearly 2000, and a street built along the side of Nash's Gully more than a quarter of a mile in length. That gully was full of life and activity from end to end. Drays were busily employed in carting the dirt from the richer or older claims to the river, a distance of nearly two miles. Great care was taken to prevent any falling out, and one of the mates always went with the dray, so rich was the dirt in nuggets. The water-hole by the roadside, where Nash had washed his first prospects, was turned to a thick, yellow mass of pea-soup consistency. Around this all day were men washing dishes of dirt from new claims. We looked in on Nash's claim. He had a large number of men at work, and he and his brother were busy on the look-out for nuggets. We passed on to other claims. We found the men all busy, elated, and reticent; these were the new chum diggers. We afterwards found the regular digger to be not at all backward in answering any civil inquiries, and often

singularly open in his revelations as to his doings. There
is a sort of freemasonry among diggers, and the old hands are
always most communicative among themselves. We noticed
that each man in digging up the dirt had by his side a
pint pannikin. This was to put the nuggets in. One man
told us on our informing him what our reason for inquiry was, that he about half filled that usually every day.
The wash dirt after this would turn out eight to twelve
ounces to the load. We visited the river bank. Here was
another singular scene. All up and down the bank were
men busy washing the dirt in cradles. The scrub had been
cut away, forming a road on the high bank. Opposite to
where each man was working was a wooden platform and
shoot; on the former the dirt was dumped from the dray,
and shot down the latter to the foot of the cradle as he
required it. The bright clear waters of the Mary were
turned to a yellow colour, as indeed they remain to this day,
for many a mile below Gympie. Here we found Mr.
Denman already alluded to, busy cradling the dirt of a claim
in which he was a mate. The cradle has rockers, hence its
name, with a long perpendicular handle to rock it with.
The dirt is shovelled on to an iron hopper filled with round
holes about half an inch in diameter. Underneath it is so
arranged as to catch all the gold on slanting shelves. With
one hand the washer rocks his cradle, and the other holds a
dipper with which he pours water on the mass of dirt. We
noticed that frequently the washers would stop to pick out
a nugget which the water betrayed. When the dirt was all
washed out, the stones that remained were carefully picked
over, and never without a few nuggets more being found.
We were shown a bag of nice shining fellows which had
been thus brought to light. The scene here was both novel
and pretty, and yet clings to memory. It was the first and

L

is still the richest washing we had seen. The busy and
eager row of men bringing to light the wealth that had so
long lain hid; the fine clear river gradually turning yellow
as it laved the feet of the gold-washers; the high and
gorgeous scrub-trees clothing the river on both banks,
until the lower branches of dark-green touched the water;
and high over all the blue sky of Queensland. Outside
the scrub it was hot and sultry, for it was the end of
October; here the air was cool and delightful. A man
might be pardoned if looking alike on the works of
nature and the work of man, as both lay before him, he
decided that there were many worse lives than that of a
digger.

Some time after Nash's Gully was opened, White's
Gully was discovered on the other side of the same ridge.
This was a far poorer gully than the former. On its site is
the far-famed New Zealand reef to which we shall again
refer. Soon after, Walker's Gully, nearer the river and
mostly covered with scrub, was discovered. This gully was
very rich, the sinking a moderate depth, and the gold well-
scattered over the ground; in other words, there was a
regular run of the precious metal, like gravel and pebbles
laid in the bed of a creek. With the exception of Nash's
Gully, no part of Gympie gave larger returns in less time
than did this. Shortly before Christmas gold was found
in the Italian Gully at the One Mile, which soon became a
town rivalling in size Gympie itself. This gully was also
very rich, as was Nuggetty Gully near it. Afterwards
gold was found in the Deep Creek, in enormous quantities
in some instances. This creek, however, was full of water,
and the sinking was wet, much water having to be contended with. One of Nash's mates was the prospector
here, and many thousand ounces were taken from his claim

alone. This man's case is a specimen one of many hundreds. Finding himself suddenly a wealthy man, he and his wife set up to lead the *ton*. They gave champagne parties again and again, and lived for some time as if their money could have no end. They were all at once people of distinction, and appeared determined to make an indelible impression on their contemporaries. For awhile all went merry as a marriage bell; but by-and-by a flood came and filled up the claims on the Deep Creek; for a considerable time no work could be done; then, when the weather and water permitted work, great expense had to be incurred to repair damages. In short, it followed in his case, as in many others, that his money was spent as fast as earned. The last we heard of him, he was working as a " wages-man " on a reef.

To a stranger it appears absolutely impossible that in a place like a diggings' township money can be so squandered as it often is. The stories of the Arabian Nights are not more wonderful than many one hears of in actual life on the diggings. There was an aged miner, who often used to visit the author's store at Jimna, and received now and then a few rations on *credit*—who was one of a party of five or six men who took no less than *one ton* of gold out of a single claim on the Woolshed Diggings in Victoria. Singular to say he was a Scotchman too. He told us that the only good he had done with his large fortune had been to visit Scotland and purchase a comfortable residence for an aged mother. There is a class of men on every diggings who are always lucky in obtaining a good claim and yet pass at least three fourths of their time in drunkenness. We have often heard it observed that this sort of people are almost always more fortunate than sober men. At any rate one meets few diggers who will not affirm it, and we

have seen many instances that give a colouring of truth to
the statement.

It is wonderful how even the sober miners manage to
let their money slip through their fingers. We remember
a journeyman printer, who told us he took 6000l. as his
share of a claim on the Lachlan, at the final settlement,
besides his weekly share of the nuggets. The claim was
nearly two years in working and every nugget found was
put into a fund which was divided between the six mates
for current expenses and pocket-money. This man had
never been a drunkard nor gambler, but by speculating in
shares in quartz reefs, &c., he had gradually lost all his
money. We mention these cases as instances of how most
diggers get rid of their wealth. A whole volume might
easily be filled with similar cases; such a work by one
who had the industry to compile it, would exhibit many a
phase in real life, of which people at home have no
conception. We have come to the conclusion that when a
miner has been fortunate and made a large sum in one
claim, unless he gives up digging at once or invests his
money, he will be certain to lose it again in the long-run.
Nash followed this wise course. When he had worked out
his claims and realized a large sum he at once took to
himself a wife, and gave up a digger's life. He had a
reward of 1000l. from Government as the discoverer of the
field. Various sums, varying from 10,000l. to 20,000l., were
mentioned as his clear earnings, but we believe that he
has never made public what he really did realize. After
visiting England with his wife, he purchased a place with a
very pretty view of the Mary River, a few miles above its
mouth and within an easy distance of Maryborough. It
is said that although he had been a digger for many years,
this was his first " rise." Very few men appear to deserve

success more, judging from the quiet way in which he has settled down, and the unassuming manner with which he has deported himself.

Of the other prospectors on the Gympie Diggings, we know nothing except Walker. This man, often spoken of as "Alligator Walker," is quite a character in his way. He earned this sobriquet by his former achievements in catching these saurians in the Fitzroy River, and for his not less interesting yarns since then, in which he fights his battles over again with sufficient gusto. Walker did not work out his claim in the gully which bears his name, but having been drinking very hard, he quarrelled with his mates and threw up his claim in disgust. With the remains of a very handsome amount of gold, he purchased a little cutter, which he called the "James Nash" in honour of the prospector, fitted her up in a first-rate style, and has since made a very comfortable income by trading in her. Since leaving Gympie he has abjured drink, and frequently spends a few weeks with his wife and family aboard, fishing for sharks in Hervey's, or Wide Bay. When last we saw him he was about to sell the "James Nash" to purchase a larger vessel. He too has become a land-owner, having selected a nice piece of land on the Burrum with a view to sugar-growing.

There have been many large fortunes made on Gympie, in the reefing line more especially. The alluvial diggings were too quickly worked out to admit of such large sums being made in them as in the larger diggings in the southern colonies, although there were not a few who did very well on Gympie. An acquaintance informed us on one occasion that two young men, friends of his, and whose claim had been contiguous to his in Walker's Gully had just left for England in a ship from Sydney. He said he would then tell me, what he had promised to keep secret as long as necessary, that they had carried away with them one hundred pounds' weight of gold each, which they had kept buried in their tent unknown to any one, only selling enough to pay their way. This was the result of about four months' work. There must have been many other claims in that gully not much behind this one in productiveness.

The Gympie Diggings had not attracted much notice beyond the colony until the finding of the Curtis Nugget. This fine piece of gold, which was worth over 3000*l.*, was found under very peculiar circumstances in a very poor claim. The claim was on the side of the ridge between Nash's and White's Gullies, in a little gully running into the former. Just as they were about to abandon the ground for its poverty, one of the parties struck his pick into this nugget, which was soon unearthed and carried in procession to the bank. Mr. Curtis, however, did not reap as much benefit as he should have done from this find. Many persons put in claims for a share in the proceeds, and much litigation followed. In the long-run, we believe it cost Curtis half as much to fee lawyers to defend his right as the whole of the money obtained from it.

But the finding of this nugget set the whole digging population of the Australias and New Zealand in motion. They had cared little for the splendid finds in Nash's Gully, that might be only a patch; but where a nugget of that size was obtained there must be more gold. A tremendous rush set in, and by the end of February, 1868, there were not less than 10,000 persons on the diggings. New buildings of a more permanent character sprung up daily, two theatres were opened, one at Gympie and one at the One Mile, as also a church or two; singing and dance houses abounded; a newspaper was started and a committee formed to improve the main street, which from the enormous travel over it had now become a vast slough. But with all this increase of population very little new ground was opened, and great was the ire of the Southerners against the "Banana men," as they choose to call the Queenslanders, for their luck in holding all the payable ground. As the population grew denser dissatisfaction began to prevail; fortunately the newspapers of Queensland had been very guarded, and care had been taken not to overrate the diggings and thus draw men on a wild-goose chase. But one mishap occurred. The local paper stated one day that a man had obtained a certain number, —five, we think,—of pennyweights of gold, by diving in a water-hole in the Mary River. This was believed to be incorrect, and although this statement appeared after all the people had arrived on the diggings and could not therefore have influenced their conduct, a *casus belli* was made of the paragraph. A "roll up" took place on a Friday evening to the *Times* office. Soon, not less than a thousand men gathered in front of the door, and loud cries were made for the editor. That gentleman evinced no anxiety to present himself. The author hearing the hubbub got up into a tree in the street near the corner of the office, to watch proceedings. Threats to pull down the place were heard and a few stones were thrown on the roof. Making a virtue of necessity the editor at last came to the door. A man who constituted himself the spokesman of the party, thrust a copy of the paper in his face and asked him if he acknowledged the obnoxious paragraph. He told him he did. He had been careful to cross-question the man who had given him the information; he could do no more. Finally it was agreed that he should have until

the morrow afternoon, when, if he produced the man at the
court-house, well; if not, he was pretty plainly informed
that his own proper person and the office itself would be in
great jeopardy.

At the time in question the editor and his authority,—a
big, heavy-faced Hungarian, whom we afterwards found
to be a great scoundrel,—put in an appearance. First,
the editor said, he had an explanation to make. A typo-
graphical error had occurred; what was printed *pennyweights* should have been *grains*—a considerable mistake
certainly, but mistakes would happen in the best regulated offices. Being an Irishman and no fool, the editor
managed to soft-sawder his hearers, themselves Irishmen
to a large extent, and when he saw neither himself nor the
office stood in much danger, he introduced the digger to
give an account of his part of the transaction. That
worthy went on to say how one day he had dived in the
river and brought up a few handfuls of sand from the
bottom, in which he had found some gold; he had repeated
this operation until he had obtained the quantity spoken of.
No one believed his story, but he got off on the ground
that perhaps he was too big a fool to know mica from gold,
and that perhaps he had found some of the latter. It is
not doubted by any that the bed of the Mary is auriferous;
it is almost certain there must be large quantities of gold
deposited there; but the gold is certainly not lying in fine
particles on the top of the gravel. In the year 1868, great
efforts were made to prospect the bed of the Mary. It had
been a dry season and the river was very low. Many
holes were sunk, in one or two of which they were so near
the bottom as to obtain a little gold. But a heavy shower
rose the river just at this critical juncture, and it has never
again been low enough to resume the works. The Mary

has so many long creeks running into it from the mountains that a heavy shower in almost any part of that district suffices to swell its waters. The last three years have been unusually moist. The season of 1871-72 promised however to be very dry. If so, we may expect to hear of mining operations being resumed in the bed of the Mary River.[1]

About the time of the greatest influx of people, the Gympie Reefs first began to attract attention. The first two from which crushings were obtained were the Caledonian and Lady Mary Reefs and the returns were highly successful. This caused a great impetus to be given to reefing. New reefs were being prospected and rushed almost daily, until reefing operations were in full swing over an area extending six miles on the south and twelve miles on the north of Gympie. Considerable capital is required in reefing, and after expending sums on their claims varying from 10*l.* to 200*l.* or 300*l.*, a very large number of the men had to throw up work, register their claims and go further afield, either to the new rushes springing up in the north, to the southern colonies, or on some station in the bush. In every direction in which one travels around Gympie may be seen these deserted shafts. On some of them extensive and substantial horse-powers and other improvements have been erected, and shafts are put down in the most approved manner, while hundreds of tons of " mullock," as diggers call clay, and stone attest to the large capital of time and money which must have been expended. Others have less work done on them, the holders having exhausted their funds more

[1] The author has not heard since leaving the colony of any fresh attempts to prospect the bed of the Mary.

quickly. There is no reason to doubt that many of those
reefs, if they had been thoroughly proved, would have
turned out as rich as those now being worked. As proof of
this we may refer to the claim number 7 and 8 amalgamated,
on the South Monckland Reef. The owners of this claim
were eight men principally from Devonshire, with the
steady industry that generally characterizes the West of
England men. They worked at their claim for over twelve
months, when the Gilbert rush breaking out, they registered
it for three more and started off to take a look at the new
diggings. At the end of their registration they were again on
their reef. Shaft after shaft was put down until three years'
time and some hundreds per man had been expended. At the
end of that time their wonderful perseverance was rewarded.
The reef was struck and the first crushing yielded them
1500 ounces of gold, worth 3*l.* 6*s.* per ounce. In this case
the men were incited to expend their time and money by the
fact that all the claims up to theirs were on the reef and
fortunes were being made by their owners. If it had
occurred that this portion of the reef had been first struck
on, the far-famed Monckland Reef would probably never
have existed. Now this claim is turning out about 1000*l.*
to 2000*l.* per share per annum and may continue to do that
for an indefinite period. We once rode with one of this
party from Gympie to Brisbane. They had then been over
a year at work, and he had expended 200*l.* on the reef. He
happened to be in our company again for some days after
he had netted some thousands from his reef. We could not
discover the least difference in his deportment. He had
still the same quiet, unassuming manner as when gradually
sinking all his hard-earned gains. One cannot but feel
pleased when fortune showers her favours in the laps of
such worthy recipients.

It may be interesting to some readers to learn how these wonderful golden reefs are found, what they are like, and how the gold is extracted from them. As a rule all auriferous reefs are of quartz. With their characteristic self-sufficiency the geologists gave out that gold could not possibly be found in any other material—just as they deny the whole Mosaic account of the Creation. For many years there was no one to contradict them in this as in many other of their assertions. Gold had never been found except in quartz, therefore it could only be found in quartz, and by no possibility could any other be a gold-bearing stone. As it takes a certain time for given causes to produce certain results now, therefore these results must always have required an equal length of time, and the first chapter of Genesis is only to be pooh-poohed by sensible men. There has been nothing to turn the tables on this last argument, nor is it probable we shall ever be able to disprove their assertions as to the Creation. But gold has within the last three years been found in reefs of other stone than quartz in Queensland. On the Gilbert Diggings none of the richest reefs are quartz; thus adding another to the many flat contradictions which the gold-digger has given to the theories of the geologists. It would be an interesting inquiry, and a very instructive treatise might be written to show in what particulars the diggers of Australia have contradicted the axioms of the geologists. We have given one instance; another occurred on Gympie, in which the celebrated green-stone theory, which was as much a truth to every geologist as the " unlimited ages" theory of the Creation, was proved to be as fallacious as we have no doubt the other would be proved, could it be done • with miners' tools. We do not wish to ignore geology. Kept within bounds it is of vast benefit to the miner as to

many others. The evil is that being almost entirely an
inductive science, its professors judging from insufficient
data, form monstrous and false theories which they
would cram down people's throats to the injury sometimes of their pockets and sometimes of their faith.
Had the repeated assertions of the geologists in reference
to the green-stone been listened to, many of the richest
finds of gold on Gympie would never have been made.
And when practical tests prove some of these assumed
facts to be false, there seems no reason why we should
believe those that they can neither prove true nor we
erroneous.

As a rule, however, all auriferous reefs are quartz-reefs;
but it by no means follows that all quartz-reefs are
auriferous. The miner in prospecting for a reef has two
tests. After having found a "blow-out" or outcrop of a
reef, he sets to work, digs down beside it for a greater or
less distance. He will generally be guided in his proceedings by the look of the quartz. If he fancies it is "likely"
quartz, he will, as we have said, sink down with a view to
finding the reef. Perhaps he may soon come on it, or
perhaps he finds he has a "leader"—a small vein of the
reef which has apparently been thrown to the surface, when
in a molten state. Sometimes these leaders connect directly
with the reef, at others they are broken off and jump as it
were from side to side, thus misleading the miner. When
he has satisfied himself that it is a leader, or the reef he is
on, the prospector collects a dishful of the "casing"—the
dirt lying close to the reef—in which there will be a lot of
loose pieces of quartz. This he washes and looks for gold
. in, just as in wash dirt. If he finds any it is almost
certain the reef is auriferous; if payable there will probably
be some of the pieces of quartz with gold in them: these

are called "specimens." In many reefs at Gympie large quantities of gold have been obtained from the casing, sometimes more than from the reef itself.

When a prospector can show "good gold" in his casing and specimens, he will be granted a prospecting claim and the reef is rushed and marked off by the commissioner. A shaft much larger than in alluvial sinking is now begun. Usually a staging of logs is raised ten or twelve feet above the surface of the ground on which the windlass is placed. This is to admit of room for the mullock and stone to be cast out as it is thrown out of the shaft. As the shaft deepens, the sides are substantially slabbed. The stone is removed by boring and blasting. At one time, on Gympie, a stranger might have supposed that a cannonading was going on, from the constant explosion of the various blasts which continued from morning till night. In some claims the reef is soon found and the stone is rich enough to enable the miners to pay their working expenses by picking out the richer part of the stone, burning it in a fire, and then pounding it in a large iron mortar. In some tents the sound of this operation might be heard night after night all the week round. For some time this was the only means of crushing the quartz, as there were no crushing-machines erected. In the meantime the reefers had to stack their quartz and in some cases fence it around to prevent the richer parts from being carried off at night. The first crushing-machine erected was the "Pioneer," which was a small and not very good one. But soon one after another was erected until there were five in full operation night and day. By this time the alluvial diggings were pretty well worked out, and the whole . dependence of this gold-field has been on its quartz-reefs since then. An attempt at deep sinking was made on the

bank of the Mary, but from insufficiency of capital or
other causes it was not attended with success.

Nothing can be more beautiful than some of the gold
specimens, as they are torn out of the solid reef by the
blastings.   We have seen some which resembled threads of
gold drawn out from the quartz.   As a rule the reefs are
not very wide, running from three or four to eighteen or
twenty-four inches on the average; a few are wider.   The
reefs do not run down perpendicularly, but on an incline.
Many of the reefs which yielded large returns at first have
since been of little value.   The Louisa, for instance, was
almost one mass of gold—more gold than stone—at first,
but of late it is never heard of.[2]   Doubtless, many
of what were called reefs were only mere leaders or
blow-outs, and, after yielding an immense proportion of
gold per ton at first, soon ran out entirely.   On one
occasion a woman going with the dinner for her husband
and mates, seeing a piece of quartz in her path, stooped and
picked it up.   It was heavy and bright with gold on the
under part.   She carried the information to her husband;
he and his mates repaired at once to the spot and laid open
a perfect "jeweller's shop."   They worked on into the
night, the woman holding candles and making fires.
Before they slept they were rich men.   It was thought
a valuable reef had been discovered, but the gold and
quartz soon ran out altogether.

In some of the reefs the gold is found in patches.   A
quantity of stone will be raised hardly worth crushing,
when all at once a few bucketfuls will be struck with
more gold than stone.   Such is the Californian Reef, in

_____
[2] This reef appears of late to have been reworked with good
results.

which immense finds have been made, almost unparalleled in the history of reefing. We remember once seeing a heap of this glittering stuff in the window of the Joint Stock Bank at Gympie, where it attracted thousands of spectators.

Other reefs, like the New Zealand Reef, carry the gold regularly through the stone, in very fine particles. These reefs are generally the most lasting, and where sufficiently wide are very wealthy. As an interesting and reliable account of what such reefs as these sometimes do for the miners of Queensland, we append an account of the Prospector's Claim, New Zealand Reef, furnished by the manager, Mr. Thomas Cockburn, under date of Gympie, 31st March, 1871, to the Hon. R. R. Pring, at that time acting as a Royal Commissioner to take evidence and examine into the working of the Queensland Gold-fields, with a view to improved legislation. We give the paper in full.

" SIR,—Acceding to your wish, I place before you a few figures and statistics showing the yield of gold from, and the expenses incurred in working the Prospecting Claim, New Zealand Reef, on this goldfield.

" Work was commenced on the claim early in December, 1867. The reef was found near the surface, and was proved by sinking shafts to a depth of seventy feet. At this depth levels were put in to the boundaries, and the ground stoped to the surface. This was completed by the beginning of October, 1869.

	oz.	dwt.	gr.
The amount of quartz crushed to that date was 1427 tons, which yielded retorted gold . . .	8,028	14	12
The loss in smelting was	162	7	1
Which leaves for smelted gold .	7,866	7	11

This gold realized 3l. 7s. 9d. per oz.,
value £26,631 11 0
Total wages to this date . £1,831 10 0
Other expenses . . 1,353 2 6
                          ——————— 3,184 12 5

Returning a clear dividend, in less than
two years, of . . . £23,446 18 7

"The average yield of the stone during this period was 5 ozs. 12½ dwts. to the ton; the total cost, including crushing charges, 2l. 3s. 3d., or 14 dwts., per ton.

"Subsequently to the completion of this work, two shafts have been sunk to the 140 feet level, proving the reef, on the underline, all the way down. Then the workings were opened out and levels put in as above. At the present time the stopes are within thirty feet of the old workings or upper level.

The quantity of quartz crushed, from this section of the
mine, up to the 22nd February, 1871, has been
1,382 tons, which yielded retorted gold . . . 10,478 5 6
Loss in smelting 309 4 16

Which leaves for smelted gold . 10,169 0 14
This gold realized 3l. 7s. 7d. per oz.,
value £34,374 13 2
Amount expended in wages £3,764 18 0
Other expenses incurred . 2,245 9 6
6,010 7 6

Returning a clear dividend, in less than
a year and a half, of . . . £28,364 5 8
"The average yield of the stone from this part was 7 ozs. 11½ dwts. to the ton. The total cost, 26 dwts., or 4l. 7s., per ton. This includes, crushing charges, erecting whim, purchase of horses, &c. The total quartz crushed (2,909 tons) has yielded 18,506 ozs. 19 dwts. 18 grs. retorted gold, or at the average rate of 6 ozs. 11½ dwts. to the ton, at a cost of 3l. 5s. 6d., or one ounce per ton.

Total cash realized . . . £61,006 4 0
Deduct wages and other expenses 9,195 0 0

Leaves a clear dividend of £51,811 4 0
"The reef has averaged throughout about one foot six inches in thickness. Before closing I beg to inform you that a new shaft, nine feet by three feet four inches, is going down, to prospect for the reef at a greater depth. It was commenced in the middle of August, 1870, and has now been sunk 130 feet, at a cost of 600l. 5s., or 4l. 12s. 4d. per foot, timber and everything included."

Many a romance might be told of reefing adventures. Speculating in this industry has all the excitement and uncertainty of gambling. It is usual for capitalists, store-keepers, &c., to " back " men working in reefs. This is done in this way. According to the present law two men may hold four men's ground until a payable reef has been struck. Thus two miners without any means, having each of them a backer, can take up a claim of 160 feet on the line of the reef. Each of these will usually receive 25s. per week from his backer, who will also pay his share of the expenses of the claim, usually amounting to 4s. or 5s. per week more, for powder and fuse, new tools, blacksmith's work in sharpening and steeling picks and gads, &c. Without a system of this sort not half the gold would be obtained that is now got. Sometimes the reef turns out well, at others and more frequently it proves a " duffer," or what is the same thing, the men grow tired of working for nothing and make a change to some other place. Every man knows he stands more chances of losing than gaining, yet nothing will prevent people from investing their money in this way. Hundreds of men have sunk their all, perhaps a few scores, perhaps as many hundreds in this backing business. The splendid fortunes that are made by it still induce other men to try their chance. We must conclude this portion of our work with an anecdote illustrative of the risks in this business.

A gentleman who had been one of the earliest successful reefers on Gympie, speculated in a great many claims, into some of which he purchased. He continued to pay into them all until his funds were nearly or entirely exhausted. On one occasion he was not able to pay his men their wages, and they informed him that if not paid the next Saturday they should work no longer. The week passed on until Friday evening arrived. Then a blast was made in one of his claims, and when the smoke had cleared away, there before the eyes of the astonished gazers was a perfect mass of gold. Bucket after bucket of the glittering ore was sent up to grass, and then the whole was conveyed to the bank. Our hero then found no difficulty in paying his men the next afternoon. Within a few days another claim struck gold, and in less than a month, from one claim and another, he was calculated to have netted over 6000l. Had not that first fortunate hit been made he would in all probability have been a ruined man.

Gympie has now settled down into a staid township of about 4000 inhabitants. The other rushes in the north have absorbed the alluvial diggers, and the place is now entirely supported by its reefs. A daily coach runs to Maryborough, and another twice a week to and from Brisbane, from which it is distant 125 miles by the new road. This latter road has been entirely opened from the Caboolture since Gympie was founded. The old road was never used for teams, passing over a steep range known as Mackenzie's Range. The present road keeps for the first part on the low coast-lands, passing among the Glasshouses, of which many lovely views are caught. It enters the coast ranges, about half way to Gympie, and opens up some splendid mountain scenery. These hills are mostly of splendid soil, and we have often thought might be turned to good account for coffee plantations. That plant flourishes well in the Wide Bay District. We have seen quite a young tree from which two pounds of coffee could be gathered about three different times in the season. We must state, however, that there has never been an attempt made in the colony in our knowledge to grow this berry other than as an experiment. About Maryborough, however, it may be found in many gardens, and always covered with berries in the season. If ever coffee growing becomes an occupation in Queensland, and we know no reason why it may not, we fancy these hills, with their splendid soil and contiguity to the sea, insuring plenty of moisture and an equable climate, will be a favourite spot for the coffee grower.

In May, 1868, Kilkivan rush broke out, and in the next month the Yabber or Jimna Diggings were rushed. The former of these places lies to the north-west of Gympie, and the latter to the south-west. Neither of them were very rich, they are what is usually called "poor man's diggings," as the work was shallow and the gold easily obtained. Kilkivan Diggings lay on a nice open creek. It was a very pretty sight to see the white tents of the diggers pitched under the green apple-trees on a slight ridge, with the high, bold hills rising directly in their rear. This country is very metalliferous, and some moderately good reefs were afterwards opened at the Black Snake, about six miles from the original diggings. There is only a small population on this place now, principally occupied on the gold-reefs and copper-mines.

Jimna Diggings are situate in a place the very opposite of Kilkivan. Instead of open flats covered with grass, were steep mountains covered with scrubs. Jimna is situated in the mountainous country in which rise the head-waters of the Mary to the north, and tributaries of Stanley Creek and the Brisbane on the south. To mend matters, it was the depth of winter, and wet weather when we first saw the place. As a rule the Queensland winter is the most lovely weather imaginable, dry and sufficiently cool to be comfortable. But on this occasion it was both wet and cold. We shall never forget the sight that presented itself to our wondering gaze when we first saw this rush. For a mile or so we had been descending the side of a steep ridge

by a narrow track cut through the scrub sufficiently wide
to admit of one horse only.   All at once we came on the
rush.   Peeping through the scrub in every direction were
the tents and fires of the diggers.   But for every canvas tent
there were at least three bark mi-mis, made of the bark of
the turpentine trees, of which the scrub was thick.   It was
a wet, foggy day, and everything was damp and unpleasant.
The rich soil was greasy, and the vines and shrubs were
loaded with moisture.   There were not less than 2000 men
crowded on the side of this wooded hill, in all imaginable
sorts of impromptu residences.   Already stores and butchers'
shops were being erected of the universal bark and leaves
of cabbage palm.   As we neared the creek the crowd grew
denser.   Here was a facetious young miner acting as
auctioneer, and selling the tools, &c., of miners, who,
already disgusted with the place, from the cheerless aspect
it presented, were about to return, but would not carry up
and down the steep mountains their heavy kit of tools.
Picks and shovels that a fortnight after would have brought
a pound a set, were sold for a shilling or even sixpence.
For so contagious is despondency that when a dozen or two
good healthy growlers declare in loud voice and constantly,
of a wet day, that the rush is a duffer, hundreds will at
once believe them without the least evidence whatever.
Hundreds were thus induced to leave this rush, and the
place was soon half empty.   The mining here was very
easy.   There was a strong flow of water in the creek.
Troughs were made of the hollow trunks of the cabbage
palms which grew in large quantities; sluices were thus
improvised, and the "stuff" quickly washed, and very good
wages were made.   So poor were many of the men that
they could purchase no rations to bring with them more
than sufficient for the journey, and had to subsist until

they had found gold, on the soft heart of the cabbage palm, found near its top, and which resembles the stump of a cabbage or cauliflower, being, however, sweeter and more nutritious. Another payable creek was found in a few days, called Sunday Creek from the day it was rushed. It is very unusual for a thing of this sort to occur and no pegging out on that day is lawful. The men slept on the ground in most instances, and thus secured their claims. These two creeks maintained a population of from 1000 to 2000 for some months. What was remarkable here was the fact, that although none of the claims were very rich, all yielded tolerable wages to their holders. Thus hundreds, who had before been in great poverty, " made a rise " on Jimna. No payable reefs have as yet been discovered on this diggings, although there can be no question that some must exist. There is still a population of about 200 here.

A later rush took place in the year 1869 to Imbil, about twenty miles south of Gympie. The character of this rush is somewhat similar to that at Kilkivan. It still maintains a small population.

The district of Wide Bay—and the same remark holds true more or less of all parts of Queensland—is not dependent for its mineral resources on its gold deposits alone. We have already referred to the coal formations, which are most extensive and of an excellent quality. Among its minerals we may mention marble, which is to be seen lying ready for the hand of man in many places. Shale is also found in some places, but whether capable of yielding kerosene has not as yet been proved. Among its metals are silver, lead, copper, and iron. This district and the neighbouring one of the Burnett, which lies to the west, are promising to become famous for their copper-mines.

At the Black Snake, Mount Coora, and many other places, very rich lodes have been found, and to some extent developed. At Mount Perry, about ninety miles to the west of Maryborough, a Sydney company has lately commenced mining operations on a large scale, having a capital of 100,000l. Already over 200 persons are employed on this mine, and the operations are all on a scale of great magnitude. Several smelting furnaces are being erected, and in the mean time the ore is exported to Newcastle, New South Wales. It is thought from the indications already existing, that this mine will soon equal in value the far-famed Moonta Mine of South Australia.[3] There are many other lodes which have been worked to some extent, but the great want of capital precludes their being developed at present. Enough is known to warrant the belief that the Wide Bay and Burnett districts will yet furnish a very large amount of copper ore.

[3] Since the above was written we have received information from Maryborough that the first year's operations of this company has enabled them to pay all their expenses in opening the mine and erecting their works, besides eturning their capital in full.

CHAPTER VII.

HITHERTO the author in his description of the colony has spóken principally of what has come under his own observation. He thinks it right to state that he can carry that personal description no further north. His remarks on the northern districts will be therefore of second-hand character, although it is hoped equally correct with the foregoing chapters.

Lying to the north of the Wide Bay District is that of Port Curtis. It comprises the ports of Gladstone and Rockhampton. There is nothing worthy of the name of an agricultural settlement in the district, although there are a few settlers on the Reserve in the neighbourhood of Rockhampton. Up to within a short time the impression has prevailed that this district was entirely unfitted for any kind of agricultural operations. But of late this idea has been somewhat modified, and we believe a company was formed in Rockhampton last year for the purpose of growing sugar in that neighbourhood.

The town of Gladstone has not at all realized the great expectations which were once formed of it. The port and harbour are excellent, the best, it is understood, in the colony. But although founded with great *éclat* in 1846, the town has never made any great progress. There are various reasons for this. There is no back country to the port, ranges cutting it off from the interior, which has for its port the town of Rockhampton. The land is apparently unfitted for agriculture, as nothing has been done in that way there, although certainly that is an insufficient reason for coming to that conclusion. The population is about 400. There has of late years a small but very lucrative trade sprung up between this port and New Caledonia in live cattle. A few cargoes were also sent to New Zealand. The facilities of this port for this business are excellent, and as most of the stations in the neighbourhood are cattle stations, the trade is carried on to the best advantage. Horses have been exported from here to India in past years, but for some reason the trade was never fully established. There is a salt manufactory here, by which salt is made from sea-water in a very ingenious manner, and with satisfactory results.

To the south of Gladstone is Baffle Creek, on which is a boiling-down establishment where a large business is done to the great advantage of the neighbouring stations. There are some small diggings near Gladstone. The Calliope Diggings have been worked for many years, and appear to maintain a small population regularly. The Raglan Gold-diggings, and the Krombit copper-mine are also in this neighbourhood.

Rockhampton, on the Fitzroy River, is in its history the very opposite of Gladstone. No well-paid and dignified officials in full dress first landed on its shores and took possession in her Majesty's name. Rockhampton owes its existence to a " duffer rush." In July, 1858, gold was found at a place called Canoona, some eighty-five miles up the Fitzroy River. A tremendous rush set in from all parts of the colonies. Fifteen thousand people are stated to have been collected on the spot only to find that the gold had been in a small patch and was all worked out. Then with that revulsion of feeling which so soon takes hold of a mining population, the crowd who had arrived big with the highest anticipations, sank to the depths of despair. They forsook the place, as rashly as they had hastened to it, and Canoona knew them no more. Recent events have shown that had they prospected the country they could have found gold enough to reward them all for their pains. But they did nothing of the sort. In fact such was the want among them, that the Governments of New South Wales and Victoria had to send vessels to bring the more destitute back. Out of the ashes of Canoona arose the vigorous young town of Rockhampton, which is situated about forty-five miles up the Fitzroy River. The town rose with great rapidity, and has now a population of 6400. The streets are a chain and a half wide, and a fine esplanade, with a row of shade trees, fronts the river, and affords a beautiful lounge for the inhabitants.

Rockhampton is, and must always continue to be a place of great importance, as the port of a vast amount of pastoral country. Many of the tributaries of the Fitzroy, as the Isaac, the Mackenzie, and the Dawson, are large and important rivers, with many large and wealthy squattages on their banks. It is the port for the far-famed Barcoo and Thompson Rivers, on which is the most splendid pastoral country in Australia. It has also a great portion of the trade of the Peak Downs gold and copper mines, although a considerable portion of the produce of the latter is sent to Broad Sound for shipment, as being a shorter route. There is a short railway built from here to Westwood, to which we have already referred.[1] There can

[1] This line of railway is now being extended towards the Peak Downs.

be no question that ere long this line will be extended to the Expedition Range, if not on to Clermont. Rockhampton is just within the tropics, and here alligators are met with for the first time in journeying northward. There is a large number of diggers employed in the country around Rockhampton, and within easy distance of it. The principal diggings are the Crocodile, Morinish, Cawarral, New Zealand Gully, and Rosewood. On all of these good finds are occasionally made, and now and then large nuggets are unearthed. Of late considerable attention is being paid to reefing, which promises to become a very important industry.

Inland from Rockhampton, 180 miles, is the town of Clermont, the centre of the mining industry of the Peak Downs. A portion of the population, amounting in all to 500, are engaged in gold mining, and the others are employed by the Copper Mining Co., at Copperfield, a rival town grown up near the mine and about two miles from the older town. The great drawback to mining here is the extreme scarcity of water. At Clermont a dam has been erected at considerable expense by the Government, and thus this evil is somewhat obviated there. But it must be evident that a business which depends so much on water, can make but poor headway where it can only be had by artificial means. Consequently very few new rushes have taken place here since the first opening of the field some nine years since. The copper-mine is understood to pay a very handsome dividend.

The town of Clermont is very liable to floods. In 1869 one took place that nearly swept away the entire town and proved fatal to some of its inhabitants. One poor old woman, seventy-five years of age, in company with a younger one, floated away on a haystack, and met her death by drowning—a unique and original mode of death, that if the old lady was at all curious in that way must have partially toned down the horror of her position. The editor of the local paper was obliged to take refuge in a tree, and had the pleasure of seeing his office gutted and his types and paper carried off, the one to be strewed in pie on the soft ground and the other perhaps to form an unwholesome meal for an alligator. By some unaccountable oversight the town was built in the bed of the Wolf-fang Creek. This stream comes down when flooded in the most remarkably sudden manner. On one occasion a solid body of water, said to be about fifteen feet high, came down like a cataract, and was the first notice the people had of an approaching flood, no rain having fallen at Clermont. Many thousand sheep were carried away in this flood, and after the waters had subsided, the trees for many miles down the creek had a crop of sheep in their branches sixty to seventy feet above the ground. The height to which these floods sometimes rise is almost fabulous. At Gympie the Mary once rose over ninety feet. A friend of ours once saw a saddled horse in the fork of a tree which he computed to be from sixty to seventy feet high. We knew an instance of a teamster who had to run for his life one night from under his dray, where he was sleeping, and leave everything to the mercy of the flood. After the waters had gone down he went in quest of his bullocks. His attention was attracted to a flock of birds over-head, and looking up he saw one of his cattle in the tree-top, off which the hawks and crows were making a feed. He found nearly all his working-bullocks, not on the ground as he had anticipated, but gibbetted in the tops of the trees. Taught by bitter experience the people of Claremont are gradually rebuilding their town on the ridge beyond, where they will be free from all danger of floods.

Excepting Broad Sound, where there are very few inhabitants, the next port to the north of Rockhampton is Mackay, situated on the Pioneer River. Some seven or eight years ago Mr. Hill, the Curator of the Botanic Gardens, visited this river, and wrote a report of its wonderfully fertile lands, lying ready for the plough and quite clear of timber. Under the coffee and sugar regulations of 1866 some of these lands were taken up for sugar growing. When the operations in the south of the colony had proved that sugar *could* be grown in Queensland, a great impetus was given to the settlement on this river, until all the lands bordering on navigation have been taken up. A town has sprung up which has now 800 inhabitants, and the foundation is laid of what is doubtless destined to be one of the wealthiest districts in the colony. Where very recently the foot of the white man had not trod, field after field of the most splendid sugar-cane is now seen. A friend of ours who visited Mackay in 1870 described the scene as most lovely. For miles before entering the town the road passes between fields of cane which droops gracefully over the fence on either side, partially shading the road. Weekly steamers connect this port with Brisbane and Sydney. In 1869, 393 tons of sugar, and 9900 gallons of rum were produced here, and, in 1870, 819 tons of sugar and 23,985 gallons of rum. 538 acres of cane were crushed in 1870 and 830 acres were under crop. The total average yield per acre in 1870 was 1 ton, 10 cwt., 1 qr., 16 lbs, being the highest in the colony. No one appears to doubt that this district will yet take the lead in Queensland as a sugar-growing district. There are several good gardens in cultivation near the town of Mackay, where all sorts of tropical fruits are grown with the greatest success. There were four mills and one distillery in this district in 1870.

Not many years since Mackay and all the country to the north was looked on as the " far north," which if not exactly *terra incognita* was still of too little importance to attract much attention. Nothing speaks more forcibly of the enormous growth of the colony than the wonderful expansion of settlement in the north. When the writer arrived in Brisbane, in 1863, Bowen, the only port to the north of Mackay, was just being settled. Soon after, a large sum of money was spent in building a long jetty here, as the water of Port Denison is shallow for some distance from the shore. We believe the growth of this town has not been equal to the hopes first formed of it. Soon after the settlement of this place Townsville was also settled, and became a very powerful rival for the northern trade. Bowen has now a population of about 700. It is the port for the Ravenswood, Cape River, and Mt. Wyatt Diggings. Of these the Ravenswood is the most important, having been worked with good results since 1869. It has many very rich reefs. The peculiarity of this field is that the gold is found in a granite formation. Squatting is the only other industry in this district; there being no agriculture worth mentioning.

Townsville to the north of Bowen, situate in Cleveland Bay, has managed to outgrow its southern rival. As the name indicates, the late Hon. Robert Towns, of Sydney, was its principal founder, and from the first it has been a spirited, stirring town. It has a population of about 1200, and is the port for the Gilbert, Etheridge, and Star, and other gold-fields, although a portion of the trade of these places finds its way to Cardwell, a port still further to the north. The trade of these northern ports rises and falls

with the condition of the gold-mines, although there is
always a natural expansion besides. As showing to what
an extent the discovery of new gold-fields affected the old
ones, at least for a time, it may be stated, that on the Cape
River Diggings a quartz-crushing machinery worth 1000*l.*
was left entirely unprotected and uncared for, on the
breaking out of the Palmer rush ; its owners with nearly or
quite all the other residents of the place going off to
try their luck on the new field. It is said that on their
return more than a year after they found their machinery
all intact, no one being in the locality but the natives, who
must have wondered to see a considerable town as speedily
deserted as it had been first created.

Of the new port of the Palmer diggings—Cooktown,
which is now said to have a trade superior to any port in
the colony except Brisbane, and where reports say a recent
fire destroyed property belonging to one firm of Chinese
merchants alone, worth 20,000*l.*, very little can be said.
When the writer left the colony there was no such town
in existence, and the mouth of the Endeavour River on
which it is situate was entirely unknown. There is now
a large population in this town ; two newspapers are
published and one of them has commenced to insert Chinese
advertisements, and announces that it has ordered a complete set of Chinese types with the view of publishing a
weekly sheet in that language. A hospital and other
public buildings are erected, and the population, which can
only be guessed at, appears to be several thousands. Two
or three lines of steamers ply regularly to the port from
the south, and hardly a week—never we believe, a month
—passes without a shipload of Chinese being landed from
their native country.

The Palmer Diggings are said to be the richest, as they

certainly are the most extensive that have ever been
discovered in Australia. They were discovered by an
exploring party sent out by the Palmer Administration,
which if not very enterprising in the construction of railways, in a great measure atoned for its laziness in that
respect by the vigour it exhibited in developing the
mineral resources of the colony. When Mr. Hann, the
leader of the exploring party sent into the extreme north,
sent down his reports, a tremendous rush set in not only
from the other Queensland fields, but from the southern
colonies and New Zealand. So many men proceeded to
this new country that food fell short, having to be carried
by pack-horses at first, and much suffering and many
deaths ensued. Roads are now being constructed with all
speed, and the diggings, which had at one time to be
almost abandoned, not for lack of gold, but for the want of
that still more valuable commodity bread, are now being
largely worked. One peculiar feature of these diggings
was the enormous influx of Chinese which set in, threaten-
ing entirely to swamp the English-speaking population,
Situate so near the Chinese ports with their teeming
populations, there really was a fear that this northern part of
the colony was about to pass out of our hands into that of a
heathen and alien race, just as its enormous wealth was
being developed. Some slight skirmishes took place
between the two races, and the Macalister Administration,
acting in the emergency thus arisen, determined to place
a tax on every Chinaman imported, and to raise their
miner's rights from ten shillings to five pounds, This in
some measure put a stop to the flood, but as before stated
they continue to arrive in great numbers. Fault has been
found with the action taken by the Government in this
matter, but it would seem that although perhaps not

strictly legal, it was yet patriotic and judicious.   In a new colony, and especially in one where the only production for the time being is gold, every one must feel the paramount importance of not allowing the country to pass into the hands of a foreign race, whose manners, laws, and language are alike alien from our own.   After all, Queensland is a British colony, and will, we hope, remain so.   There are now said to be from 7000 to 8000 Europeans and from 18,000 to 20,000 Chinese on the Palmer Diggings.   The Chinese are not allowed by the other diggers to mix with them, but work principally ground that has already been run over by the white men.   Unfortunately the blacks of the Palmer, who are a much more warlike race than those further south, have developed a taste for roasted Chinese, and several of them have fallen by their spears, to be at once roasted and eaten.

The Palmer Diggings lie between the 15th and 16th parallels of latitude.   It does not appear too sanguine to hope that this discovery will soon be followed by others further north, and that thus that great *terra incognita* of our boyhood, Cape York, will soon become as well-known and as populous as the southern districts of Australia.[2]

---

[2] Under Government auspices the first prospectors of the Palmer Gold-field were lately fitted out for a fresh trip of exploration, and news from them is to hand.   They have penetrated into pastures new. Seeking for the rocky country where gold spangles the soil, they are "greatly disappointed" in where they expected to get rough country by finding level, deep, rich alluvial soil, well-grassed and well-watered, over three thousand square miles in extent, interrupted by mountains further south, where they found extensive scrubs, estimated at over one hundred and twenty square miles, containing very large cedar and kauri pine.   They crossed the Main Range into the heads of the Herbert River, where there is another large extent of very good level country.   They obtained prospects of stream tin here, and then crossed the range again into the western waters.   There are,

Recently a very important discovery of another kind has been made in this northern territory. In 1873 an exploring expedition known as the Queensland North-East Coast Expedition was equipped by Government and placed under the command of G. E. Dalrymple, Esq., to which Walter Hill, Esq., Curator of the Brisbane Botanical Gardens, was attached as Botanist. This expedition explored the coast-line from the 18th degree up to 16° 20″. No less than seven principal rivers were explored, with as many excellent harbours, and an almost unlimited amount of the very richest and most valuable agricultural land was found on the navigable portions of these rivers—beyond which the expedition did not ascend further than to find that most of the rivers flowed with fresh, above the tidal waters. Both Mr. Dalrymple and Mr. Hill speak in the most enthusiastic terms of this new land. At the head of navigation on the Johnstone River, Mr. Dalrymple, ascended a hill, from whence he describes the prospect as follows : —

" At a rough calculation, not less than half a million acres of soil, unsurpassed by any in the world, all fitted for tropical agriculture, and fully 300,000 acres of which are suitable for sugar, spread far around us, penetrated in three different directions by navigable rivers, with a fine harbour and river estuary visible on its sea-board. We had suddenly come face to face with a true tropical Australia, with a vast and hitherto hidden region, the qualifications of which for every description of tropical cultivation at one stroke places our noble colony not only far beyond all Australian competition as an agricultural country, but—the vexed

we imagine, few other countries on the face of the globe so rich in all the products of nature, that a discovery such as this could be announced as a great disappointment.—*Brisbane Courier*, July 10, 1875.

labour question settled—on a par with older tropical countries, the names and products of which are household words." From the descriptions given we learn that this new region has great natural beauty with many excellent sites for towns and cities. Speaking of the Daintree River, the writer says that " no .river reach in North Australia possesses surroundings combining so much of distant mountain grandeur, with local beauty and wealth of soil and vegetation." In the not distant future this district will doubtless be the home of a prosperous and extensive agricultural population, and the wonderful development of Cooktown, in the very midst of this district, offers a ready market for its produce, while the great influx of Chinese will in some measure settle the labour question.

At the very extremity of Cape York is Somerset, a small establishment supported by the Queensland Government, more for the benefit of shipwrecked mariners and in the interests of commerce at large, than for any advantage accruing to the colony. Here are a police magistrate and boat's crew, who, when they have had nothing to occupy them, have on one or two occasions visited the opposite shores of New Guinea and established friendly relations with the chiefs and their tribes. At the bottom of the Gulf of Carpentaria are Burketown and Normantown, two small townships of which there is nothing remarkable to relate.

CHAPTER VIII.

WE have now spoken of all the ports and settlements on the coasts of Queensland, and have treated more particularly of its agricultural and mining pursuits, these being all carried on on the eastern sea-board or at no great distance from it. Normantown is about 300 miles from the nearest point on the eastern or Pacific coast. Supposing a traveller were to start from there and keep at an equal distance from the coast until he reached the borders of New South Wales, on the McIntyre River, a distance of nearly 1200 miles in a straight line, he would, after leaving Normantown, which for the purposes of the Land Act is supposed to be in the Settled district, through all the remainder of his long journey, be in the Unsettled or pastoral districts. In the settled districts free selection for cultivation is lawful, while in the unsettled the land is entirely in the hands of the lessees of the Crown as pastoral country, although large tracts, especially in the districts of Burke, Cook, and Gregory, remain open to occupation. The terms on which a squatting property can be acquired are very easy. Not less than twenty-five square miles can be taken in one block : but for this area the annual rental is only 6l. 5s. for the first seven years, 12l. 10s. for the second, and 18l. 15s. for the third ; the lease being in all cases for twenty-one years. At the instance of either the lessee or the Government, the rental for the second or third term may be appraised and either raised or lowered.

The squatting business has always been lucrative, but in Queensland, which is so eminently adapted for cattle, a great impulse has of late been given to this pursuit by the introduction of meat-preserving and the enhanced price of cattle consequent thereon. Mr. Daintree, the Agent-General for Queensland, himself a squatter and therefore speaking by the book, in his excellent handbook gives a statement which shows that on a capital of 21,600l. there is an annual profit of 3795l., or 17½ per cent. on fat cattle sold, without any calculation as to the natural increase, while on a larger capital the profits would be considerably more. The expansion of this interest is something wonderful; while in 1861 there were 28,983 horses, 560,196 cattle, and 4,093,381 sheep, twelve years after, in 1873, there were 99,243 horses, 1,343,093 cattle, and 7,268,946 sheep in the colony. It will thus be seen that horses and cattle have relatively increased more than sheep, arising doubtless from the great superiority of the new lands in the unsettled districts for fattening cattle. Yet although grazing has expanded so much, out of 364,360,000 acres in the unsettled districts there were only 132,121,030 acres under lease in 1873.

In following our suppositions line of travel from Normantown through the interior of Queensland, the traveller would leave the district of Cook to his left and cross the splendid prairies of the Flinders, said to be among the best grazing lands of Queensland. Still further to the south is the far-famed Barcoo River with its rich plains, where the fattest cattle in Australia are said to be raised. Further to the south is the Warrego and Maranoa Districts, which are principally occupied by sheep.

Striking eastward from the Maranoa, the Darling District is entered, which by many is considered the finest district in Queensland. In it are situate the Darling Downs, occupied largely by the wealthiest squatters in the country, some of whom number their sheep by the hundred thousand—one firm alone is said to have shorn 210,000 in 1862. For many years there has been great difficulty in obtaining good farming land here, the Crown lessees having managed to retain the more valuable portions in their own hands, as elsewhere stated. The Macalister Ministry has entered ejectment actions against many of these gentlemen, and the result is likely to be the throwing open for selection of very large tracts in this most favoured district. Railroads now intersect this district in two directions, and a great impulse will doubtless be given to agriculture by the completion of the main line from Ipswich to Brisbane. Here are produced all the products of the temperate zone. Wheat, barley, oats, maize, potatoes, are the principal crops in the field, while the gardens produce grapes, apples, pears, peaches, nectarines, plums, oranges, lemons, almonds, melons, and other fruits. Flour mills have been erected; breweries are at work, and here under the most favourable terms is likely to be reproduced the agriculture of Great Britain. There are agricultural and horticultural societies holding annual shows and giving prizes as at home, and doing much to foster farming pursuits. At a late gathering of this sort his Excellency the Marquis of Normanby, the Governor, remarked that before long Queensland " would be enabled to furnish so great an amount of ingrown produce as would make her independent of the sister colonies, both in the matter of the necessaries and the luxuries of life."

The wheat grown here is of the very finest quality.

From a return furnished by the proprietor of the Allora Mills, to the Minister for Lands, of the result of the harvest of 1873, we learn that the average yield in that district that year was no less than 38 bushels $32\frac{2}{15}$ lbs. per acre. Much of the land in this district is entirely free from timber and only needs fencing to be ready for cultivation.

There are many flourishing towns on the Downs. Too-woomba, noted for its ale, Drayton, Warwick, Dalby, Condamine, and the new and flourishing capital of the tin-mining country, Stanthorpe, are the principal towns, besides many other flourishing townships. So great is the change taking place yearly in these districts that any attempt to furnish statistics appears useless. To those interested in the subject and desirous of further information we recommend the publications of the Queensland Government Agency, 32, Charing Cross, London, or for the most exact information on every subject connected with the colony up to the latest date, to that excellent publication, "Pugh's Queensland Almanack," than which there is nothing more reliable. This almanack is a publication of which Queenslanders are justly proud; perhaps there is no better almanack published in the English language.

CHAPTER IX.

CLIMATE AND CROPS.

WE have been comparatively brief in our description of the pastoral districts for various reasons. In the first place, we have seen less of them than the coast country and are anxious, as far as possible, to have this work reflect our own observation and experience. Then there is less opening in this line than in agriculture in the colony now, in consequence of most of the country within a payable distance of the coast being taken up. Another reason is that the mass of readers are not likely to require information on this point so much as in reference to the selection of a farm or plantation. There is in the breast of almost every man a desire to be the possessor of a freehold of his own. In Great Britain, this is for most an impossibility. There society appears to be fast dividing itself into two classes as far as farming is concerned, large land owners and land occupiers. It is in the Colonies or the United States that the man who wishes to live on his own land and see his family do the same must look for the accomplishment of his wishes.

To such persons the colony of Queensland presents advantages at the present time, far superior to those offered in her earlier history, and far superior in every respect to either of the other Australian colonies. For whatever may be the opinions entertained as to the relative advantages to be found in New Zealand or America as compared with Australia, there can be no question whatever, that there is no comparison between Queensland and the colonies of New South Wales, Victoria, or South Australia, either as to their climate, seasons, soil, or productions. We unhesitatingly affirm without fear of contradiction, that in all these Queensland is far superior to any of the others; while, since the passing of the Land Act of 1868 and the Homestead Act, in no part of the world can land be obtained so cheaply and easily as here.

Queensland, as lying further to the north than any of the sister colonies, has of course a greater degree of the sun's heat. But this is more than counterbalanced by the sea-breeze that invariably blows inland every day in the summer season. We were for the greater part of our residence in the colony working in the open air, and always noticed that there were never more than two or three days in any summer, and none in some, in which this sea-breeze did not blow. It usually begins to be felt about nine a.m., before which time it will be hot. But as soon as the toiler feels the cooling breeze playing about his forehead he is sensible of a wonderful change. Although the sun rises higher and higher until it shines down the chimneys into the pots on the fire, the cool breeze tempers his rays and makes them bearable. Were it not for this breeze, we believe it would be almost impossible for the European to do much manual work in the Queensland summer. As it is, he can work with as much comfort and more safety than in the more southern colonies, or even in the fields of Upper Canada, or on the prairies of the Western States. We are aware that many will be inclined to doubt this statement. But we have found the summers of Queensland more endurable than those of Upper Canada,

frost-bound region as many suppose that to be. As to
safety, it is only necessary to compare the number of deaths
from sun-stroke in those places to prove the truth of our
assertion. We have known ten or twelve cases of sun-
stroke in New York in one day. We never heard of half
that number in eight Queensland summers. Probably
this arises from the care taken by the inhabitants to guard
themselves from danger, but the fact is patent to all
residents in the colony, that people engaged in open-air
occupations carry them on throughout the summer without
any ill consequences. There is to this rule, as every other,
a slight exception. As we have said, there will be an
occasional day when no sea-breeze blows ; then the weather
will be close, sultry, and oppressively hot, and most people
will find it impossible to continue working for five or six
hours in the middle of the day. But these days are of
very rare occurrence.

In the southern colonies, the inhabitants suffer greatly
from hot winds, "brick-fielders," &c., which render life
burdensome during their continuance. During our residence in Queensland a hot wind blew once, and old inhabitants spoke of such a thing having once before occurred in
their memory many years since. Certainly no terms would
be too strong in which to speak of the discomfort of that
day, and after it was experienced Queenslanders felt how
much they had to be thankful for in being exempt from
this scourge. If only in this respect that colony would be
far superior in point of climate to the southern ones. It
has often struck us, as an instance of the kindness and
wisdom of Providence, that this country, lying so much
nearer the sun, is by its cooling sea-breeze rendered so
much more endurable than the countries lying in a more
remote and generally speaking more temperate latitude.

It is a very common thing for persons coming from Melbourne or Adelaide to express their wonder at finding the climate so fine. Coming from a country so much further south, where they suffer so much occasionally from the heat, they anticipate being almost roasted in Queensland. Their surprise is great to find the heat less oppressive than with them.

Another thing which assists in making this climate so enjoyable—and it is doubtless among the finest in the world—is the fact that the rainy season is usually in the latter part of summer, thus shortening the hot season very materially. The rains continue as a rule from February to April, commencing sometimes a week or two earlier or later. Then begins the Queensland winter, than which it is scarcely possible to conceive a more lovely season. There are slight frosts in the months of May, June, and July or August, sufficient in some cases in the East Moreton and Wide Bay Districts to form thin ice, which is looked upon as a curiosity, and, as it is usually found in some zinc or tin vessel, is carefully preserved for a few hours to show any friend who may call in. These frosts, however, are sufficiently severe to injure the sugar-cane, in some positions, as well as to cut up the leaves of the bananas and other tropical trees. The effects of these frosts are sometimes very curious. We remember on our last journey up the Brisbane River, a few days before leaving the colony, being struck with the appearance of the bananas in some places. Here was a grove in which the frost had killed every leaf, turning them all dry and white as if every tree were dead. Directly opposite on the other bank was another grove where scarcely a leaf had been touched, but all were green and flourishing. Were it not for an occasional new leaf shooting up its pale green foliage amid the dry leaves, one might have thought the whole grove had been killed by a fire running through it. The sheltered position of the one grove, or the lighter nature of the soil will account for this difference. When the bananas are thus affected by the frost it will be many months before they again come into bearing. There are many positions in the south of the colony where we opine the frosts, slight as they are, will prevent sugar-canes being grown to advantage.

Thus it will be seen that Queensland is highly favoured in her climate, so far as its relation to health is concerned; but we do not wish to convey the idea that it is therefore equally superior in an agricultural point of view. So far is this from being the case, that the climate is what the farmer has to fear most. If he is a man of sense, and is not in too great a hurry, he can find a piece of land as good as is to be had in any other spot on the earth's surface; but he cannot command the fruitful showers to fall as he wants them. The very fineness of the climate is at times a great disadvantage. He has, indeed, two evils to contend with—droughts and floods. Were it not for these, we should say emphatically that Queensland was, without exception, the finest country for farmers in the world; as it is, these must never be lost sight of in any calculations connected with this matter.

Every place has its advantages and disadvantages. In Canada and the States farmers have to house-feed their cattle for five or six months, and the crops they grow will not return anything like the same sum per acre as in Queensland; but, on the other hand, in the open season their crops grow twice as fast, and the seasons are so regular, that when the seed is put in they can to a large extent rely on a harvest at a certain time and to a certain amount. This the Queenslander can hardly do; there

may be a drought and nothing grow, or, if he is on a scrub-
farm, a flood may come just as his crop is ripe, and destroy
the whole.   Then he has the advantage of being able to
grow two or even three crops in a year, while elsewhere
farmers have to be content with one.

As to floods and droughts, it is not at all certain that
the settlement of the country may not in a great measure
modify these evils.   Certain it is, that old residents will
tell you they observe the weather to be more showery than
formerly, and the seasons have of late been very favourable
in that respect to the farmer.   There is another cause
which ought to be considered in a Christian country, but
the mention of which we are aware in this age of ratio-
nalism will lay us open to the charge of superstition or ignorance.   We allude to the effect which the settlement of a
Christian population should have in ameliorating the evils
of drought or flood.   Nothing is more clearly laid down in
Holy Scripture than that the rainfall should be withheld or
given as a reward or punishment for national sins.   We
should not have adverted to the benefits that a nation
which has its recognized prayers for rain and fair weather
might reasonably anticipate from their regular use, did
not the history both of Queensland and New South Wales
afford pleasing instances of the good effects which the use
of these prayers by Christian congregations has had on
the country.   It is related by all the old residents of
Sydney that many years since a great drought brought
the country to the verge of ruin.   A day of fasting and
prayer was appointed by the Governor, to pray for rain.
The day came, and was strictly observed.   While the
various congregations were in their churches in the evening, the clouds began to roll up, the thunder came nearer
and nearer, until it broke with its deafening sound directly

over the heads of the worshippers, who soon heard the welcome sound of the first drops pattering on the roofs. The congregations were dismissed, but could hardly reach their homes before the rain came down in torrents. It is said to have been many years before a drought again occurred in the colony.

Precisely similar was an instance in the history of Queensland. In the early part of 1866 the colony was suffering from a drought of ten months' duration. The greatest distress prevailed; cattle and sheep were dying in all directions. It was painful to pass by a water-hole and see the poor cattle in dozens lying dead all around its margin, where they had come to drink and been bogged in the mud before being able to reach the shrunken water. All vegetation was dry and burnt up. For a long time all agriculture had been virtually suspended; only those plants and vegetables which were watered, or are from their nature impervious to drought, were to be seen flourishing. The drought was alike fatal to animal and vegetable life; ruin stared every one in the face. At this time the Governor in Council proclaimed a day of fasting and prayer. Strange as it sounds, a large portion of the population actually laughed at the idea of obtaining a change of weather by recourse to such an old-fogy method as prayer. To have heard the sneers that were nearly everywhere thrown out, a stranger would have supposed Christianity was entirely exploded, and that the men of this generation were vastly too well informed to stoop to such a prejudice. But the day was observed, and we believe in every place of worship of all denominations services for the special purpose of imploring a change of weather were held. The consequence was the same as in the former case. The rain at once came and saved the

country, which from that time to 1870 has never suffered
from a lack of rain to any considerable extent. To us it
appears more philosophic in a Christian community to
ascribe these results to their true cause, the goodness of the
Almighty, than to attempt in what appears to us both a
mean and short-sighted manner to find some cause for
these results other than the obvious one. Why should we
not in our calculations take into account the data which
may be gathered from such facts as these?

As we have before said, bad as are the floods in Queensland, they by no means equal in their destructiveness those
of New South Wales. Indeed, such is the character of
most of the scrub country in Queensland, that with proper
precaution taken in the selection of sites for houses, &c.,
much less damage might be done than is at present. It
was natural for the settlers when first entering on their
land to build their houses close to the water, which was
their only highway; but as the land gets cleared they have
an opportunity, as their means increase, of building on the
high land further to the rear, where floods can never
reach. There is this great advantage of floods to land—
that each flood will leave a rich deposit of manure, thus
renewing the land. It has been found, too, that sugar-
cane is very little injured by the floods, so that this crop
has the advantage of suffering little from drought or floods,
a fact that points it out as extremely suitable for the
climate.

The crops that up to the present are most cultivated in
Queensland are the following :—in the coast country, sugar,
cotton, maize, oaten and lucerne hay, English and sweet
potatoes, oats, sorghum, tobacco, arrowroot, pumpkins, and
wine. On the Downs no sugar and little cotton is grown.
The principal crops there are wheat, barley, oats, maize,

hay, potatoes, and pumpkins. Wine-making is also being commenced here too.

Sugar is a crop of which a very large number of varieties are grown and the manner of cultivation differs somewhat with different sorts. The principal canes at present cultivated are the Bourbon, the ribbon, the yellow Otaheitian, and the purple Java. Other varieties are, however, being constantly brought before the public, some of which are considered very superior. In the Botanical Gardens at Brisbane, there are, as before stated, thirty-six varieties, many of which will doubtless be found valuable. We have already shown the average yield of cane in each district of the colony. The yield on certain estates of course often exceeds very largely this average. Some pieces of cane have been said to yield three tons per acre. That the poor machinery in use in many places has much to do with the smallness of the returns is doubtless the fact. Great improvement is being made by the experience gained as to the varieties of cane best adapted for certain situations. We append an article on this subject from the pen of Angus Mackay, Esq., the Agricultural Editor of the *Queenslander*, a gentleman who has done much for the improvement of agriculture in the colony, and whom immigrants will find most ready to yield them any information they may require. In an article published in Slater's *Almanack* for 1870, he says,—

"Great strides have been made during the last year in the growing of sugar-cane, and the manufacture of sugar. There is no longer a difficulty felt in making, all the mystery engendered by the different notions brought from most of the sugar-producing countries of the earth, have been exploded. It is known now, with as much certainty as man is permitted to entertain upon such subjects, when the canes are ripe; when they are at their best; the weight of cane to an acre; and close calculations are made of the probable yield in sugar; and all this has been done, in not a few cases, by men who, two years ago knew little or nothing of either the growth of the cane or the manufacture of sugar.

"There have also been adverse occurrences during the year; occurrences unusual to this climate, but which sugar growers and makers have surmounted. The best proof of this is found in the fact that the demand for sugar is now largely met by the produce of Queensland plantations. A serious check was experienced upon low and badly drained lands from frost, which upon three occasions visited the southern section of the colony more severely than during the preceding ten years. The canes in many places were bitten severely, and as a consequence decay set in. This was promptly met by the use of bi-sulphate of lime, which, diluted with four times its bulk of water, enabled the boilers to turn out good sugar when, but for this ready aid, all might have been lost. But the great majority of planters, especially in the north, know nothing of frost; they have gone on unchecked, and return from one and a half to three tons of sugar to the acre. The quality of the Queensland sugar is very even, varying only about 10l. per ton—30l. to 40l.—being the figures. Nor do these figures show a proportionate loss or gain to the producers, but arise from the simple or more expensive modes of draining out the molasses and preparing the sugar for sale. By the general employment of the centrifugal machine an almost uniform range of qualities might be obtained; but as the demand is heavy for sugar at about 34l. per ton (that is brown table sugar), and as it is made with inexpensive appliances, the smaller mill-owners find it pays best to supply that demand.

" Many canes new to this section have come into notice during the year, prominent amongst which are Chigaca and the green or yellow (from New Caledonia), the first of which gave 1 lb. 8 ozs. of sugar from 24 lbs. of cane, and the latter 1 lb. of sugar from 20 lbs. of cane; the Diard (from Mauritius), 2 lbs. of sugar from 50 lbs. of cane; the Poetii (from Java), 1 lb. 5 ozs. of sugar from 38½ lbs. of cane; the Dijong-jong (from Java), 1 lb. 10 ozs. of sugar from 51½ lbs. of cane. Each of these canes is found superior to the ribbon or Bourbon, which have been amongst the most extensively cultivated hitherto.

" The ' labour question,' with the many difficulties surrounding it, in the eyes of interested or impulsive men, is rectifying itself. It may with some confidence be asserted that the small plantations· are the most successful, and that the presence of coloured or any particular species of labour is not a necessity in sugar cultivation here. With an average of about six men (white), cultivating from thirty to forty acres of cane and with complete manufacturing plant, costing from 200l. to

500*l.*, from 1½ to 3 tons of sugar to the acre, and worth 30*l.* per ton at least, has been made. Leaving a wide margin for all expenses, 15*l.* per ton comes to the growers and makers, and this fixes the industry as one of the safest in which intelligent men can engage. Brains tell in Queensland, and we have men amongst us who knew nothing of sugar or sugar machinery until all was ready for setting to work upon their own plantations; then they went in and did the work themselves, and have since sold their produce. The process is simple, but can be learnt only by actual work; no secret is made of anything, so that any one can learn who tries willingly.

"Some of the large plantations have done well under the care of skilful managers, and the country is much indebted to those gentlemen for the freedom with which they have made known items of the utmost importance to the development of the sugar industry. The Curator of the Botanical Gardens has been busy as usual; he has grown and tested in various ways the merits of sixteen varieties of cane, and the results are offered freely for the benefit of all interested.

"Almost every conceivable distance has been tried for planting cane. The distances now followed are 7 × 4, 6 × 3, and 6 × 2, according to the strength of the soil. The plants are laid in after ploughing, harrowing, and cross-ploughing, at a depth of 10 to 14 inches, by opening holes at the distances mentioned. The holes are about 18 inches square, and about 8 inches deep: sets of the canes are laid flat if the soil is dry, and slightly set on angle if it is damp—the eyes at the sides—and then covered over with one or two inches of soil. Where teams are available, deep furrows can be run out with the plough; and by returning in the same furrow with the plough body only, a depth of eight inches can be obtained; in such furrows, the plants are set upon large plantations. The four top joints make the best plants: they can be bought at the plantations at from 1*l.* to 1*l.* 10*s.* per 1000. When the soil is moist, the plants send up shoots in eight or ten days. In dry weather the shoots take longer to come up; if they appear not in fourteen days, it is well to look and see if the plants are all right. Soil is generally filled into the holes as the shoots grow, until they are nearly level with the surface. The soil must be kept stirred and free of weeds until the plants are strong enough to take care of themselves. The lower leaves are stripped from the canes as they become ripe—this stripping or trashing hastens the ripening, and the leaves, &c., are buried between the rows; by such means the soil is kept clean and comparatively mulched."

There is at the present time a good market for standing

cane growing up in most places. On the Mary, in 1871,
when on a visit among the farms, we found the owners of
mills rowing about on the river from one farm to the
other, examining the cane, and offering from 12l. to 14l.
per acre for it as it stood, their own men to cut it and
place it on board the punts. We knew an instance where
20l. per acre was given for a fine field in 1871. It is
unnecessary to say that with such an opening as this few
places offer greater inducements to the farmer. It is
our opinion that at the present time Queensland offers a
field to the farmer not to be excelled, if equalled, in any
part of the world. It must be remembered that when
cane is once planted, that process has not to be repeated
every year. The first crop is called the " plant " crop, and
the following " ratoon " crops. These ratoon crops may
be continued for several years, before a fresh planting takes
place; experience has not yet settled how many. When
the labour required for maturing a crop of cane is
considered it will be seen that even to the poor farmer this
crop offers great inducements. Of course to him who can
erect his own machinery the profits will be vastly enhanced.
In 1870, 2854½ tons of sugar were made in Queensland,
while 2090½ tons were imported against 1½ tons exported [1].

Cotton, as we have already indicated, after having been

---

[1] We learn from Pugh's *Almanack* for 1875 that the following were
the statistics of Sugar-growing in Queensland in 1873 :—

Land under cultivation with cane	14,495 acres.
Sugar mills	66
Distilleries	10
Rum distilled (proof gallons)	164,413
Sugar manufactured	7,987½ tons.
Molasses manufactured	412,253 gallons.

Showing an increase of nearly 300 per cent in three years in the
quantity of sugar grown, a fact that must be almost unparalleled in
the history of agriculture.

lauded to the skies as a certain fortune for all embarking in its cultivation, fell for a time to be considered unworthy any one's attention. When we reached the colony there was scarcely a cotton-gin in it, and those who grew a little had to hawk it about to obtain a market at any figure offered, or had to send it home and wait for the returns—a process not convenient for new beginners. This state of things too has passed away, as one of the early evils the farmer had to contend against. In this, as everything else of the sort, the supply has created the demand, and no difficulty exists in disposing of the crops, for which most likely several competitors will visit the farm, and offer the highest price possible. One advantage of this crop is that it can be grown on light soil, another is that everything connected with its growth and preparation for market can be done within the family, especially where there are a plenty of children, the most delicate of whom can pluck the beautiful bolls of cotton. If sugar and maize are beautiful crops, and they are doubtless among the loveliest sights in the agricultural world, cotton too has its beauties. When the plants are young, their straight rows of green leaves are worth looking at. In bloom, covered with yellow flowers they have another beauty, and to the eye of the owner no sight will be more beautiful than when the white cotton is everywhere bursting from the pods and transforming what was lately a green field into a sea of billowy whiteness. This plant too can be cut down and allowed to bear again without replanting. But the pruned cotton, as it is called, does not appear to be in so much favour as formerly from the difficulty experienced in keeping the land clean. Where this is effected the pruned cotton is preferable, there being no danger, as with the young seedling plants, of suffering from droughts.

The cotton crop of 1871 was, we believe, about 6000
bales. We again copy from Mr. Mackay :—

" Notwithstanding adverse seasons, the cultivation of cotton goes on
extending in Queensland. The quality of the staple has proved to be
first-class. As the seasons are better understood, and the varieties of
cotton best adapted to the climate develope themselves, cotton cultivation is carried on with greater confidence.

" The one great hindrance to the cotton of the colony taking that
rank to which its merits entitle it, springs from the bad way in which
the seed is mixed. Scarcely a handful can be taken up amongst which
cannot be found almost every sort. The result of this mixed seed is
a staple of unequal length ; or as the brokers term it, a ' broken-
staple,' believing as they do that an inequality is caused in ginning, an
idea for which there is no foundation, as the ginning is as well done as
that of any other sent to Europe. As growers get acquainted with
the plant, the mixed seed fault will be remedied ; but it certainly is
the duty of those in authority to do something in a case fraught with
such importance to the colony.

" The Sea Island cotton is a free black seed. It has proved rather
delicate in the colony.

" The planting season extends from September to the beginning of
December—cotton has been planted successfully up to Christmas. The
planting is done by drawing shallow furrows, at from four to six feet
apart, with plough or hoe. The seed is scattered in almost as thick as
it can lie, and then covered over with two or three inches of soil, and
manure if possible, which ought to be made fine. The plants come up
in about eight days, and are thinned out gradually until some six
inches apart, and about six inches in height. The soil is then hoed
about them and a little scraped up to the plants. As the strong plants
show themselves, the others are thinned out until a distance of from
two to four feet between plant and plant is obtained.

" The after cultivation consists in keeping the plants clean—which
must be attended to, or they will not yield a paying return. If they make
too much wood, it is well to pinch out the ends of the leading shoots.

" In February and March the plants begin to ripen, by the bolls
containing the wool opening and exposing their contents, which must
be picked as soon as the seed is hard. From sixty to one hundred
pounds per day is considered fair work. One penny per pound is paid
for picking ; occasionally less. The aborigines are occasionally found
useful at this work.

"After being picked, the cotton is either sunned or aired—the less sun it has the better—until the wool is quite dry and the seed is so hard that it cracks between the teeth. The cotton is then fit for the gin, which machine separates the wool from the seed. The ginning houses charge about one penny per pound. The usual proportion after ginning is one-third wool and two-thirds seed, in weight. Dealers in the colony buy up the cotton either in the seed or after it is ginned. They give from twopence-halfpenny to fourpence for the former, and from seven-pence to eleven-pence for the latter. Cottons of the descriptions mentioned sell at from eleven-pence to fifteen-pence per pound, in England. In a few instances higher prices were obtained—as much as two shillings and sixpence per pound in some cases. The lower figure may be taken as the average until an improvement takes place by picking and selecting the seed.

"A fair weight of clean cotton to the acre when manure is used, is about three hundred pounds, and a fair figure for total returns per acre 10*l*. Much higher returns have been given. The Government grant a bonus in land for every three hundred pounds of clean staple. As the labour connected with cotton growing is not excessive, and considerable help can be afforded by the younger branches of a family, it is a favourite crop with the small farmers, and perhaps the safest and most remunerative they can put in. In several farming districts the cotton crop of last year put more money in circulation than any previous crop had ever done. The return is immediate, directly the crop is grown."

The maize crop was for some years the main stay of the Queensland farmers. It is still and must always continue to be a very important item of the agricultural produce of the colony. Although this crop in Queensland does not yield so well as in some others—the crop averaging from thirty to seventy bushels per acre—yet it has the advantage of affording two returns in the year. We have seen three crops taken off the same piece of rich scrub land; but in that case the one crop is planted between the rows of the other while yet growing. Two crops are easily to be obtained, or one crop of maize and one of potatoes, or oaten hay, may be taken off the same land. Formerly, as we have said, the settlers endeavoured to compete with the Clarence

farmers in the growth of maize by the use of the hoe, and of
course they were worsted. As long as maize stood at 5s. to 6s.
per bushel this sort of thing would pay; but maize now
sells at from 1s. 8d. to 4s. 6d., though it is occasionally 5s.
yet. These prices would sound fabulous to the maize
growers of the Western States, where 1s. 6d. is a high
price, and 10d. or 1s. a good figure. But the Americans
are far in advance of Queenslanders in one respect—their
use of horse-power instead of man-power. The Americans
are also far in advance of the colonials in another matter—
they have the sense to know that maize makes capital food,
and, therefore, it enters largely into their diet, appearing constantly on their tables in a variety of excellent preparations.
By-and-by, we hope, as the old "lag" element dies out,
that Queenslanders will be equally sensible with their
American cousins. We see no reason why, by the use of
the plough and horse-hoe, maize may not always be a fairly
paying crop. Up to this time it is the exception and not
the rule to see it cultivated in this way. This crop has
lately been grown with great success on the Downs, where
the most superior maize we have seen in any part of the
world has been grown. With increased facilities of carriage—when the railway is carried through to Brisbane, and
thus saving the costs of change of carriage, commission, &c.,
at Ipswich—we anticipate that this will be a very important crop in that neighbourhood. Up to the present time,
large quantities of maize are imported to the colony,
yearly, from the northern districts of New South Wales.
Queensland maize has, on the other hand, been exported
with good results to Melbourne, where, were the supply
sufficient, a large market might be obtained, that cereal not
growing so far south.

Hay is another crop which was in great favour before

sugar and cotton were cultivated. It is usually a good paying crop. Oaten hay yields two harvests, while lucerne can be cut from four to seven or eight times in a year. Oaten hay was formerly 10*l.* to 14*l.* per ton, but it is now about half that price, when well pressed in bales. The crop is from one and a half to three tons per acre. The oats for hay are cut just as the seed is forming. A great evil in much of the Queensland-grown hay is, that it is too strong and coarse in the straw, arising from the richness of the soil, and being sown too thinly. Hence the imported article from Sydney is always sold at a higher price. It would be very easy to remedy this evil; but of late too little attention has been paid to this crop. In some places it is scarcely grown at all, or if so, is so badly managed as to produce very unsatisfactory results. Lucerne hay is probably one of the most paying crops grown in the colony. Once put down on good, clean land, it will after the first year—during which the growth is very slow and the returns comparatively nil—return from five to eight tons per acre for an indefinite number of years. This hay finds ready sale at from 4*l.* to 6*l.* per ton, thus leaving a very handsome profit indeed. Perhaps the reason why this crop is not more extensively grown is to be found in the fact, that the seed costs a considerable sum, the cultivation must be of the best description, and no return will be obtained for some length of time. Of neither of those crops is there enough raised to fill the home market, a large quantity being imported from New South Wales.

English potatoes is a crop which returns twice a year in Queensland. It is not the most certain of crops, sometimes turning out very well and at others but poorly. The winter crop is usually a good one, but the summer crop is frequently a comparative failure on some land. These potatoes

are also liable to have a disease called "the blacks;" the
exterior of the root will be all right, but on cutting it in
two the centre will be found black.   In these instances the
outer portion of the potato is eatable.   Potatoes used to be
much higher in price than now.   They vary of late from
3l. 10s. or 4l. per ton to 7l. or 8l., averaging about 6l. per
ton to the farmer.   Large quantities of potatoes are yet
imported from New South Wales, Victoria, and Tasmania.
Both the imported and local grown are generally of very
excellent quality.

The sweet potato is grown very extensively in the colony,
and supplies, in a great measure, the place of the English
potato.   It is a species of yam, and being unknown to the
British public we will give a short description of the root and
its production.   It is not propagated by planting the root,
as with its English namesake, but by a slip of its vine-like
top, which runs over the ground like a convolvulus, to which
family it belongs.   A cutting of this vine, containing six
or eight leaves and buds, is taken and placed in the earth
in a slanting direction, half of the buds being above and
half below the surface.   These cuttings are placed in rows
about a yard apart, and from two to three feet apart in the
rows.   When the plant has shot out a few inches, which it
will do from each of the buds above ground, the earth on
each side is drawn up around the plants, thus forming a
high ridge.   The roots are propagated from the buds underneath, and if the soil is rich and light will grow to a large
size.   We have seen a specimen of the red variety weighing 16 lbs.   The white variety is most usually grown, and will
often weigh 3 lbs. to 4 lbs. each, although there are many
smaller ones.   This root takes from five to eight months
to come to maturity, which must be before the frosty nights
come in, as it is very susceptible of cold.   During the

summer the tops can be cut for fodder; horses, cows, and pigs are all alike fond of these tops, which are sometimes eaten as a vegetable. Pigs thrive well on them, and are often fed on them in the summer. The crop is highly suitable to the climate; for if the cuttings have a few showers to start them at first, they will do with very little rain subsequently. We cannot say what weight they yield per acre, as we suppose no one ever did or will dig half or a quarter of an acre at once, as they will keep for any length of time in the ground, but only for a short time when once dug. But the yield is very large, and as they are far more nutritious than the common potato, and are eagerly eaten when raw by every animal on a farm, dogs and poultry not excepted, we look on them as one of the most valuable products of the land. When raw they taste like ground nuts somewhat. Cooked properly they are dry and sweet —too sweet, perhaps, for some palates at first. There is nothing which can be more easily spoiled in cooking, most cooks treating them as they do English potatoes. They require almost as much care in boiling as an egg. Baked with a roast of meat we esteem them one of the luxuries of Queensland diet. They can be cooked in a variety of ways, and are always nice. Nothing has ever been done, so far as we are aware, in exporting these roots to Sydney or Melbourne. Yet, in New York and other northern cities of America, they are imported largely from the Bermudas and the Southern States, and meet with a ready sale. We see no reason why a similar trade may not spring up in Queensland, when she has farmers enough to do more than serve her own local supplies. Oysters are largely exported from Brisbane, and the sweet potato is far less perishable than these. We would advise every new settler to put in a small patch of this excellent root as soon as possible. The seed costs nothing, and when they are once grown the family will never lack for healthy and nutritious food.

The sorghum, or Chinese sugar-cane, is a small species of sugar-cane which is propagated from seed. It is a most excellent green feed, for which purpose it is alone grown. It is planted in rows a half-yard apart or sown broad-cast; the former is the better plan; it soon runs up, if permitted, to a height of six or eight feet, producing a quantity of black millet-like seed, excellent for poultry. This crop is not a very important one, except to market-gardeners, who cut it when four to five feet high and sell it in bundles as " green-stuff." No farm should, however, be without it, as it grows well in all weathers, can be cut every few weeks in the summer season when other green feed is scarce, and produces a greater weight of long food per acre than any other crop. Those few farmers who have made a trial of it for feeding their cows in the dry summer months when grass is scarce, have had no cause to regret the experiment.

Tobacco is a crop which grows to perfection in Queensland, but has never been largely cultivated. Enough has been done to prove that it can be grown to any extent there, and that is about all. A few persons only, grow it as a staple crop, but those few have no reason to be dissatisfied. Some years since when neither cotton nor sugar were grown as they are now, a good deal of tobacco was raised. But the market at that time was very limited and, worse still, was in too many instances in the hands of unprincipled persons, who cheated the farmers. This dissatisfied them, and, cotton and sugar at that time beginning to attract attention, very few have done much in this crop since. A few manufacturers still obtain enough of the leaf to carry on business, but the industry is by no means in the position it should be. According to all accounts we have gathered and from the experiments we have ourselves made, the growth of tobacco will pay better to the small capitalist than any other crop. The dried leaf will sell readily at 1s. per pound if well cured, at which rate the return per acre would not with a fair crop fall short of 40l. and might reach half as much more. There is, however, considerable labour attendant on this crop. In its early stages the plant is treated very similarly to the cabbage, and there is no more trouble with it. Subsequently the plants have all to be examined daily to remove any grubs, which would otherwise destroy the leaves, and also when the proper quantity of leaves, eight to ten, are developed, to pinch off all shoots as they come out. When cut, the plants are dried a short time in the sun and then hung to dry in an open shed. After this they are placed in heaps to sweat them and it is this part of the process only which requires the exercise of any skill whatever, more than the growth of turnips or potatoes. A very large sum is annually spent in tobacco in the colony. What tends to make this sum so large is the considerable quantity used in washing sheep, and which as the number of sheep increases will become still more considerable. With the large local demand existing and the advantage afforded by the customs duty of 2s. 6d. per pound, any one who goes into this business for some years to come cannot fail to meet with great success. The men who have engaged in it up to this time have been not only ignorant of the plant but in needy circumstances. To one who would, as the Virginian growers do, not only grow the plant but press it himself, a splendid field is here open.

Of arrowroot a considerable quantity has been grown for many years. The Messrs. Grimes of Boggo have paid particular attention to this article. They grow the arrow-

root, grind it down by horse-power in the open air, and
when manufactured, paper it in 1-lb. and larger packages
for sale. Other growers also now produce an excellent
article, and it is admitted that the Queensland arrowroot
is equal to the West Indian. The growth of this plant is
very simple. It is propagated by planting the small
roots, which are saved for that purpose and treated somewhat similarly to potatoes. It is a crop eminently suited to
the climate of Queensland, and never fails of a return.
The method of manufacture is simple in the extreme.
Any ordinarily handy man can master all the process
in a few minutes and make all the apparatus in his
leisure hours, unless he proposes growing it on a large
scale. Arrowroot not only forms a pleasing change in
domestic diet, but sells readily at from 6d. to 9d. per pound,
if properly manufactured.

The growth of the vine on a sufficiently large scale to
admit of the making of wine has now become a regular
industry in the neighbourhood around Brisbane. Much of
the soil of the ridges and hollows in the district appears
well fitted for this interesting pursuit, which is also very
lucrative. To Mr. Lade of the Surrenden Vineyard belongs
the honour of having, amid the sneers of his neighbours,
persisted in his experiments in this direction until he had
established the reputation and character of the Surrenden
wines. He has now a vineyard of several acres, as has also
each of his sons. Many other vignerons have since then
gone largely into the business, and it seems certain that
not many years will pass before Queensland wines will be
both plentiful and excellent. It is not only in the East
Moreton District that vines are being cultivated. On the
Downs and in the north good results are being obtained.
A few days before leaving Maryborough we paid a visit to

the well-built and ventilated wine-cellar of Mr. J. Dowser, where we tasted different wines that gave promise of yet establishing a reputation for their grower. It is calculated that a vineyard will take five years to come into full bearing from the planting of the cuttings. Hence, as considerable outlay must be gone to in trenching and preparing the land, fencing, &c., it requires a moderate capital to enable one to embark in this business with success. But for people possessed of sufficient means it offers a very pleasing and remunerative occupation, and the power of indefinite extension. There is a drawback or two in this line also. Sometimes tremendous hailstorms have been known to sweep over a vineyard and almost entirely destroy its crop. There is also a disease, called *oidium tuckeri*, which, if not watched for and nipped in the bud, will sometimes devastate the vineyard. This scourge, which has only been known of late years, can be successfully resisted by the use of sulphur applied with a pair of bellows constructed for the purpose.

These are the principal productions of Queensland at the present time on its coast range. The crops of the Downs being such as every British farmer understands, appear to require no particular mention. There are a variety of crops, however, which experiment has proved can be advantageously grown in the colony, but which have not as yet received any practical attention. Of these coffee appears to be the most important, and to its successful growth we have alluded in a former chapter. Tea also has for many years been successfully grown in the Botanical Gardens, but has, so far as we know, never been tried outside them. The same may be said of madder, which is of easy growth and cultivation and appears well suited to the climate. The growth of the mulberry and the production of silk has had just sufficient attention to prove how much might be done in this way. At every agricultural show some beautiful specimens of silk are shown, but the industry does not appear to have gone beyond this stage. Some years since we met with an American gentleman in Brisbane who had introduced to the colony direct from the Levant large quantities of mulberry seed and silk-worms with a view to entering largely into this business. He very properly asked Government to grant him a piece of land to carry on his experiments. This was refused him, and we believe he afterwards fell among thieves, who robbed him: we have heard nothing of his enterprise nor himself for two or three years. Of ginger about the same thing may be said. It is occasionally grown, you see it in every Chinaman's garden, every one knows it can be grown, but no one has yet been found to attempt its cultivation on a practical scale. There are a variety of fibrous plants which grow to perfection, but of which no use has ever yet been made, Of these we may mention in particular the banana, of which Manilla rope is made, the *sida retusa*, a common weed, but which produces splendid fibre, and the currijohn, from which the natives make their nets, dilly-bags, &c. All these grow in abundance and could be had in any quantity. There are other fibrous exotic plants which have been tested at the Botanic Gardens, such as the China grass-cloth plant, jute, &c. At some future time large fortunes will probably be made by those who shall open up these sources of wealth now lying dormant.

There are some other crops, which are very generally met with, which often bring in considerable sums to those farmers living near a market, such as bananas, pine-apples, &c. It is said, on the authority of Humboldt, that more human food can be grown per acre in the shape of bananas than in any other product. It is certain that it is a very prolific fruit, and both pleasant and nutritive. It has the advantage, too, of being pretty well impervious to the effects of both drought and flood. These plants are propagated from suckers which grow out around the parent tree in considerable quantities. These are easily removed, the roots being very few and small; they are planted in rows, when forming a plantation, about four or five yards apart. The plants thus set out come into bearing in from fifteen to eighteen months; by that time about half a dozen young suckers in various stages of growth will be clustered around the parent stem. The fruit, like the leaves, comes out of the centre of the plant, and hangs down in a large bunch, containing more or less fruit according to the variety and the richness of the soil. In good land, and it cannot be too rich for these plants, the common banana will average five or six dozen in a bunch. The Cavendish, a thick dwarf plant, not attaining a height of above four or five feet, frequently produces double and even treble this number of fruit. When the "bunch" is nearly ripe it is cut down for market, as they ripen quickly after being cut, and are carried much better green than ripe. The plant is then cut down and allowed to rot on the ground or in a dunghill, and its room is soon filled up by the young trees. These will now continue to bear every few months; and if care is taken not to allow too many suckers to grow up, restricting each group to about six or eight, according to the richness of the soil, there will in a plantation of half a rood be always ripe bananas after the grove is two years old. Where there is a family of children, nothing more economical can be grown than bananas for domestic consumption, as all children are fond of the soft, pulpy, farinaceous fruit, and will almost live on it. In the summer time, when they are most plentiful, nothing

can be more healthy as a food. As the trees soon grow to
a height of from sixteen to twenty-five feet, and have
broad green leaves of four to six feet in length, they form
an excellent shade, and, from their very graceful appearance,
very soon give an air of beauty and prosperity to the
homestead. They are everywhere in use as shade-trees,
for which purpose they answer admirably, the clumps of
thick stems and broad leaves always affording shade and
coolness. We have seen in some places considerable taste
displayed in forming avenues of these fine plants, which
were something to be remembered for a lifetime. The
stem of the banana is a series of soft cellular layers or
rings, with a large quantity of fibrous matter which makes
excellent rope. The Manilla rope is usually manufactured
from one particular variety; but every kind has the same
sort of fibre, although, perhaps, not equally good. As
before stated, no use is made in the colony as yet of the
vast amount of banana-fibre which is grown there. Because of the universal growth of this fruit, and because it
will not grow in the southern colonies, some witty digger
from New Zealand or Victoria nicknamed the Queenslanders "banana men," a term which soon became very
popular, and seems likely to be perpetuated. Certain it is
that from the beauty of this plant, the ease with which it
can everywhere be propagated, its prolificness, and the
palatableness of its fruit, it is, as it well deserves to be, a
universal favourite. Considerable numbers of bananas are
exported to the southern colonies. They are usually sold
by the growers at 4d. per dozen, each bunch being counted
and the number of dozens marked on the stem. At that
price they return as much as 40l. to 60l. per acre.

The pine-apple is another very hardy fruit in general
cultivation. These, like bananas, are propagated by suckers,

and are planted in rows a yard apart each way. They soon close up and become a complete mass of vegetation, and have to be regularly thinned. The pine-apple is of very prolific growth, and is now sold around Brisbane very cheap. Formerly they were sold by the farmers from 3s. to 4s. per dozen in summer, to 12s. and 18s. in winter. Now the price is not more than half that, or even less. A lady of our acquaintance had a sackful delivered to her for preserving purposes for 1s.; and on our expressing surprise, she said a neighbour sent a dray to a farm at the German Station, and was allowed to fill it for eighteenpence. In other neighbourhoods the price is better; but it cannot be long before this luscious fruit will be very cheap in all parts of the colony. Great numbers of pine-apples are also exported.

There are many other descriptions of fruit which are grown for the market. The commonest of these is the peach, which grows in great variety, but as a rule is not equal in flavour to those found in older countries. Yet it has been proved that excellent peaches can be grown in Queensland if only proper attention is paid to the choice of variety. The usual plan is to let the stones lie on the ground around the tree and produce plants in this way, which are transplanted as required. The finer varieties fetch a good price, but the commoner are a mere drug on the market.

Much attention is paid to the growth of the orange, and several very fine oranges are already in existence. This tree has a deadly enemy in a small parasite, which is known as " the blight," and which often destroys the young trees. When, however, they have arrived at maturity they produce largely, and are a great source of wealth. Some varieties of Queensland oranges are superior to those from New

South Wales; and there is every indication that many
years will not elapse before the present large importation of
this fruit will cease.   It takes about five years' time and
great attention to bring an orange grove into bearing;
when once this is done, the returns will be regular and nearly
certain.   There are still many openings for the cultivation
of this fruit without any danger of overstocking the market.
Lemons, citrons, shaddocks, &c., grow without any trouble
whatever, but have only a limited market.

We have thus enumerated and described the principal
crops which do or could occupy the attention of the Queensland farmer to advantage.   There are many others of minor
importance which we have not thought it necessary to par-
ticularize.   Enough has been said to show that there are
many branches of agriculture and horticulture which may
be entered on advantageously, and that in none is there an
overstocked market.   The farmers of Queensland are not
nearly enough to supply the local consumption, to say
nothing of the export market, which in sugar, cotton,
tobacco, flour, and many other articles, is always open and
profitable.   The emigrant landing in this colony has the
great advantage of choosing among many different kinds
of occupation; he can go on the Downs and grow the crops
of his fatherland, with the additions of maize, grapes,
pumpkins, melons, &c.; or he can, by selecting his land
east of the coast range, devote himself to those products of
warmer and more favoured climes, of which he has hitherto
only read in books.   He has not now, as former settlers
had, to spend his means experimenting on the nature of the
soil and climate: the experiments of others have smoothed
his path for him.   He has not to experience the dissatisfaction of raising a crop and then learning that there is little
or no market for his produce: that state of things is among

the past. He has not now to select his land from a given reserve, that some ignorant or misdirected surveyor has chosen for him, but which is entirely unfitted for cultivation. Nor has he, on the other hand, to purchase his land at an auction sale, where there are so few agricultural buyers that one is immediately spotted by the "land sharks," and run up to an enormous price, or obliged to resign his choice farm altogether. Under the new regulations he can, when sufficiently experienced, strap his "swag" on his saddle and ride over the whole country, and choose his selection from the best lands in the colony.

There are drawbacks to agricultural life in Queensland, and we have faithfully and fully pointed them out. To the intending emigrant, who surveys the various colonies and dependencies of the British Empire and the United States, it is a matter of great importance where he directs his steps. The author knows by experience too well the vast capabilities and advantages of the American continent to hold them cheaply, or in any way decry them. A seven years' residence in that part of the world has impressed him with the wondrous resources it possesses, and its fitness for the Anglo-Saxon race. There are there many advantages which Queensland does not as yet possess. On the other hand, Queensland has a far better climate, and resources equal if differing from the other. It must be a question for every one to decide for himself as to which way he will turn his footsteps. The colony of Queensland, like a gigantic infant, has passed through those earlier and tedious phases of life incidental to such an existence, and is now in its boyhood. The earlier settlers have borne difficulties and overcome obstacles which future comers must benefit by. The author's own opinion is, that no part of the world affords a better opening to the agriculturist at the present time than this colony. It has advanced sufficiently to have established regular industries and markets, and is not so thickly populated but that thousands of new settlers may yet reap the advantage to be gained from taking up new land at first hand, and at a nominal price, and thus benefit not only by their own industry, but by the certain and rapid increase of value in real estate in every new country.

It may not be uninteresting before closing this chapter to give some account of the way in which a farm is taken up, and of the process of settling down and improving it. We remember reading such a sketch in the work of Mr. Wight. The whole of his plan of settlement rested on finding a neighbour to lend a dray, which was to be drawn by a hack mare *and her foals*. It is needless to say that such an idea as that would never be realized. It is one of the evils of Queensland social life that people are far too selfish. The difference a new arrival experiences in his treatment by his neighbours in Queensland and Canada is marked and striking. In the latter he will receive offers of service on all hands, and ten to one but the neighbours turn out and assist him at a " bee." We are sorry to say there is none of this neighbourly assistance, so useful to the new arrival, in Queensland. We have always looked on it as partially the result of the selfishness engendered by the squatting life, and partially the leaven of the old convict system still working; but there is no doubt that the old residents regard the " new chum " more in the light of a person to be swindled with a bucking horse, or a vicious unbroken cow, than in that of a person who may need any assistance. It is true, this custom of seeing a stranger and taking him in is being, to some extent, modified by the increase of an agricultural population from home. But there is still very much improvement to be made in this respect. Queenslanders might well take a leaf out of the book of their fellow-subjects in Canada. In our opinion, the wonderful improvement of that province, and the almost certainty with which a person commencing farming obtains a competency, is to be ascribed to the assistance he almost invariably receives from the neighbours, who, by all turning out and giving him a day in raising his house and barn, and clearing his land for his crop, assist him at the very time when that assistance is of most use to him. As yet there is no habit of this sort in Queensland.

The farmer having selected the land he likes,—we will suppose part scrub for cultivation, and part forest for his homestead and paddock,—calls at the land office of the district and makes his selection. Perhaps the land is already surveyed and he has chosen it with the assistance of a map of the locality which he has purchased at the office for 1s. In that case he has only to indicate the number of the lots on the map; or it may be a piece that has not yet been surveyed and he has the advantage of making his own choice. The land, however, must be in rectangular shape, with not more than one-half as much frontage to the creek or river as it is deep. In this latter case it is well to take a licensed surveyor on to the land and have him survey it at once, marking the corner trees and side lines by "blazing" or notching the trees, and drawing up a description for the land office. If this is not done, the selector marks out his own corner trees and makes such a description as will enable the land agent to identify the selection. But as the survey fee has always to be paid on the land surveyed at the selector's expense, it is better to make one's own bargain with the surveyor and have his assistance at the land office.

If the selector is a sensible man, he will see that his selection is not too small. The idea of small, that is forty or fifty acre farms, is pretty well exploded, as they offer no facilities for keeping any stock. Although the bush is open for the farmer's horses or cows to graze on, he will find it practically impossible to keep either without a paddock of his own, which requires to be of some size, or he will have no grass in the Summer months, when he needs it most. Our selector therefore takes up, under the conditional purchase clause of the Land Act, a farm of 350 acres, of which 100 are good scrub or agricultural land, and the rest either first or second class pastoral. If he is fortunate it may be 100 acres first class and 150 second class. He also selects in addition to this, under the homestead clauses of the Land Act, forty acres of scrub or agricultural land, and eighty acres of first-class pastoral land, making a total of 470 acres—a very respectable block of land certainly. For this land he has to pay as follows:—the homestead will cost him 9*d*. per acre per annum for the agricultural, and 6*d*. per acre for the pastoral land, for five years, when if the terms of settlement are fulfilled he will obtain the deed in fee-simple. He may select eighty acres of agricultural land as homestead, or 160 of pastoral or, as we have supposed, a portion of each. Then for his selection, under the conditional purchase clause of the Act he will have to pay as follows:—for the agricultural land 1*s*. 6*d*. per acre for ten years; for the first-class pastoral 1*s*., and for the second-class pastoral 6*d*. per acre for the same length of time. He will also have to pay with the first year's payment the survey fee, or it will cost him the same if done by himself. Tabulated then, this will be the position :—

		Acres.	Per Acre.	Rent.		
Homestead Agricultural	.	40	9*d.*	£1	10	0
,,	Pastoral . .	80	6*d.*	2	0	0
Purchase Agricultural	.	100	1*s.* 6*d.*	7	10	0
,,	1st Class Pastoral	100	1*s.* 0*d.*	5	0	0
,,	2nd ,, ,, .	150	6*d.*	3	15	0
	Total . .	470		£19	15	0
	Survey Fee			£7	0	0

Thus for an annual payment of 19*l.* 15*s.* for five years, and a further payment of 16*l.* 5*s.* for five years more, making a total of 180*l.* (besides survey fee), an estate of 470 acres of fine land may be secured. But it will cost the immigrant who pays the passages of himself and family considerably less than this. He will be entitled to a 20*l.* land order for each adult member of his family, and a 10*l.* order for each child over twelve months old; so that a man with a wife and three paying children will be entitled to land orders worth 70*l.*, which would reduce the sum he has to pay in cash to 110*l.* In fact, many men would look on the quantity which 70*l.* would pay for as a sufficiently large farm of itself; but we would, if the settler's funds permitted it, advise him to take up at least double that quantity, which could be all pastoral land. Certainly no country offers lands to the immigrant on such easy terms as these.

His land secured and the land-agent's receipt in his pocket, our selector's next business will be to get on his land as soon as possible. If it is on navigable water and there is not a good road to it, he will probably find it best to purchase a boat as his means of communication. At any rate he will need a dray and one or two stout horses. If his land is scrub, ploughs and harrows will be of no use

to him the first year. If it is open plain, he will find his
best plan will be to purchase a team of bullocks or hire a
team to do his breaking; if this latter can be done it will
be cheapest, unless he has by living in the country a year
or so learnt to manage cattle, when he may think it best
to purchase a pair of leaders and a few young steers, and
break them in himself. This latter plan has the great
advantage that by using these steers to break up his
ground, he will double their value in the course of one
season. A person proceeding in these matters must be
dependent entirely on the amount of his capital. If he
has only from 200*l*. to 300*l*., or less, he had better be very
careful in his outlay, and not go in for both bullocks and
draught-horses and drays. A team of ten bullocks usually
costs from 90*l*. to 120*l*., with dray and gear. In some
places they will be even more than this; but a pair of
leaders can be purchased for about 20*l*., and young steers
at 4*l*. to 4*l*. 10*s*. per head. A dray will cost from 20*l*. to
30*l*. If it is open land, bullocks of one's own or on hire
are a *sine qua non* for breaking and bringing the land in
cultivation at first. It is usual to charge from 1*l*. 10*s*. to
2*l*. per acre for breaking and cross-ploughing with bullocks.

But as a rule the agricultural land will be scrub, and we
will proceed on that supposition. A good pair of draught
horses will cost, with harness and dray all complete, about
75*l*. or 80*l*.; these will be got if money is plenty, or
otherwise one horse will have to answer the turn. In the
dray the tools and a supply of rations will be put. These
tools are a cross-cut saw, a couple of American axes, a
morticing axe, two pairs of mall-rings, five or six iron
wedges, a hand-saw, a few augers, a tomahawk or hatchet,
and a few other carpenter's tools, and half a dozen heavy
hoes, and a gun and a supply of ammunition for shooting

game. The rations will probably be a 200 lb. bag of flour, some tea and sugar, beef, salt, &c., with a few pickles, jams, and tobacco. Then, with his hired man, our selector sets off to drive his team to the place of his future labours. It will probably take a day or two to reach the spot if the road is unmade and the distance considerable; but the dray and horses are necessary, and have to be taken up, although many a farmer has taken up a scrub-farm without horse or dray or even a cow. Arrived at the spot, the horses are hobbled out after having had a feed of corn; the dray, with its tarpaulin, forms the temporary residence, and our friend sets to work. First a few sheets of bark will be stripped, and in this sort of work a native black is very useful, and a bark hut is soon run up, which will serve for a house in the meantime and for some other purpose afterwards—perhaps a stable or tool-house.

Selecting the site of his residence, our friend and his man begin by cutting down any trees which may be growing there. Perhaps some of these are of iron-bark or blue-gum and will split. It is not by any means every tree that will split. There are many that from their crooked growth or twists in the grain will not "run." These will have to be cross cut, their tops chopped off and rolled in heaps with handspikes and then burnt. But straight trees are found and these are cut in lengths of eight to nine feet and split up into slabs. The former experience of the settler has taught him this work, and if he finds a good tree or two the slabs for his house will be "run out" in a couple or three days. Then the timbers for corner-posts, wall-plates and sills will have to be squared out of saplings of iron-bark, gum, or blood-wood, and morticed together. If he intends to put up a good house the settler will place his frame on short stumps let into the ground and fit his slabs into the frame. This house, admits of a floor of pine boards, or of hard wood slabs smoothed off with the adze, but many settlers simply fix their slabs into the ground and fit them to the wall-plate above. The first description is always to be pre-ferred. The frame being raised and bolted together with iron-bark trenails, the slabs are dressed or squared at the edges, any splinters or roughness removed with the adze from their surfaces and then placed perpendicularly on the sill. The walls of the house are thus quickly formed, the necessary openings being left for the doors and windows. The chimney is built in a similar manner at one end of the house, and is always of considerable dimensions, and a par-tition or two runs across to form the different rooms. An addition is made of one or two lower rooms at the back, the verandah posts are fixed in the front and perhaps at the end opposite the chimney, rafters of small saplings are placed for the roof, and the whole is covered in with large sheets of bark of the stringy bark, turpentine, black-bull, or apple-tree, or in default of all these of the tea-tree, or iron-bark dressed down. The dray being made use of to bring all these materials from the places where they are procured, a good substantial four-roomed house, with one or two chimneys and a verandah of eight feet or more in width, will very soon be erected by two good bushmen. The roof is tied down to the rafters with strings of bark or vines from the scrub, and kept from curling up or being blown away by three or four stout saplings fastened on the top. The timber for the floors, and the doors and windows are brought from the town in the boat, or, if economy is studied, a pine-tree can be felled in the scrub and split into thin slabs or palings suitable for these purposes and dressed off very neatly with the adze. In this way a very comfortable and

tolerably commodious house can be put up at very little
other outlay than that for labour.

The house being finished, the wife and family, who have
up to this time been lodging in the town or living in a
rented cottage, can be brought up in the boat together
with the household stuff, and an air of home will at once
be given to the bush homestead. If the selection has been
judiciously made it will often have such a shape that by
running two lines of fence from the scrub to the creek at
another point it can be permanently enclosed. If this be
the case or not the fencing of the lot should be at once
proceeded with, unless the season of the year renders it
imperative to fell some of the scrub at once with a view to
a crop. It is always the best economy to enclose the land
as soon as possible. This is a work of some time, and is
justly considered one of the most laborious jobs which
befalls the new settler. Fences in Queensland are put
up on a farm with posts, and either two or three rails, the
latter being preferable. The posts are split from blood-
wood ten inches wide by four thick, and are let in from
eighteen to thirty inches in the ground—two feet is a good
depth—and stand about five feet out of the ground. Three
holes are morticed in each, in which are placed the rails.
These are cut in such lengths that two panels make a rod;
they should be two inches and a half at least in thickness
and vary in breadth from six to twelve inches, the middle
one being the broadest, and the top one the narrowest. A
fence of this sort properly constructed of blood-wood and
iron-bark or blue-gum should last a lifetime. Many
settlers find it suit them better to let out this part of their
work, which will be taken at from 4s. to 5s. per rod for
three-rail fencing, according to whether the contractors have
to draw their own materials from the tree to the fence or not.

There are several other sorts of fencing, some of which
are cheaper than three-rail fencing, while others have the
extra advantage of keeping out bandicoots and kangaroo
rats, and being therefore well adapted for a garden or
cultivation paddock. Of these latter, one of the best is
formed by placing the posts and the top rail in the usual
manner and then excavating a shallow trench, and placing
short slabs in it, on a slight incline, with their tops resting
inwards on the rail; the trench being then filled in again
firmly, a close fence or wooden wall is obtained, through
which even a snake cannot pass, if care is taken in fitting
the edges of the slabs, or by allowing them a little lap.

Of the cheaper and more expeditious fences suitable for
outer fencing, that known as "chock and log" fence is
the best. Mr. P. R. Gordon, Chief Inspector of Sheep in
Queensland, gives the following description :—

"This fence is composed of chocks laid across the line, on which logs
or rails of any length are made to rest in notches cut in the chocks for
the purpose, so that each chock supports the small end of one and the
butt end of another log. Thus, supposing the fence to run in a north
and south direction, the north or small end of each log would rest on
the west end of one chock, and the butt end of the same log on the
east end of the next succeeding chock. The chocks of the second tier are
made to rest on the ends of the first logs, exactly perpendicular to the
bottom chocks, notches being cut in the lower sides corresponding to
the logs in which they rest so as to bind them firmly. The second
tier of logs are placed in exactly the same manner as the first, and so
on until the fence has been piled up to the desired height."

By a careful selection of the saplings, this fence may be
erected, with the assistance of a team of bullocks, very
rapidly, and of nearly or quite equal permanence to a three-
rail fence. It will not cost the selector who has his own team
and plenty of saplings within easy distance over 1s. per rod.

The fencing being completed, the stock-yard engages
attention. This is a most important matter in the

economy either of a farm or station. Nothing in the way
of live-stock can be done without it, and care is always
taken to have it very strong and as high as possible. Of
course a farmer does not need a very large yard. It is
well to have it large enough to admit of subdividing.
There are four rails in a stock-yard fence, with a heavy
sapling let into the top of the posts, this forming a fifth
rail. It should never be less than six feet high, and the
rails must be wide enough to prevent a calf getting his
head between. In one corner of the yard the " milking
bail " is put up, which consists of two strong posts with a
cross-piece on the top, and a thin rail, fastened to a bottom
cross-piece, and working on a pin, about eight or ten
inches from the inner post on a slott morticed out of the
top cross-piece. The cow puts her head inside this moveable
piece against the post, it is then pushed forth close to her
neck behind the ears and secured by a peg running through
it and the cross-piece. The cow is thus prevented from
moving her head while being milked. She is in fact
" bailed up," a foot-rope with a noose is passed around her
right hind-leg and fastened tightly back to the fence,
drawing her leg so far back as only just to admit of the
foot touching the ground. By this means all sorts of
cows, whether quiet or vicious, are prevented from either
moving or kicking. " Breaking in " a cow or heifer is
accomplished in this wise. She is " run in " to the yard
with her young calf by her side, by one or two men on
horseback, with stock-whips, the sound of which all cattle
know too well to wish to come too close to them. Then a
" head rope " is dexterously placed over her horns at the
end of a long pole; this rope has its end passed through
the bail where the cow has to come, and is then taken
round the corner-post of the yard and hauled on by a man

or two on the outside. One man with a whip in his hand urges the poor creature to " bail up," and at every run she makes the slack of the rope is pulled in until she is hauled with her head through the bail close up to the corner-post. The man inside then pushes forth the rail and fastens it with the peg. There is always just enough room left between the bail and the fence for the cow's head. The rope is now taken off her horns by climbing on the fence; the leg-rope is carefully got on her leg and fastened back, and she is ready for milking. It often occurs that an unbroken cow will not yield her milk, without the calf being placed beside her. A small yard is made for the calves just in front of the cow's eyes, and they are admitted by a little gate. The plan is adopted in this exigency of bringing the calf with a rope round its neck and fastening it alongside the dam's head, when she usually yields her milk freely. It is a usual, though a poor fashion, to take a portion of the milk from the cow and then let the calf have his share, by which means he has all the richest portion. Others again let the calf suck awhile first, which is a better plan, and then tie her up at the cow's head while the milking is performed. As soon as the cows are milked they are let loose with their calves with them for a few hours in some cases; in others, the cows are put outside the fence in the bush, and the calves are kept in the paddock. An unbroken heifer will need to be hauled up to the bail a few times in the way mentioned, after which on hearing the cry "bail up" she will walk up to the bail of her own accord. It is wonderful, where kind treatment is shown the cows, and they are patted, scratched about the ears, and otherwise fondled, how quickly they will become quiet. There are some, however, that are perfect brutes; they will rush out, or "charge" a man on horseback, and can be only got into the yard in company with others. Once there, they place themselves in a corner ready to meet all comers, and if a man on foot enters the yard they are down on him at once. We have seen some pretty tall jumping done under these circumstances, and cows have been known to break a rail of a fence with the strength of their blow. A cool hand will often await his antagonist with a short stout stick, and jumping aside as she comes up, hit her behind the horns with sufficient force to knock her down. This treatment will soon bring the wildest beast to her senses. It often happens that the wildest cattle before breaking make the most docile when broken in; this is true both of bullocks and cows as well as horses. Care has to be taken when drawing in cows given to charge, that they do not rush on the horse one rides, or they may do serious damage. The cows are sometimes no worse than their calves as far as the will is concerned. If a few weeks old before being brought in, these will often charge too. We once saw a heifer bailed up and leg-roped, the milker adjusted his stool, and with pail in hand was about to begin operations, when the calf, which had been stamping and pawing on the other side of the yard, suddenly made a strategic movement on his rear, and in a second man, pail, and stool were flying in different directions to the great amusement of the onlookers.

A new beginner will generally find it better to purchase broken-in cows rather than those unbroken, having plenty of work else on his hands. Quiet cows with young calves will cost from 5*l.* to 6*l.*; unbroken heifers can be had about 2*l.* cheaper.[2] With paddock fenced in, the stock-yard and calf-pen up, he will at once obtain a couple or three cows,

---

[2] Since the above was written the price of cattle has advanced from 1*l.* to 2*l.* per head.

and from that time a great saving in rations will take place. The dairy, with the produce of a dozen hens, will supply many a meal, and make an agreeable change in the diet. The hens will quite keep themselves on the seeds and insects in the grass. He will also erect a "gallows" in the yard, and at the same time the cows are driven home from the station, a fat bullock or cow will be fetched, and at once killed and salted for use. This is done in this way, every one being his own butcher. A ball is discharged from outside the fence at the animal's forehead, which thus stunned has its throat cut and is skinned. To complete this operation the gallows comes into requisition. It is formed of two stout saplings with forks at the top, set four feet into the ground, with a roller on the top working in the forks; a cross piece is morticed into one end of the roller outside the upright, and a rope fastened to each end of this transverse piece enables the bullock to be hauled up above the reach of dogs, where it hangs until the morning. A fat beast which will weigh 700 lbs. or upward can be purchased for 4l. 10s. or 5l., so that meat will not cost our friend very much; and he has the skin besides, worth 19s. 6d. or 20s., which he can sell if he does not want it for domestic purposes.

By this time a sow or two will have been purchased and brought home, and as these animals will pretty well get their own living if allowed to run in the paddock or scrub, no expense will be needed to be gone to on their account. The slops and milk they receive daily will keep them about the house, or else they might perhaps take to the scrub and return no more. This often happens, as they find ample sustenance from grass in the forest and roots in the scrub. In many places, miles from any house, fine pigs may often be seen. We have had more than one exciting pig-hunt, which has ended in bagging one or two fine animals, the meat of which was of the very best quality. It is curious how quickly the finest breeds of pigs will degenerate on becoming wild, and develope the points of the coarsest breeds—the long snout, big tusks, coarse hair, red colour, and flat sides. But by being daily fed pigs will visit their pens daily and sleep in them at night. In Queensland, as in every place else, pig-keeping is among the most lucrative branches of farming business. Pork will always sell readily at an average price of about 6d. per lb., and as the sweet potatoes, pumpkin, and many other coarse and unsaleable products of the farm, which grow in profusion, are excellent food for pigs, on which they can be fattened with the addition of very little corn, we have often marvelled why farmers do not more frequently turn their attention to this business. There is a large quantity of bacon and hams imported, although there is a duty of 2d. per lb. in favour of the local article. It is true bacon cannot be easily cured in the summer season, but there need be no difficulty with it in the winter.

The homestead being completed, a fruit-garden paled off, and a selection of trees and plants set a growing, it will be time to turn the attention to the clearing of some land for a crop. Where a man is not driven, by shortness of cash, to put in some crop before anything else is done, it will be good policy to make his place secure; and by the addition of a few cows, and the means of killing his own beef— which he cannot well do without a stockyard—diminish very materially his weekly expenses for rations. These, in the way we have indicated, may be reduced nearly or quite one half. The paddock secures his horses from straying away and being lost, which, otherwise often occurs, and enables him to separate his calves from the cows, and thus

obtain much more butter and cream; while his pigs will
be increasing by the time he has some green stuff growing
to feed them on.   He is thus in a position to turn all his
attention, with his man, to clearing the scrub and putting in his crop.

Selecting a piece of scrub land on the banks of the stream,
and in front of his house, so that his crops may be under his
eye and the view be opened to the river from his door, he sets
to work at a clearing.   It is hard work, but not nearly so
hard as chopping forest timber would be, being much
softer.   By the time a few acres are cleared, the first
chopped growth will be getting dry and ready to burn off.
It will often happen that a neighbouring tribe of blacks
will do this part of the work if found in a ration of flour,
with the promise of a pound or two on the completion of
the job.   We have often known them employed to great
advantage in this way, the work being of a class that they
appear to like.   In burning off large heaps are made of the
logs cut in lengths, with the branches placed on the top.
It is hot, dirty work; but there is a keen feeling of en-
joyment in thus mastering the giants of nature, and preparing land for cultivation, which never fails to solace the
labourer.   If ever the hope of reward cheers the workman it
is in clearing land; and although the hands are growing
hard and horny, and the sweat pours in rivulets over the
blackened face, or drips on the soil as the workman stops
to breathe, the day always appears too short, and the settler
will be seen far into the night rolling the logs together,
or throwing the burnt ends on the glowing embers.

As soon as a piece is thoroughly cleared it will be time
to put in a crop.   There is no difficulty in settling what
will be first planted.   A small piece of ground will be
certain to be devoted to potatoes and other crops for domestic use, and no less certain will a patch of maize be put in

for the horses, pigs, and poultry. If it is the season of the year for sugar-planting, and there be a mill in the neighbourhood, and there will soon be few places where this is not the case, our settler will doubtless determine on placing most of his land under this crop. All the work on scrub land has to be done at first with the hoe, as it is impossible to use the plough until the roots have had time to rot out, and the smaller stumps can be removed. But the ground is soft, and the work is easier than it would be when the timber had not grown so thick. The plants for the canes at some near neighbouring farm in the crushing season will cost 1l. to 1l. 10s. per 1000.

It will be fifteen or eighteen months before any return can be expected from the sugar-cane. Hence it will be necessary to look to other crops for a first return. Most likely when this stage has been reached another man or two will be hired, and the work of clearing and planting will go on with double speed. Three or four acres in cane the first season will not be a bad beginning, although of course double that quantity can be got in if necessary, by hiring the extra hands sooner. But the judicious man will husband his resources. He will get in, if possible, a patch of tobacco, which will certainly take some labour, but will also turn in a very handsome sum in eight or nine months. An acre or two of potatoes will also assist in making the returns equal the disbursements. Thus, as the domestic expenses will be very light and, as the crops grow, decreasing regularly, if all goes well, at the end of a year from first commencing to clear his scrub, our farmer will find his income becoming sufficient to pay his way. He will by that time have his first crop of cane nearly ready for the mill, and several acres more he will now begin to plant. He will manage to grow enough potatoes,

maize, tobacco, &c., to pay his men's wages and his store
account, and retain the balance of his original funds at his
banker's; or if this is expended, he is yet able to meet his
payments. His cane plantation will regularly increase
every year, and as soon as he sells his first cutting of cane,
he will have plenty of tops of his own to plant extra
ground without any further outlay in this direction. He
has perhaps laid out what means he had to spare in purchasing a small lot of breeding heifers, which, as they drop
their calves, are broken in and placed under the charge of
his own boy or a hired lad, and grazing in the open bush
will not cost a shilling a year for food. Thus he lays the
foundation of a good dairy at a moderate expense, and if
the milch cattle are also fed on the leaves stripped from the
sugar cane, with green sorghum, pumpkins, &c., which
latter take up no ground, as they are always grown among
the cane, the produce of the dairy will be quite doubled. He
will soon have pork enough for his family and a few hundred-
weights over to balance his account with his grocer. His
bananas, peaches, pine-apples, and other fruit begin to repay
him for their cultivation, and even should a flood come down
and destroy his standing crops, his sugar will still grow on,
and the returns from his dairy and pork will be undiminished.

Thus by degrees, by hard work and due precaution in
starting, a person with a moderate capital may gradually
accumulate a small herd of cattle and bring his scrub land
under sugar, until the annual returns will be sufficient to
induce him to erect a small mill for his own use, when
each acre of cane will not fail to return him from 25l. to 40l.
By this time his own family will, perhaps, be grown up to
render assistance, and our settler may look forward with satisfaction to a competency in his old age, spent in a delightful
climate, literally under the shade of his own vine and fig-
tree, and with his family prosperous and happy around him.

There is one error that we must combat here. It has been a favourite remark with lecturers and writers on Queensland, from Mr. Jordan downward, that the less a man knew about farming at home the more likely he is to succeed in this colony. A tailor or linen-draper, a clerk or a factory operative, was more likely to succeed than a man who had spent all his life on the soil, because he would bring no old-country prejudices and ideas with him. His mind would be a perfect blank as to all agricultural knowledge, and he would be more likely on this account to pick up the right mode of procedure. Nothing can be more prejudicial to the interests of colonial agriculture than this idea, which is entirely erroneous. Mr. Jordan acted honestly on this belief and introduced people of every calling except farmers. A few of these certainly came, but they were the exception and not the rule. Instead of hard working-men accustomed to out-of-door work and inured to hardship, delicate operatives and people of in-door and sedentary occupations came to the colony. A majority of them were men who would have been knocked up in a day's harvesting in the old country, and had not the stamina needed in farming pursuits. These people would not have earned a labourer's wages in England, where the weather is cool; how then could they be expected to earn 35*l.* or 40*l.* a year and their rations under a Queensland sun? Had the same class of people been sent to Queensland as usually settle in Canada, we believe there would have been no outcry for coloured labour, and that not a Kanaka would have ever been imported. It is true that the system of agriculture is very different in Yorkshire or Devonshire and Moreton Bay or the Mary River; but the grand principles of cultivation are the same in every part of the world. Soil needs the same treatment every where. Crops differ, as do the seasons, and in these respects one's ideas have to be entirely reversed. But no man who knew what agriculture was himself would ever have ventured on such statements as we have seen published to the detriment of the mere farmer. We do not mean to say that no man but a farmer will succeed in Queensland as a sugar, or cotton, or tobacco grower,— quite the reverse; but at the same time the practical farmer will always have an advantage over others, partly from his present knowledge, but more from being accustomed to open-air employment and from possessing the robustness of body consequent thereon.

Queensland is everywhere overrun with artisans,[3] clerks, and people of that class. Much too large a proportion of her population consists of consumers. What is wanted is a few thousands of farmers and farm-labourers. For these there is no end of room, and the more that arrive the more will be required. But were her population double what it now is, we fancy there are enough people of nearly every other class but these and female servants. The great want of Queensland is the yeomanry class—men with a few hundreds or thousands of pounds, the ability to work hard, and the requisite knowledge how to use their strength. Could ten thousand men of this sort be introduced in one year they would all find ample room, and not only make openings for many more of their own class, but for tens of thousands of labourers and artisans. With the inducements offered in the way of free land and the splendid crops that land will bear, we repeat that no part of the world is more worthy the attention of the British farmer at this time than the colony of Queensland.

[3] This must have been some two years or more since; a reference to the official "Rates of Wages" at 32, Charing Cross, will show that mechanics of almost all kinds are in *great demand*. [ED.]

CHAPTER X.

WE have already spoken of the various kinds of timber growing in the scrubs. There are also some very valuable timbers growing in the forests, but up to this time there has been very little done in the way of an export trade for any of them. A great many trenails have of late years been exported from Brisbane, but we believe this is nearly the only shape in which the excellent hardwoods of Queensland have been introduced to Great Britain, and from wooden shipbuilding being abandoned this has ceased. Yet there can be no question that were the iron-bark, the blue, spotted, and red gum, the black-butt, turpentine, and many others, once known, they would realize good prices and become a very important article of export. The only drawback, perhaps, would be their great weight. These timbers, when seasoned, are often so hard as to turn the edge of an ordinary axe, while the limit of their power of endurance has never as yet been ascertained. We should think that in ship-building or as beams for large buildings these fine, straight, long poles would be invaluable. They enter largely into the construction of buildings in the colony, but for the most part they are cut down and burnt or allowed to stand in their primeval grandeur.

There are many curious trees in the colony, which are of no value and appear only intended to diversify the scenery.

Of these are the bottle-tree (so called because it resembles
nothing so much as a lemonade-bottle placed in the ground)
and the grass-tree, from whose top long pendants (trian-
gular blades of grass) project. This tree sometimes attains
a considerable height, but is now usually seen, stunted and
blackened by fire, covering wide plains of barren soil.
This tree has one great use; the smoke arising from it,
although pleasant to human beings, appears to be highly
obnoxious to the mosquito. If some of it is burnt in a
room, not one of these pests will be found in it. Another
tree avoided by every living thing is the dreaded stinging-
tree. This, although called a tree, is more properly speaking a shrub. It grows from a foot or two to ten or even
fifteen feet in height. It has broad leaves, and might be
easily mistaken by a stranger for a variety of mallow. If
once stung by this bush, the sufferer will never need to be
again cautioned of its proximity. The pain it inflicts is
most excruciating, and nearly drives one mad. The worst
of it is that this pain does not die away and cease; every
time the part stung becomes wet, for many months afterwards, the pain will return in full force. One can scarcely
conceive a greater infliction than to be struck on the naked
body with a branch of this tree and then driven into a
water-hole. It would probably be more than the human
frame could endure. These trees grow usually on the
borders of scrubs.

One of the most remarkable trees in the colony is the
Bunya-bunya (*Araucaria bidwillii*), a species of pine
which towers like a pinnacle above all other trees of the
scrub to a height of 200 feet and upwards. When young
it is a peculiarly handsome tree, throwing out branches all
around close to the ground to a distance of many yards,
and smaller branches rising in regular gradation to the

top, thus forming a perfect cone and so dense in foliage that scarcely any animal can penetrate it. There is a splendid row of these young trees in the Botanical Gardens in Brisbane, which are justly esteemed one of the finest sights in the gardens. But the beauty of this tree is not its chief peculiarity. When full grown it produces on its very top a large cone of fruit which is esteemed a great dainty by the blacks and is eagerly eaten by the whites. This cone will contain a bushel or two of the fruit, about the size of the chestnut, which it somewhat resembles, but is more farinaceous and better eating. The trees bear the largest crop once in three years, which has led Mr. Hill into the error of supposing that they only have fruit on them triennially. This, however, is not the case. It is true that one year there are only a few comparatively, the next year more, and the third year a full crop. But each year they are in large quantities and supply the blacks with food for many weeks. When in bearing the branches for probably eighty or one hundred feet will be all gone and the rest of the tree like a thicket of prickly fronds. Yet the blacks find no difficulty in reaching the summit.

The bunya season is the blackfellow's harvest. Then from all parts the tribes flock to the bunya scrubs, situated principally in the countries drained by the Mooloolah, Marovaby, and Upper Mary waters, usually arriving a week or two before the fruit is ripe. This time is spent perhaps in a corrobboree and in hunting. When the bunya is ripe there is no confusion. It might be reasonably supposed that as this fruit is so highly prized, and so many tribes meet in one scrub to eat it, quarrels and fights would be continually arising. But the opposite of all this is the fact. These people set us an example that with all our boasted civilization we might well follow.

Every tribe has its own clump of trees, which are again
divided so that every member of each tribe, males and
females, old men and piccaninnies, has his or her own tree
or trees. Each tree is marked or branded with the peculiar
crest of its owner and no other blackfellow would for a
moment think of infringing on his rights. Every little
baby is allotted its tree, which of course the parents retain
until the youngster is old enough to climb it for himself.
The bunya scrubs are of considerable extent in many parts
of the coast country as well as further inland, and as it is
a finable offence to cut down one of these trees, their
number is not lessening, which is more than can be said of
their owners. We never remember to have seen but one
of these trees which had been cut down, and that was on
the Mooroochy River. This tree had been cut for the
purpose of a portion of its timber being sent to the Inter-
national Exhibition of 1862. The timber is said to be
equal or superior to any other pine in the colony, but we
doubt if any one is competent to pass an opinion on this
point. Another tree, if indeed there be not a number of
varieties of it, is a small shrub-like tree which supplies a
very bitter bark possessing the properties of the cinchona
and, by some, said to be that tree itself. Its bark has
the properties of quinine, and Dr. Bancroft, of Brisbane, has
obtained that drug from it. It grows in many parts of
the colony and is sometimes made use of by the inhabitants, who make a decoction from the bark which has been
found very useful in fever and ague.

Of the kangaroo it is unnecessary to say much. Every
one is well acquainted now-a-days with the principal characteristics of these curious animals, which afford so many
days' sport every season to those fond of the chase. They
are everywhere to be met with and are usually of the

ordinary dull brown. We have seen in the country about the Durham Bay Lagoons kangaroos of a light grey colour, with streaks of a dull white. They were very pretty, but whether another variety or only singularly light specimens of the ordinary sort, we know not.

It is not always safe to get too close to an old man kangaroo without being well armed. We were once chasing a tremendous old man in the country near the Glass Houses, when he was pulled down by a fine big hound. The dog was not large enough, however, for this monster, who after rolling over picked himself up and stood on the defensive. Coming up we noticed that he had already given the dog one severe gash and was preparing to rip him open by holding him up with his fore paws in order to give him the *coup de grâce* with the enormous claw of his hind foot, which cuts like a knife. Jumping off the horse, we ran to him stock-whip in hand. What was our surprise to see him drop the dog and come towards us with a cry between a scream and a grunt. Rising on his long hind legs, he endeavoured to grasp us with his fore paws, showing his teeth at the same time, as if inclined to bite. A heavy blow with the short handle of the stock-whip rather confused him, although by no means stunning him. Just then the hound sprang on his back, which gave us an opportunity of seizing a fallen limb of an iron-bark tree and bestowing a few hearty blows on his head. A stab with the sheath knife finished the business; but we thought it might have fared worse with us but for the intervention of the dog, as we were taken completely off our guard, never before having seen a kangaroo show fight. We have since heard of a case in which an old man kangaroo tried to jump into a water-hole with a young lad, who also had jumped off his horse to assist his

dog, and was only prevented from drowning the youngster
as they do dogs, by the arrival of his elder brother. We
may mention here that the idea that the kangaroo uses its
tail to assist it in running is erroneous; their tails never
touch the ground when they are running. Young kangaroos can be easily tamed. We had one that delighted
very much in going with the stockman to assist in yarding
the horses or cows. He would run along with his enormous jumps by the horseman, keeping up to him all
around the flat until near the yard, when he would make a
bolt for the house. He was on very good terms with the
dogs,—much better than with the cook. He would wait
till the latter had his back turned, dart at something or
other on the table and be out of the house too quick for
foot or hand. He had so many cunning ways that he was
generally forgiven his peccadilloes. Milk was his favourite
food and a slight call or whistle would at any time bring
him leaping out of the long grass where he was sleeping,
to his milk-pan.

There are several varieties of the wallaby, which is a
smaller animal than the kangaroo, but of the same
description. The paddy-melon is still smaller than the
wallaby, and much better eating. We have never been
able to discover how this little animal became possessed of
such an extraordinary name. It would seem as if a Paddy
had at first mistaken one for a large melon, but there is no
tradition on the subject that we could ever hear. Paddy-
melons are not so plentiful as wallabies, which in some
places exist in millions, impoverishing the country by
denuding it of grass. Of late it has been found that their
skins are marketable, and a large trade has sprung up
about Roma in catching them for their skins, which are
being sent in bales to Sydney. We were informed just

before leaving the colony that almost all the people in that
township were turning their attention to this business. We
promised a young man who was engaged in it to pay him
a visit about Christmas and spend a week or two in the
chase, but we left the colony too quickly. Stock-yards are
erected with long wings of brushwood running out, and
the wallabies are chased in flocks into them by men on
horseback and kangaroo dogs.

The flying-foxes are a great nuisance to the fruit grower.
These animals will sometimes invade a garden in such
numbers as almost to destroy everything green in the
shape of a tree. About sunset heavy clouds of them may
sometimes be seen darkening the air, continuing their
flight in one direction for an hour or two, until one is led
to wonder where such myriads can bestow themselves by
day, or where they can feed at night. The leaves of the
gum-tree appear to be their principal food, and on moonlight nights they can be shot in great numbers. Only
those which are killed outright will fall to the ground, as
the wounded ones cling with great tenacity to the branches
by means of the sharp hook attached to their wings.
They are greedily eaten by the blacks; we were once
offered some hash of flying-fox at a bush tent and being
hungry after a long ride we essayed to taste it. But the
flavour was by no means enticing, and we left the dish
unfinished. Our experience might be summed up in that
of the man who ate a skunk for a wager in Canada. "We
could eat it, but did not hanker after it." The flying-
squirrel is a pretty little animal, with beautiful fur, which,
unlike the flying-fox, makes an excellent dish. They can
be easily tamed and are very amusing pets, the only
objection to them being their nocturnal habits, which induce them to be rather too lively at night to suit light

sleepers. Like the flying-foxes, these little creatures prey on the fruit-trees and gardens of the settlers.

The dingo, or native dog, is the only carnivorous animal in the colony. Their numbers are very large and the depredations they commit among sheep and calves is often very serious. They occupy a position between the English fox and the prairie wolf and the dog. In the pure bred animals the tail approximates to the brush of the fox, the colour is a dirty yellow or red, and their size about that of the prairie wolf. Like these they usually hunt in mobs, but hunger scarcely ever drives them to attack a human being. There have been cases in which they have killed and eaten shepherds, but it has been thought that in those instances the poor fellows have been caught lying asleep, or been suffering from sunstroke. Of late years the native dog has been so often crossed with the domestic animal, that in the more settled districts wild dogs of all colours and nearly all breeds may now be seen. Great expense is often incurred on various stations to exterminate these animals by means of poisoned baits, and considerable success has in many instances followed. On many sheep stations a man is employed expressly to lay baits for them. On the other hand the absence of the dingo is balanced by the wonderful increase of kangaroos and wallabies which, not suffering from the ravages of their natural enemy, in some of those stations threaten to drive off both sheep and cattle by eating up all the grass. This state of things doubtless arises in part also from the diminution of the aboriginal race, who formerly lived on the marsupials. When he first settles in the bush, the immigrant hears with surprise, often not unmixed with consternation, the howling of the native dogs, which night after night assemble around his dwelling and make night hideous with their noise. They are as great thieves as foxes and like poultry quite as well, so that great care has to be taken to secure them from their fangs. They have another peculiar taste which will often cause much annoyance at first. This is an apparently irresistible *penchant* for walking on newly dug soil, perhaps looking on it as a curiosity and wishing to examine it, or perhaps looking for worms or grubs. We have often been greatly annoyed when, after nicely raking and finishing a bed in the garden overnight we have come out in the morning to find it trodden all over by these brutes. They are so very crafty that if one watches up ever so late, lying in ambush to have a shot at them, they take good care not to put in an apppearance until you have retired for the night.

The bandicoot and kangaroo-rat are too pretty little animals, which hide in hollow logs and graze principally at night. Like the kangaroo, wallaby, paddy-melon, flying-fox, and flying-squirrel, and oppossum, they are marsupials, carrying their young in a natural pocket. Both these are excellent eating, the bandicoot especially furnishing many a meal to the blackfellow, who traces it to its home in some log by the aid of his dog, and then chops it out. We have enjoyed many a night's keen sport hunting these little fellows on moonlight nights, in which the fun is almost as good as bear-hunting of nights in Canada, although not attended by the same spice of danger. The bandicoot is plump and fat, about the size of a rabbit and better eating. It is in fact the only quadruped in Queensland in which any fat can be found. The kangaroo-rat is simply a miniature kangaroo, and the name rat is a misnomer. It runs, or rather leaps, remarkably fast, and doubles in its track without slackening its speed. Very few dogs are swift enough to catch one.

Of pigeons there are a vast variety, all of which are good eating, some of them being of extremely delicate flavour. The painted pigeon is of gorgeous plumage and large size, equal to a small chicken. It would be useless to attempt an enumeration of the varieties, for we never yet found out how many there are. The pretty little zebra-dove cannot, however, pass unnoticed. It is to be found everywhere, and is always tame and trustful of mankind; in size it is somewhat less than a thrush. There is another very tame bird, known as the shepherd's companion or robin. It is not unlike a wagtail, and is always very inquisitive and friendly. It peers in at the door of your humpy, stands on the horse's back as he eats his corn, picks the flies off the bullock's horn as he stands in the team, and runs along the back of the cow as she chews her cud in the yard. In fact he is always at hand, always busy and vastly interested in all your proceedings. The solitary shepherd throws him a few crumbs of his damper, and no bushman would hurt a feather of his long tail.

There are many other birds which always live on friendly terms with mankind. Chief among these is that early-rising, merry old chap, the laughing-jackass. Like many another person of sterling merit, both his name and appearance are against this bird, but these are his only bad qualities. Certainly his grey speckled plumage, big head, and monstrous beak forbid his being looked on as a beauty by the most sanguine of his friends, and he has many. But he is a deadly enemy of the snake, which he kills with his powerful beak, and for this reason he is specially pro-tected and petted. We never knew but one instance of a laughing-jackass being shot, and that was by a red-hot Irish new-chum sportsman. There is probably more humour in this than any other member of the feathered or quadruped tribes. He gets up very early in the morning, before the crow, and soon after the little chirping finches, which are awake with the first peep of day. He seems to look on it as a capital joke that he is up before everybody else, and he sits on a tall limb to see the sun rise, chuckling and laughing in the jolliest way. Like Falstaff, he is not only merry himself, but provokes mirth in others, for no one can help laughing when he first sees this uncouth fellow sitting on a limb of a gum-tree nearly bursting with laughter. But he comes out strongest when he happens to light on the camp of some traveller or bushman, and spies him asleep, rolled in his blanket, or perchance just awoke, sitting up to light his pipe in the embers at his feet. Every laughing-jackass appears to think this the most ludicrous sight in the world; it is to him a never-failing source of the most explosive and violent mirth. His harsh yet funny laughter now breaks out in peal after peal; all the rest of the family in that part of the bush hasten to join in the fun, and soon the camp is enlivened with their united laughter breaking out overhead in all directions, until the traveller, if he be a new chum, begins to fear that his friends will burst themselves and fall dead at his feet. The only time when our jocose friend feels dejected is during wet weather or on its approach; the fall of the barometer is not more certain than that of his spirits. He may now be seen sitting on a branch or fence in the most abject state of melancholy. His head is buried deep between his shoulders, his feathers are rough and dishevelled, and you are prepared to go bail that he will never laugh at anybody again. Either fearing no harm or grown reckless as to what becomes of him this miserable weather, he allows you to come close to him before he flies dejectedly away a short distance, only to perch himself down in the same position. The moralist might, perhaps, draw a lesson from his woful state, as to undue merriment being naturally followed by a corresponding depression of spirits ; but his disconsolate condition disarms even the moralizer, and he leaves him to condole his lot until the weather changes.

Less known than this huge goat-sucker are some other very merry birds which enliven the camp of the solitary bushmen. In some parts of the country, especially in the Wide Bay District, we have been startled when lying in the tent half awake by hearing one of these impertinent rascals vociferate, " Get up, get up !" while another, as if to put a finishing-stroke to the insult, would say in a deeper tone, " You lazy rascal !" Perhaps it may be the same bird that makes both these little speeches, as they are usually to be heard in the same place; but, if so, he has a power of wonderfully changing his note. We have often thought the distinctness of expression of the " get-up" bird to be fully as remarkable as that of the " whip-poor-will " in America. There is a bird in the Barcoo District which strenuously advises the traveller or stockman to "quit the Barcoo ;" and in many places one is startled, when perhaps resting for a few minutes under the shade of a tree, at hearing a bird overhead threaten to " tell your father." The woods of Queensland have many birds which tend to enliven their shades and beguile the bushman as he rides along. Many of them have harsh and grating voices, but others have very sweet notes, only they are never sustained like the songs of English birds. Such as they are, there is no lack of songsters, many having notes so novel and curious as to make amends for the want of the thrush and the lark.

Of parrots there are many varieties, all with lovely

plumage. Perhaps the prettiest of these are the long rosella and ground parrots, but all are very beautiful. The ground parrot is rather scarce. He makes his nest in deserted ant-hills, and, though very lovely, has colours very similar to the brown tint of the ground. There are white cockatoos in enormous quantities; they are a terrible scourge to the farmer on new farms when surrounded by scrub. When the corn approaches ripeness they descend upon it like a cloud of snow. Posting sentinels on high trees around the plot, they fall to with energy, and soon make sad havoc among the cobs of maize. On the approach of danger a sharp cry from the sentinels is the signal for all to retreat to the tops of the high trees, where they are safe from shot. The black cockatoo is a very handsome bird, very shy and much more scarce than the white. Both these and all the parrots have very discordant, harsh voices, making a terrible din both mornings and nights. As stated in a previous chapter, the songs of all the birds are silenced in the heat of the day; but the woods are vocal with them at other times.

The scrub turkey is larger than a domestic hen; its flesh is excellent. The plain turkey is larger, but not so good eating. The scrub turkey is plentiful in most scrubs. It builds its nest in a very peculiar manner, in which both sexes take a part. This nest is nothing more or less than a large heap of small twigs and leaves, consisting often of several dray-loads, and rising when new to a height of three or four feet. In this heap all the hens deposit their eggs, which are apparently hatched by the heat thus engendered in addition to the heat of the weather. We have had two or three large zinc buckets of eggs out of one of these nests, all eatable; besides more lower down, too far advanced for eating. Snakes and other vermin prey on these nests and thus prevent the too great increase of the race. Otherwise, from the number of eggs laid, the scrub would soon be alive with turkeys. The plain turkey makes no nest, we believe.

There are a number of ducks, grey, black, and black and white. Some of these roost on trees, having claws to enable them to make good their hold. There is something very queer to an Englishman in seeing a covey of ducks rise from a water-hole and perch among the trees, but one soon gets used to this as well as other novelties. One species of duck, known as the diver, is so rapid in its motions that it is impossible to shoot it on the water. It dives on the flash and escapes unhurt. A friend of ours used to relate how he had determined to shoot one on the water; for this purpose he took with him two double-barrelled guns. After the bird dived and rose to the surface, he fired again, and at the fourth shot managed to kill his bird, which had now become somewhat exhausted. These birds will swim with their bodies under the water, showing only their heads and necks, in which posture they are often mistaken for snakes, which may often be seen swimming across rivers.

The common crow is found everywhere in Queensland; he partakes of the characteristics both of the rook and crow of the old world. The blackfellow dislikes him for his prying habits and thievish propensities. He will hold a conversation with him for some time, then order him off, and, when he fails to go, pepper him with stones and waddies. He is quite as sagacious as his English friend, and we should not be at all surprised to learn had a fair knowledge of the black's language, as every boy knows his cousin at home has of English. At least every blackfellow will assure you he knows very well what is said to him.

There are a variety of marine birds, prominent among which are the pelican, the native companion, and the ibis. The two latter of these visit some distance inland, and the ibis is often shot on fresh water. The native companion stands five or six feet high and is easily tamed, but is always mischievous. It is a white and very stately creature, frequenting the sand and mud flats near the coast.

On the sea-coast in the northern parts of the colony considerable quantities of *bêche de mer* are found. We have seen it as far south as Freecan Bay, but they are here small, of too light a colour. This little creature is not only a curiosity in itself, being a large hollow snail or slug, which ejects its entrails and a quantity of water on being removed from the rocks or flats on which it lives; but the trade in it and sandal-wood, which are usually carried on together, afford one of the most curious incidents of commerce. What do our English friends think of large fortunes being made by their countrymen, by procuring snails for the tables of the middle and upper classes of Chinese, and by furnishing sandal-wood to be burnt as a perfume in their joss-houses? It does appear curious that British colonists should gather wealth in this manner, yet such is the case. Various Sydney merchants have for many years employed small fleets of light schooners in this trade—one noted merchant alone having fitted out scores to cruise on the shores of Northern Queensland and among the islands, for the purpose of gathering *bêche de mer*, sandal-wood, pearl, and tortoise-shell. The *bêche de mer* is picked up by numbers of Kanakas, shipped for this trade; they are split open, cleaned, parboiled, and then dried in the sun, after which they are packed away for sale. So fond are the Chinese of this luxury that it is said they readily purchase it at its weight in silver.

Sandal-wood is not plentiful, if found at all in Queensland. Recent discoveries have been made of considerable deposits of pearl-shell on the more unfrequented parts of the coast north of Rockingham Bay, and many vessels are now engaged in the trade of procuring it, and are said to be doing remarkably well, although nothing can be said with certainty of their actual earnings, as each vessel makes efforts to carry on its business unknown to the rest of the world. The pearl-shell lies on banks in considerable beds, and as the better sorts are worth 70l. to 120l. per ton, it can be seen at once that the sole knowledge of the existence of a bed is very valuable. The fish have more or less pearls in them, which are carefully saved, and are said to average about 1000l. per quart. Some of the shells are very large, thick and heavy, weighing at times from 4 lbs. to 5 lbs. The beds are occasionally dry at low water, but more generally have from one to three fathoms of water on them. As yet very few, if any, vessels belonging to the colony of Queensland have been engaged in this lucrative trade. That lack of capital and enterprise which has retarded the development of its other resources has also kept its waters, in a great measure, a sealed treasure to Queenslanders. The Sydney merchants have entirely monopolized the trade on the coasts of this colony, as well as in the neighbouring islands. Yet Queensland, with the splendid ports all along its coasts, seems as if intended by nature for the seat of a vast maritime trade. Occupied by an offshoot of the great Anglo-Saxon race, were her sons only true to their destiny, there is no reason why she should not sit as a queen upon the placid waters of the Pacific, and reap enormous wealth not only from the Polynesian islands, which lie in endless numbers contiguous to her eastern coast, but also from the great Eastern Archipelago, some of the vast islands of which can be seen seated amid the blue waters from her northern shores. The vast island of New Guinea, second in size only to Australia itself, awaits occupation and civilization. It seems very singular that, amid all the missionary efforts in nearly all parts of the world, no Christian missionary has ever set up among its tribes the standard of the Cross;[1] and equally singular that in a land, only divided by a narrow channel from five English colonies, and passed weekly by British shipping, no commerce or trade has been attempted. For some years it has been proposed to form a colonizing company to settle there, with a view to opening up its gold-fields; but whether the British race is growing effete, and decay is already affecting the extremities as well as the ancient seat of the race, or from some other reason, nothing has been done. Lately the police magistrate at Somerset, Cape York, paid a visit to the island and inspected one of the villages. He speaks of well-tilled land behind the belt of jungle on the shore, where land is so valuable and so well cultivated that the paths are only wide enough to admit of people walking in single file. The village was well built on tall piles to avoid the noxious malaria of the night, and its inhabitants, which numbered some hundreds, appeared to be gentle and hospitable, though by no means unwilling nor unable to defend themselves against aggression. Their ornaments of gold and copper and strings of pearls testified that their land is not wanting in those riches which usually entice the merchant. As the Dutch have recently ceded a fort of some sort, which they possessed at the north end of the island, to Great Britain, we may suppose that something will soon be done in the

---

[1] We believe the London Missionary Society has now a Mission established in New Guinea.

way of opening to civilization this vast island, and making
us acquainted with its resources.² To the east of this lies
the smaller, though very considerable, islands of New
Britain and New Ireland, also *terra incognita* to us. The
trade of the more northern islands also lies open for Queenslanders to share with the rest of the world, for which her
unrivalled climate, geographical position, fine harbours, and
great resources, her timber, coal, iron, and other minerals,
admirably fit her. Here indeed are fields of adventure and
speculation which will yet make this colony a pride and
glory of the British race. Almost the first steps in seizing
on this vast destiny have yet to be made.

Of all the resources of Queensland waters, none is so
extensive or valuable as its flocks of dugong, which abound
in all the northern waters, and are found at certain seasons
as far south as Moreton Bay, although they are here in
much less profusion than further north. The *Halicore
Australis* is an animal around which hangs a halo of
romance, so strange are its habits and such singular
properties has its flesh. Until lately very little was done
to make any practical use of the vast wealth which
Providence has thus spread out on the shores of this colony,
and which may perhaps be found equal, when well developed,
to any other of its means of wealth, not even excepting its
sheep or its sugar. It is true that some years ago attempts
were made to establish dugong fisheries; but for certain
reasons, such as the intemperance of the men employed,
who were able to earn several pounds per week, the specula-

---

² We notice that an address to her Majesty in favour of the
annexation of New Guinea has recently been passed in the Queensland
Legislature. Although the matter has attracted but little attention in
England, it is of vital importance to the Australian colonies that this
fine island should not be held by any nation but Great Britain.

tion proved an unprofitable one. Recently several fishing
stations have been established for catching dugong, and
boiling down their carcases on Tin Can, Wide, and Hervey's
Bays ; and as great care is used at these establishments to
boil at a proper temperature, and also to prevent anything
like adulteration, the oil manufactured there has already
taken a high stand as a medicine, and obtains a ready and
extensive sale.

The dugong is not confined to Queensland ; there are
other kinds known to naturalists as the *Halicore dugong*
and the *Halicore tabernaculi*, but we are not aware that
either of these has the peculiar medicinal properties of the
Halicore Australis. Knight in his " Animated Nature "
says :—

"This species is a native of the Indian seas, being common among
the islands of the Indian Archipelago, and visiting also the coasts of
New Holland. Its favourite haunts are the mouths of rivers and
straits between proximate islands, where the depth of water is but
trifling (three or four fathoms), and where, at the bottom, grows a
luxuriant pasturage of submarine algæ and fuci : here in calm weather
may small troops be seen feeding below the surface, and every now and
then rising to take breath. The position of the mouth, the muscular
powers and mobility of the lips garnished with wiry bristles, and the
short incisor tusks of the upper jaw, enables these animals to seize and
drag up the long fronds of the subaquatic vegetables which constitute
their nourishment.

" The dugong is in high esteem as an article of food, its flesh being
tender and not unlike beef; hence it is hunted assiduously by the
Malays, who attack the animal with harpoons, in the management of
which they are very dexterous.

" The mutual affection of the male and female is very great, and the
latter is devoted to her offspring. If a dugong be killed, the survivor
of the pair, careless of danger, follows after the boat carrying the body,
impelled by an overmastering passion, and thus often shares the fate of
its partner ; indeed, if one be taken, the other is an easy prize.

" The dugong attains to the length of seven or eight feet ; its caudal
paddle is crescent-shaped ; the large thick upper lip hangs over the

lower; the skin of the body is thinly set with very short prickly bristles; the anterior limbs, or flippers, are destitute of nails. The ventricles of the heart are not united together, but form as it were two distinct hearts joined at the top: this separation of the ventricles does not alter the routine of the circulation. The eyes are very small."

Dr. Hobbs, who first discovered the curative properties of the fat or oil of this animal, says :—

"The dugong resembles somewhat in shape and size the porpoise, but is unlike it in having no dorsal fin. The hide or skin in its dried state, although much thicker, partakes of the character of pig-skin, and, if tanned and prepared, would, doubtless, make good saddles. The bones are very heavy, of the same specific gravity as ivory, and take a beautiful polish; when struck together they give out a metalliferous sound. indicating the density of their structure, and reminding one of the bones of Behemoth, which were 'like bars of iron.' The eyes are very small and deep-set in the head, like those of a fat pig. The ears also are very small. The tail is like that of a whale; and as the fins, one on either side, are so very small in proportion to the size of the animal, it is evidently the principal propelling power. The dugong is a graminivorous ruminant; by means of its large lips the long blady grass growing on the banks in shallow water is plucked off and conveyed to the mouth, the roof and floor of which are curiously covered with circular tufts of short bristly hair, resembling two shoe brushes which have been almost worn down to the wood. The design of this is very evident; the thin blades of grass could not be retained in the mouth were it not for this arrangement. The tongue is short, thick, and small; in the upper jaw the bulls have two front teeth or tusks; the females (cows) have none: the grinders are like those of the ox. The stomach is precisely similar to that of ruminant animals in general, full of grass, of various degrees of fineness, indicating more than one mastication, and innumerable long worms, like those found in horses occasionally. The heart is like the whale's, double. The lungs are of great length, and of great capacity. The mammæ are beneath the fins, as in other mammalia of that class. In rising to blow, the dugong exposes less of the body than the porpoise, and at a distance might be mistaken for a turtle. The meat of this animal when fresh is very tender and savoury; its muscular fibre is very short and easily masticated. To persons suffering from weak stomachs the dugong meat would prove a very nutritious and easily digested article of diet.

"The mode of capture for commercial purposes is by long nets; but when sport is the object, the harpoon is used.   It is whaling, in fact, on a small scale; as a sport, it is as exciting as fox-hunting, without the noise.   The oil procured from this animal is very sweet compared with other animal or fish oils; and although no one would take oil from choice, yet, compared with cod-liver oil and other medicinal remedies, it is palatable."

In an article entitled "Submarine Squatting in the New Colony of Queensland," published in 1862, we find the following sketch of the fisheries then in existence :—

"Upon the island of St. Helena, in Moreton Bay, the first submarine run has been formed, and is now in the second season of its operations, under the superintendence of an experienced person formerly engaged in the seal trade in Newfoundland.   Around this lovely island, for miles in every direction, are extensive submarine pastures of great luxuriance, affording a never-failing supply of long grass, and upon which the herds of dugong feed and fatten like oxen on the plains; yet unlike them in requiring no stockman to tail them, no stockyard to confine them, and no driving to the abattoirs.

"The habits and physical conformation of this curious marine animal, corresponding in so many particulars with the description of Behemoth by the patriarch (Job xl. 15), have led some to the belief that the two are identical.   Such belief, however, is not without some show of reason.   The Egyptian word from which the name is derived (Bo-he-mo-ut), signifying water-ox, strongly supports such an idea, and this is coupled with the facts that the digestive apparatus of the dugong is precisely alike in every particular to that of the ox, and the bones so heavy, that, from their great weight and density, when struck together they give out a metallic sound, thus closely agreeing with the Scripture description before referred to, 'He eateth grass as an ox,' 'his bones are like bars of iron.'   Whether this supposition be right or wrong, the dugong has as good a claim to the honourable mention of the patriarch as the hippopotamus (sea-horse), which animal has generally been considered the behemoth.

"For seven months in the year at least, from September to March, these animals are taken almost daily, by means of long nets set across the channels leading to and from their feeding-grounds.   The nets used are of considerable length and depth, and of large mesh, such as were formerly used by deer-stealers in days gone by, and such as were probably used, if there be any truth in the legendary story, by Henry VIII. in securing the portly old friars of Waltham Abbey on their midnight travel to Cheshunt nunnery, and who, when captured, were complimented by the royal polygamist as being the fattest *bucks* he had ever taken.

"The boiling-down operations are continued without any interruption during this period. A large boiler, capable of holding one of those monsters, is continually steaming away, and the oil flows away from a tap in the upper part of the boiler in a clear limpid stream, of the colour of pale sherry wine. Upon cooling, the oleine and stearine separate, the latter being retained in the flannel bags through which it is filtered, and is sold to the soap-makers for about 40*l.* per ton; while the former is used for medicinal purposes, and is consequently of great value, being used by Dr. Hobbs and other medical men as a substitute for cod-liver oil, and has been found as serviceable in every malady attended with debility as that popular remedy. The steady and continuous demand for this oil, both from England and the neighbouring colonies, is sufficient proof of its utility, and of the position it is likely to assume in the catalogue of our colonial exports.

"The flesh of the dugong is considered by those who have tasted it a great luxury. From the same animal can be procured flesh resembling beef, veal, and pork. It appears to be a highly nutritive kind of food, for not only do the natives, but the white people also, who engage in the pursuit of capturing them, and consume it in the absence of beef and mutton, become remarkably fat. Upon a submarine station there need be little expenditure for beef and mutton. The submarine squatter who can dine off a veal cutlet fried in oil every day cannot complain much of his cuisine, for even Soyer, with the most perfect gastronomic arrangements, would fail in supplying a more dainty dish, concerning which an American writer has said, 'It was a dish of which Apicius might have been proud, and which the discriminating palate of Heliogabulus would have thought entitled to the most distinguished reward!'

"There is no part of the animal which does not possess a commercial value. The bones, particularly the ribs, eighteen in number on each side, when carefully boiled and freed from the oil they contain, cannot fail to be of considerable value from their great weight, density, and resemblance to ivory, being free for the most part of cancellated structure."

An article contributed to the *Brisbane Courier*, in 1869,

on this subject by the author is perhaps worth republishing ; we therefore give it entire :—

"The dugong (*Halicore Australis*, of Cuvier) belongs, in common with the whale, to the great family of mammals. The class *cetacea*, to which it belongs, is divided into carnivorous and herbivorous *cetacea*, the dugong being the principal of the latter genus, subsisting, as it does entirely, on a species of sea-grass which grows in those shallow waters which are its regular feeding-grounds. The whale and dolphin are carnivorous *cetacea*, and have many things in common with it ; yet, as Professor Owen remarks, 'The whole of the internal structure in the herbivorous *cetacea* differs as widely from that of the carnivorous *cetacea* as do their habits ; the amount of variation is as great as well could be in animals of the same class, existing in the same great deep. The junction of the dugongs and manatees with the true whales cannot, therefore, be admitted in a distribution of animals according to their organization. With much superficial resemblance, they have little real or organic resemblance to the walrus, which exhibits an extreme modification of the amphibious carnivorous type. I conclude, therefore, that the dugong and its congeners must either form a group apart, or be joined, as in the classification of M. de Blainville, with the pachyderms, with which the herbivorous *cetacea* have most affinity.' The thickness of the skin in the dugong, varying from three quarters of an inch to over an inch, together with the very great similarity of some portions of its flesh to that of the pig, would seem to lend some colour to the opinion of M. de Blainville ; yet, on the other hand, all the knowledge we have of the animal leads us to conclude that Professor Owen is nearer the truth in believing it to be an entirely separate and distinct group. Singular as it may appear, there are very considerable reasons for believing that our Queensland dugong is nothing more or less than the principal representative of that mythical creature—the mermaid—that it is, in fact, the veritable mermaid itself. It is true that the fact of its being confined principally to the Indian Ocean and Australian waters would appear at the first blush to place an insurmountable obstacle in the way of this theory. But it must be borne in mind that the manatee, an animal which differs from the dugong only in the slightest degree, is an inhabitant of the West India seas, and we have records of specimens of this animal having been washed ashore in Newhaven, in the Frith of Forth, and also at Dieppe, in France. In the latter case a mother and her cub or calf were secured, and it is not to be wondered at if an ignorant population, seeing an animal with a countenance which might be imagined to bear a considerable resemblance to that of man, with flippers, in which not only fingers, but nails also, can be easily discerned, and above all, with breasts bearing more closely still a likeness to the mammæ of woman, should at once set it down as a real mermaid and her infant. The dugong has the same hand-like flipper as the manatee, lacking only the nails, which are replaced by a horny substance. So great is the resemblance to a human being of this animal, when seen at some little distance, that the Dutch have given it the name of BAARDMAENETJE, or LITTLE BEARDED MAN, arising doubtless from the fact that the muzzle, being thick-set with hair, has, at a short distance, somewhat the effect of a human beard. This is not the only point of resemblance they possess to mankind. The dugong is an inhabitant of the Indian Ocean, and is found principally amongst the islands of the Archipelago, and the north-eastern coast of Australia. As far as we are aware they are not found south of Moreton Bay, and even here they are not by any means as numerous as in the bays and shallows further north. In the waters of Wide, Hervey, and Rodds' Bay they are far more numerous. But their cheif *habitat* is the tropics. There they may be found at all seasons of the year in almost incredible numbers, coming in and going out with the tide, just like huge mobs of cattle at a mustering on a large cattle station. Dugongs, being obliged to come to the surface to breathe, are rarely found in deep water, but usually in from two to four fathoms, where grow the grass and weed which is their sole food.

" In length they vary from six to fifteen feet, the average probably being about nine feet. The weight of an ordinary specimen will be from four to six hundredweight, although we have heard of individuals weighing something like a ton, and producing no less than twenty gallons of purified oil. We have already adverted to their peculiar flippers. Directly behind these are situated the mammæ, or breasts, which are not of very large proportions. The young are born singly, and are here known as calves. When killed and opened, a dugong is about the size and appearance of a bullock, except that the skin is thicker, the fat more like that of the pig, and that the tail-part assumes the shape of a fish.

" Everything connected with this animal is strange and wonderful. Its human-like appearance and cry, and the touching affection exhibited to its young, are by no means the only peculiarities it possesses. Its skin is probably capable of being manufactured into a gelatine of great value as a food for sick and delicate persons. Its bones are heavy and perfectly solid, and would be an excellent substitute for ivory of a second-rate quality. Its flesh is excellent, and is esteemed as a delicacy by all the nations who are acquainted with its use. The adept knows where to cut to obtain either beef, or veal, or pork; and, if properly prepared, the best judge would scarcely be able to distinguish it from these.

" Sir Stamford Raffles states that during the summer of his residence at Singapore, four of these animals were taken, but that the greatest number is said to be taken during the northern monsoon, when the sea is most calm. He adds, ' They are usually caught by spearing, in which the natives are very expert, during the night, when the animals indicate their approach by a snuffing noise, which they make at the surface of the water.' In the Singapore seas the dugong is usually from seven to eight feet in length.

" A French writer, M. Leguat, writing about the year 1740, speaks of their being found in the Isle of France waters at that period in great numbers. He describes them as being twenty feet in length, and feeding in flocks like sheep. They made no attempts at escape when approached, and were sometimes shot with a musket, and at other times laid hold of and forced on shore. Three or four hundred were met with together, and they were so far from shy that they allowed themselves to be handled, and the fattest were thus selected. The larger ones were avoided, not only on account of the trouble they gave in the capture, but because their flesh was not so good as that of the smaller and younger ones. We have never heard of such unusual tameness among the dugong of these seas, except in the case of a mother whose calf has been taken. In this instance the parent will follow the boat to which her offspring is lashed to the shore, and make no attempt whatever to avoid the fate that soon befalls her. Her moans under these circumstances are so human-like, and the tenderness and appealing look of her eyes and whole countenance is so touching, that the fisherman has need to steel his heart against all sentiment, who does not almost condemn himself as a murderer. Nor is this feeling of attachment confined to the parent. The young calf, in like manner, will follow the dead body of its mother, crying out with a human-like utterance. The Malays in the islands to our north are said to collect the tears of the dugong as a charm, under the belief that they will secure the affection of those they love. Sometimes this feeling of intense regard is shown by the male for the female, and *vice versa ;* it having been known, in the experience of fishermen in Queensland and elsewhere, that, when one is caught, its partner will blindly follow the boat, and thus give an opportunity, readily seized by the crew, for its own destruction.

" Sir Stamford Raffles describes a piece of the flesh which he ate, roasted, as ' excellent beef ; ' while on the other hand, a French author, who ate of the animal in the Mauritius, describes it as ' well-fatted pork, of pleasant flavour.' Dr. Hobbs again describes to us a dish from which he ate as being ' splendid veal cutlets ; ' while Mr. E. Wilson, in a letter written from Cleveland to the *Melbourne Argus*, says the salted meat so nearly resembles bacon, that he ' unconsciously ate it at friend Cassim's for bacon, and was rather startled by his assurance afterwards that the morning's rasher consisted of the flesh of a " young-un." ' The explanation of this singular diversity of opinion is, that from various portions of the animal, meat of different descriptions can be obtained. The Malays consider it a royal dish, and the king has a prescriptive right to all that are taken. In this colony, blacks and whites are alike fond of dugong meat, which, whether fried in its own oil, or salted and preserved as hams or bacon, is no mean dish.

" Another peculiarity of the dugong is the hairy palate it possesses, of which we can give no more accurate idea than by describing it as a large scrubbing-brush, in which the bristles are fixed with all the regularity and strength of the manufactured article. Ruppell, the naturalist, describes a variety of the dugong—if, indeed, it be other than the *H. dugong*—as the *Halicore tabernaculi*. This variety is found in the Red Sea, and Ruppell was led to give it this name from a belief that it was with the skin of these animals that the Jews were ordered to veil the tabernacle. It would be interesting to know by what process of reasoning he arrived at this conclusion, but we have not been able to obtain any particulars.

" It remained for a prominent citizen of Brisbane to discover the chief and peculiar value of the dugong. To Dr. Hobbs, M.L.C., who was at that time the Health Officer of Moreton Bay under the New South Wales Government, belongs the distinction of first conceiving the idea of making use of dugong oil as an article of medicine. In a lecture which he published on the subject of his discovery, in 1855, speaking of the therapeutic qualities of the oil, he says :—' The beneficial effect of dugong oil in chronic disorders in general may be attributed to its nourishing properties ; the blood being supplied through the chyle with absolutely necessary ingredients, without the stimulation of the system which almost every article of diet will more or less produce. But in chronic disorders of the digestive organs, in the treatment of which it is peculiarly valuable, I am inclined to the opinion that, in addition to its emollient action upon the digestive mucous membrane, the unusually large proportion of glycerine this oil contains, exerts its peculiar solvent powers upon the crudities and inspissated bile locked up in the alimentary canal, which, by their presence, keep this highly sensitive membrane in a perpetual state of irritation.'

"Dr. Hobbs further tells us, what the later experience of many others also confirms, that 'so sweet and palatable is the oil procured from the dugong, that in its pure state it may be taken without disagreeing with the most sensitive stomach, and also used in a variety of ways in the process of cooking; so that this potent restorative remedy may be taken as food, and many ounces consumed almost imperceptibly every day, thus furnishing the system with the requisite amount of carbon for its daily oxidation.' For many years Dr. Hobbs continued to prescribe the dugong oil for his private patients before he took any steps to place the article before the public. At length, in conjunction with the late Mr. T. Warry, he commenced the manufacture of the oil on a considerable scale. A fishing station was formed on St. Helena, at considerable expense, and means were adopted for bringing the oil before the public. An exhibit of the article was made at the Sydney Museum in 1854, by the Commissioners of the Paris Exposition of 1855, and it was afterwards sent to that Exhibition. This was so highly prized that Dr. Hobbs received a silver medal, and, as a consequence, considerable orders were received for the article. A branch of trade sprang up, which promised to add considerably to the wealth and resources of the colony, while at the same time conferring a priceless boon on thousands of sufferers in all parts of the world. Soon the demand was far larger than the supply. The principals in the concern being unable to bestow a personal superintendence on the manufactory in the Bay, irregularities which could under other circumstances have been easily prevented rendered the supply both uncertain in production and inferior in quality. These irregularities, through certain causes, at length became so glaring that a stop had to be put to the proceedings as far as the original projectors were concerned. One or two parties, however, continued for some time to follow the pursuit; but another blow was struck at this struggling industry, which resulted in its practical annihilation. Orders had been received by certain houses in Melbourne, from Paris and London, to a considerable extent. Unable to fill these orders with the unadulterated article, it is said that recourse was had to shark oil to make up the requisite quantities. The result is easy to foresee. Dugong oil, only on its trial as yet, was pronounced anything but what it was represented to be ; authoritative opinions of an adverse nature were given, and the trade and consumption entirely ceased in Europe.   Thus the cupidity of an over-smart set of men was the cause of putting a stop to the production of what promised to be, in the words of a prominent writer, 'a valuable and peculiar nutriment to the great Anglo-Saxon army,' as well as to all Europe and America.

"There can be no question, however, that the dugong oil possesses every valuable quality inherent in cod-liver oil, in at least equal proportions with that popular and widely-used medicament, while having the superlative advantage of being quite pleasant to the most delicate palate.   According to Dr. Hobbs, not only has it been highly successful in the cure of consumption, that great foe of the human race, but also in the treatment and cure of many other chronic diseases."

Other evidence might be adduced as to the peculiarities of this wonderful denizen of the deep—fish, strictly speaking, it is not.   The proprietor of the *Melbourne Argus*, writing soon after separation, to that journal, thus speaks of the dugong:—

"But an animal more interesting even than the turtle to all but aldermanic tastes is that which I have already alluded to as the 'young-un.'   This is, of course, its vulgar colonial name.   It is also called the sea-cow, or dugong.   Scientifically it is the *Halicore Australis*, described, I believe, by Cuvier and other naturalists.   It seems to be something between the whale, the porpoise, and the seal. It frequents the shallow waters of the bays along this part of the coast, browsing peacefully upon the marine herbage that grows upon the flats.   It is usually, when full grown, ten or twelve feet in length ; it rises to the surface to breathe, is generally found in pairs, and suckles its young with great tenderness.   It is caught with the harpoon, but with difficulty, as its sense of hearing is excessively keen.   The value of this animal is peculiar   Its flesh is not only palatable and nutritious, but actually curative in a very high degree, and is particularly good for all forms of scrofula and other diseases arising from a vitiated condition of the blood.   In its fresh state it is something like tender beef, and salted it very nearly resembles bacon— so nearly, indeed, that I unconsciously ate it at friend Cassin's for bacon, and was rather startled by his assurance afterwards that the morning's rasher consisted of the flesh of 'young-un.'   But the principal value of this animal consists of the oil which is extracted from it in large quantities.

An intelligent medical man, in long practice in Brisbane, has found that this oil possesses all the virtues, and more than all, of the celebrated cod-liver oil of the pharmacopœia. When properly prepared. the dugong oil is almost entirely free from all unpleasant odour or flavour, and the quantities which can be administered are, therefore, very much greater than is the case with the cod-liver oil, without risk of offending the most delicate stomach. Dr. Hobbs assures me that he has used it for some years, and in great numbers of cases, and that he has every reason to be satisfied with the results. With a little management it could be obtained in large quantities, as each full-grown animal will yield from eight to twelve gallons of the oil.

"As I sat luxuriously lounging in the spacious verandah at Cleveland, or floating over the placid waters of the Bay, I could not help thinking that, whatever other good qualities this neighbourhood might hereafter prove itself to be possessed of, at all events it should be confessed the true refuge of the consumptive. With a climate which, even in the depth of winter, was not only the most bland and genial I ever witnessed, but absolutely challenging imagination to suggest improvement, and with a valuable and peculiar nutriment, such as I have described, floating past the very doors, where could the afflicted turn with a readier hope of relief? I would commend this considera- tion to those who watch over the health of your community; for well I know that you have no immunity from that fatal disease which hangs upon the skirts of the great Anglo-Saxon army wherever it strides along in its energetic march. I see instances of the importance of this suggestion everywhere around me. There are now living, and going about their daily avocations here, persons who ten years since were pronounced incurable with you; while a quiet grave here and there in this very cemetery tells a sad tale of premature loss, which would have been prevented had the steps of the destroyer been earlier arrested."

The Gympie *Times* also adds its testimony as to the excellent quality of the oil in the following terms:— "Candidly, it was with considerable hesitation that we accepted this assertion that the article was 'not in the least nauseating,' but now we can vouch for the fact; the oil compares very favourably with a great deal of the substance described as 'butter,' and in truth it is not at all unpleasant."

With all these properties—a fat which is equal if not
superior to the best cod-liver oil in consumptive cases, and
superior to it as being useful in many other diseases of the
human frame, with the great advantage of being sweet and
palatable as a food—with a skin which may either be
boiled down to a jelly for children or invalids, or cured
into the stoutest and most durable leather—with bones
that equal any other ivory, while its flesh can be eaten
either as fresh or salt meat—the dugong must play an
important part among the future products of this highly-
favoured country, especially as this is the only portion of
British territory where it is found. As the shores of
Queensland abound with large shallows with mud bottoms,
on which grows the grass eaten by these animals, their
feeding-grounds are practically unlimited, occupying probably over 3000 miles of coast. The immense herds which
frequent these shallows appear almost fabulous. One of
the fishermen in Wide Bay told the writer that a few days
before he had seen a mob which appeared to fill the water
with their bodies. He computed this "school" or mob to
be half a mile wide and from three to four miles long. It
is usual for the dugong to come in with the tide, feed on
the flats, and then retire with the receding waters. The
writer's boat was once anchored in Hervey's Bay, in one of
those channels through which the tide passes when running
off the flats. For between three and four hours there was
a continuous stream of dugongs passing while the tide
went out, which those in the boat could only liken to the
rush of cattle out of a stock-yard after a general muster.
Some of the men in the boat said that millions of dugong
passed, which was of course incorrect; but some thousands
must have gone out with that tide. As the dugong does
not eat the top of the grass, but bites off about an inch or so

which it rejects, it is very usual to see on those seas large
quantities of these grass-tops floating on the water, covering
acres in one mass—thus showing what large quantities
of animals must have fed on the grass below. Another
evidence of their vast number may be seen on the beach
inside these grass flats when the wind is blowing in-shore.
Then the whole beach will be loaded with their excrement
for two or three miles at a stretch. A friend of ours once
told us he was entirely at a loss, when on a visit to the
sea-coast, to account for the large quantity of cow-dung
which bestrewed the beach, and which he thought must
be evidence of large mobs of wild cattle in the opposite
islands. He was ignorant of the natural history of the
dugong, and, when we explained the matter to him, was
filled with surprise at the existence of such marine monsters.

Although a very inoffensive animal, never turning on
its captors, the bulls often have severe fights among themselves. A timber-getter related an instance of this sort.
When lying one night at anchor in Wide Bay, in a boat
alone, he was greatly frightened by the struggles of two
huge fellows which he thought as long or longer than his
boat. Unfortunately they had chosen that precise spot for
their duel, and often rose to the surface so near to the boat
as to cause great apprehension on his part that it would
either be upset as they rose fighting to the surface, or be
smashed by a blow from one of their huge tails. He
described the water as being perfectly white with the froth
they made. Having no gun, he was fain to halloo at the
top of his voice and beat the water with an oar, in order, if
possible, to frighten them to a distance, in which he at last
succeeded.

There are two methods by which the dugong are captured. In some instances a party of six men, furnished

with harpoons, lances, lines, and floats, track them to their
feeding-ground, where the harpooner, usually a blackfellow,
strikes the prey as it feeds quietly below. In this case
great care is requisite in consequence of their very delicate
hearing. The oars are muffled, not a word is said nor a
foot moved, and the harpooner directs the steersman by a
motion of his hand. It often happens that a dugong will
escape through being struck in a fleshy part of the body,
from which the iron easily draws. If otherwise, the poor
creature rushes wildly away, the line is paid out, with an
oil-can or some other article attached as a buoy. The
boat's crew pull vigorously after it, to be at hand, when it
comes up to breathe, to strike it a second time. This
second harpoon or "iron" has a shorter line, as the dugong
will sooner be exhausted and rise to breathe. It is then
struck with a lance, if not already dead. The water will
be dyed with its blood for a long distance.

The other method of catching is by netting. In this
case a net with a very large mesh is stretched across the
channel through which they have to pass to their feeding-
ground. The rush of water in the tide-way soon strangles
them, and they are easily removed from the net. From
lack of capital, very little has as yet been done in this way.
The natives are extremely fond of the dugong's flesh,
esteeming it above all other food—as indeed do white men
when engaged in catching them. They think the skin the
most delicate part, which they roast on the coals, as they
do all their food. When hot through, it looks like a nice
jelly, and is by no means bad eating. Some dugong will
turn out twenty gallons of oil from the fat of the flesh,
independent of the belly and kidney fat. A fair average is
about five or six gallons, besides from a hundred to two
hundred pounds of lean meat. It is, however, understood

that further to the northward the animals are much fatter, as they certainly are more numerous.

The late police magistrate at Somerset, Cape York, paid a visit to the island of New Guinea. He found there, in each village, towers built as a sort of trophy, of the ribs of the dugong. The method of catching them there attests their great plenty. In a shallow part of the sea a light platform is erected, where a man, armed with a spear, seats himself, and, calmly awaiting the arrival of a dugong, "piths" it while feeding, as cattle are pithed in a slaughter-yard, by passing the spear through its spinal vertebræ. Among the natives of Queensland the plan adopted is very similar to that by which they catch mullet, only the nets they use are very much larger. Their nets are bags, having a crescent-shaped mouth extended by a tough stick exactly like a schoolboy's bow, and, like it, having a stout string. It is evident, if small fish once get into a bag-net of this sort, their chance of getting out is remarkably small. With a number of these nets they form a semicircle around a shoal of fish, and gradually approach each other and the shore, shouting and holloing and splashing the water. The noise they can make in this way is something wonderful. Of course, when they have once formed a line with one of these nets in each hand, there is not much chance for the fish to get away, and large numbers are often caught. When catching dugong, the nets are so large that each man only holds one. When a dugong is caught, the fish and blackfellow both make a dive, and the one stops down as long as the other. On rising to the surface, another black relieves the one who holds the net, the others all striking the poor dugong with their spears. Every time it rises to the surface, this is repeated until the dugong is either drowned or bled to death.

Like many other valuable discoveries, the value of dugong fat or oil in consumption was made by a very simple circumstance. About the year 1849, Dr. Hobbs, the health officer at Brisbane, had noticed a blackfellow, with whom he was well acquainted, as being far gone in lung disease. After awhile he was missed, and of course was looked on as being dead. A few weeks after, the worthy doctor was surprised at meeting the man in question, not only alive, but stout and hearty, without any trace of disease. He naturally felt great interest in the case, and questioned the black as to what he had done to obtain a restoration to health. He replied that he had been to the Bay, eating "young-un." This put the doctor thinking. He had frequently noticed, he recollected, that blacks in rather poor case would leave the town, and, after a short stay at the Bay, return in robust health, with great increase of flesh. He had always considered this as merely the effect of change of air and diet, and of abstinence from alcoholic drinks. From what he gathered from this man he formed a different opinion, and, with a view of testing his idea, he obtained a few gallons of the oil from a fisherman, and also tasted the meat. Soon after this he had an opportunity of trying the oil, which we will let him relate in his own words :—

"I was first led to the use of this oil by having under my care a young man who had suffered from an obstinate obstruction in the bowels, terminating in acute inflammation, for which he had been bled five times, and otherwise extremely reduced, leaving him in an exceedingly debilitated condition. His illness extended over a period of eight months, and the debility attending the stage of convalescence was very protracted, notwithstanding the administration of all the usual remedies prescribed in such cases, together with every necessary comfort. Feeling assured that, owing to the irritability of the stomach of my patient, cod-liver oil could not be retained, if administered, I resolved upon trying the dugong oil as a substitute, telling him not to expect any great improvement until he had taken it for a month. At this time he was so weak he could not walk from his chair to the verandah of his house, a distance of a few yards only, without experiencing the distressing feeling of exhaustion. In a fortnight, under its use, he could take short walks ; and in a month could leave his house for several hours, walking a considerable distance without feeling much fatigue. He then went to the Bay, and amused himself in fishing and procuring this oil, which he used freely, not only in its pure state, but also frying his fish and flour cakes, and other articles of food in it. He returned to see me in perfect health, and quite fat. It was not the mere recovery of this patient that so much surprised me, but the *rapidity of the change* from complete prostration to perfect health and vigour."

The writer had a conversation with the gentleman here referred to a few days before leaving Brisbane. He is now a man in middle life, with a wife and family, and occupies a very important official position. He assured us that his health had been good ever since the time spoken of, although he was then so unwell as to have given up all hopes of recovery, and had actually made his will and arranged for his funeral. There are many persons moving in the first circles in Queensland who have to thank this wonderful remedy for restoration to perfect health. Dr. Hobbs received a medal from the Sydney Exhibition of 1854 for a sample of the oil he forwarded there, which has been the only recognition he has received of his great service to humanity by introducing this article to the pharmacopœia. We believe that such measures are being taken for extending the production of this oil as will enable it to be introduced to the British market, which has up to the present time been impossible in consequence of the small quantity procured. There seems to be no reason, when the enormous stretch of coast, the plentiful numbers of the fish, and their great value is considered, why the dugong fisheries of Queensland should not equal in impor-

tance the cod-fisheries of Newfoundland, and furnish
employment to thousands of seamen. When we recollect
that the dugong is found on all the coast-line stretching
from Wide Bay to the island of Finior, including the
shallows of the New Guinea coast, some idea may be formed
of the enormous source of wealth which here awaits but
the introduction of capital. Here indeed we see, in the
words of Dr. Johnson, "a potentiality of acquiring wealth
beyond the dreams of avarice."

The insect life of Queensland is a matter of no small
importance to the resident. If it is not plagued with as
many venomous flies and reptiles as Mexico, Africa, and
other tropical and semi-tropical countries, Queensland has
quite enough torments of this nature to cause one to wish
their number less. Flies, mosquitoes, sand-flies, and fleas
abound in some localities during the summer months.

One variety of dun-fly is so numerous in some localities,
and their bite so sharp, that horses cannot be pastured there
in the summer season without loss of flesh. These flies will
bite through a thin pair of trousers so sharply as to cause
one to start. They are, however, only occasionally met
with, and, unlike the little black fly, are easily caught or
driven away.

The mosquito is the great enemy of the new chum. It
appears to delight in the thick blood of the European, and
soon tells its tale in the swollen and discoloured features of
its victim. The old resident certainly feels its bite to a
greater or less extent, but no swelling or redness shows
where he has been bitten. Not so with the new arrival.
Every mosquito-bite causes a hard lump of red flesh to rise,
until the whole face is one swollen mass. Thus is the "new
chum" who arrives in the summer-time branded, if he
happens to be exposed to the depredations of those little

fellows, who sing their blythe tune while they suck their victim's blood. By care, in sleeping only in beds protected by mosquito curtains, this painful and unsightly ordeal may be avoided. Even then, however, it will be necessary to be very careful to brush out all intruders with the towel before turning down the curtains, and to tuck these well in after getting into bed, to prevent their coming in from underneath, which they will otherwise certainly do. Any one who has been in bed and watched these rascals, minutely examining the curtains in every part to find some aperture by which they can get at their prey, and the celerity with which, when such unhappily presents itself, they rush in like a flock of sheep through a gap, will be prepared to admit that the faculty which naturalists term instinct in the inferior creatures differs very little, if at all, from reason in man. If the sleeper will rest in peace he must look well to the state of his bed-curtains; in this instance, also, " eternal vigilance is the price of safety." Certain positions are more infested by mosquitoes than others. As they breed in water, it follows that low, damp situations, near rivers and lagoons, are more subject to them than dryer places, where they will often be entirely wanting. On the other hand, many places on the banks of rivers. if near mangrove or fresh-water swamps, are so plagued by them that instances have occurred where they have actually driven away settlers. Cultivation and clearing the land soon diminish their numbers; and it is customary, meantime, to burn cowdung in order to smoke them out. We discovered, a year or two before leaving the colony, that the smoke of the grass-tree is highly efficacious in driving them away; it has the advantage, too, of yielding an aromatic and agreeable odour by no means objectionable. No mosquito will stop within smell of this perfume. As at sea it is the fashion to laugh at every one who is sea-sick, so we have noticed it is considered the correct thing to "chaff" the new chum whose countenance is disfigured by mosquito-bites. Each habit has always appeared to us as being alike senseless and ill-natured, and nearly every one suffers at first from both inflictions. There are various kinds of mosquitoes in Queensland; the principal sort is the small black one. A much larger greyish mosquito is occasionally seen, whose sting is very acute. Old residents grow impervious to their attacks, although we remember having to clear out of a camp near the coast swamps, bag and baggage, in the dark, to escape from the multitudes of these insects. The mosquito rarely bites during the daytime.

The sand-fly is not nearly so generally met with as the mosquito. It is a very minute fly, a mere speck, scarcely discernible, and yet it has the power of inflicting the most excruciating pain. Every bite of this little insect raises a large lump, and continues to pain for hours. Fortunately its haunts are prescribed, and it bites only an hour or two in the mornings and evenings, and never where a breeze is blowing. When unfortunate enough to have been attacked by them, the sufferer feels as if he had been bathed in fire, and for a time can hardly endure the torment they inflict. We have seen a party of men driven off the shore to their boats by the attacks of these diminutive assailants, before they had time to boil a billy of tea, as quickly as if set upon by a human foe. Like the mosquito, the sand-fly haunts low and damp situations, or sandy tracts near the sea.

The flea may be said to have its home in Queensland. Every old hut and camp swarms with them. If one goes into a deserted hut, dressed in a pair of white moleskins, he will soon see them change from white to speckled and then to black, and hordes of fleas crawl over him. Woe to the unsophisticated traveller who essays to sleep in such a place! The night will be for him one vast horror, unless he has the hide of a rhinoceros. Old stagers avoid these places and camp in the open air. In some few places the very ground teems with these sprightly fellows, and you may see them jumping about in all directions, by simply drawing a groove in the sandy soil with a stick. The heat of the climate is very favourable to their propagation, and great care is needed to keep them out of the dwellings, which on light sandy soil is often difficult.

There are many varieties of wasps and hornets, some of them of vast size, and proportionately venomous. The writer was once stung in the back of the neck by a hornet about an inch and a half long. Before he could reach the house his legs became paralyzed, and he had to be carried the rest of the way. In this case three half-tumblers of Hennessey's brandy were drank without producing any effect, so potent was the poison; another draught, however, had the desired effect. In all cases of snake poisoning the free use of strong spirits is highly advisable if no other remedy is at hand. If the ordinary effects of liquor can be produced, the virus has been overcome. Some of the wasps' nests are very curious and interesting structures, although they do not, as far as we have observed, equal in beauty those found in America.

There are many very splendid butterflies to be seen nearly all the year round. Moths of scores of patterns and hues, each more lovely than the other, abound everywhere, and may be caught in large quantities in the evenings, or by a visit to the scrubs at any hour of the day. Some of the collections of moths and butterflies which we have seen, caught in Queensland, were beyond description lovely and beautiful. Lovers of conchology, also, may find here ample fields for their favourite pursuit. The collection of our friend C. Coxen, Esq., Land Commissioner for East Moreton, comprises several hundred different shells, many of them exceedingly rare and valuable.[3] In fact, whatever portion of the great field of nature the student or collector may wish to explore, this great colony furnishes for him inexhaustible resources, among which he will be constantly falling in with some novelty.

Among its insect life Queensland has nothing so valuable and important to its inhabitants as its bees. Before the settlement by whites, the aboriginal had two varieties of honey-bees, which yielded him a very considerable amount of food. In the language of the Wide Bay blacks, these are known as " cobboy " and " gidla." The latter is the more plentiful, and is that usually spoken of as the native bee. It is a small black insect, very similar in shape to the house-fly. Its comb, like that of its congener, is found in the hollow of a tree, usually a small one, such as the she-oak, honeysuckle, or tea-tree : sometimes, however, it will be found in the gum or ironbark, and at a considerable elevation ; but this is the exception, so far as our observation has gone. The comb can usually be put in a two-quart billy, and often is not above one half that size. It is quite black, and divided into large, roundish, irregularly-shaped cells, two or three times as large as those of the English bee. The honey is very nice, having a slight and pleasantly acid taste, besides the usual sweet taste of honey. Many people prefer it to English honey on that account. It is also much more liquid than the latter. " Cobboy " differs from " gidla " both in the colour of the

---

[3] Mr. Coxen has, we believe, presented his very valuable collection of shells to the new museum, in the management of which he takes a very prominent part.

bee and the appearance and taste of the honey. This bee
is a little larger than the other, and of a reddish colour.
Neither of them has any sting or other means of defence
against intruders. The "cobboy" honey is contained in a
lighter-coloured comb than "gidla;" the cells are more
cylindrical and larger, and the honey itself is of a thicker
consistency, being very gummy and thick, and tasting
very much like sugar-candy. There are few Europeans
who do not relish this dainty at the first taste, and eat it
with great avidity. Unfortunately "cobboy" is scarce,
and, when found, is equally diminutive with the other
native comb. Of all the benefits conferred by Englishmen
on the Australian black, none equals in importance the
introduction of the English bee; in fact, the bee and the
iron tomahawk are perhaps the only benefits our enlightened race has conferred upon these poor people. The
English bee may be said to have wrought an entire change
in their domestic economy wherever it has found its way.
It flourishes in Australia in a way that is quite impossible
in the cold and wintry climate of Great Britain. Instances
have been known in which a hive of bees has increased
nearly thirty-fold in one year; we once knew an instance
in which a stock of bees in England increased nine-fold in
one season, but two or three of the swarms were too weak
to stand the winter. But in Queensland there is no winter
as far as the bees are concerned. They appear to gather
enough for present consumption every day of the year,
especially in severe rain. Swarms are thrown off nearly
all the year round, and these again soon begin to colonize.
It is obvious, therefore, that this must soon be a country
flowing with honey if not with milk—and there is no
scarcity of the latter—and such soon comes to be the case
wherever the white man plants his foot. It is impossible, if

one has a hive of bees, to prevent many swarms from escaping. We once had a block which soon increased to eight or nine, and we were kept in a perfect state of bewilderment by the increasing outcome of new swarms. Every day and at nearly all hours the loud hum of the young colonies could be heard, until it seemed quite useless to attempt to save them. Working in the field, a swarm would be seen careering overhead, making for some tall tree, where they had selected a roomy hole as their future home.   While riding in the bush, a swarm was frequently seen passing overhead or clustering on a limb.   In the course of two years the bush in every direction was filled with bee-trees, until it became almost less troublesome to obtain the honey from them for domestic use than to look after one's own hives.   Bees are never killed; the box, usually a gin-case, is turned up, and the larger portion of the comb cut out, which is quickly replaced by the busy occupants.   On felling a bee-tree to obtain its contents, known in colonial parlance as a " sugar-bag," it is not unusual to obtain four to six buckets of honeycomb, while some will have much more.   Great fun is often had when three or four men thus rob a bee-tree—the enraged owners often showing fight desperately.   But smoke soon drives them away, and the poor creatures may be seen high up in the air, looking in the vacant space for their old home. The natives have another and better way of getting the honey, described elsewhere.

The rapid spread of the honey-bee is something wonderful.   They appear to advance both northward and westward with a certain and regular yearly march.   When we first knew the Neusa River, the nearest bees were about twenty miles distant.   That season the blacks found them half-way in the bush, and, on cutting into their nests, found little honey, a sure sign they were but just swarmed. The next year a bee-tree was found on the river. In a year they were tolerably plentiful, and the workmen saw bees fifteen miles to the northward. Now the bush teems with honey-trees, and a white man, if accompanied by a black, can live there very comfortably on honey alone. This may appear a singular statement to people accustomed to eat it only as a sweet. But the hungry bushman or black sits down to a large mass of honey in the comb and makes a hearty meal off it, and we know from experience that such a meal is fully as strengthening as when made on more solid food. With the addition of a small slice of damper an excellent meal may be made of honey-comb. We were once much amused at a remark from a friend, an old resident in the bush. Speaking of the satisfying and strengthening properties of honey, and the quantity a man could eat, he said very naively, that when he had not been in the habit of eating honey for some time he could not eat much at first. "The first day," he said, "I cannot eat over a quart-pot full, but the next day I can eat that billyful easily," pointing at the same time to a three-quart billy containing the tea with which we were regaling ourselves. We thought at the time, his idea of a very little and that of many people might somewhat differ. As a rule we have not been in the habit of measuring our stomach; sitting in front of a sheet of bark piled up with the white and luscious comb, we cut it into squares, corresponding to the capacity of our mouth, with a sheath knife, and then deftly pass it under our moustache with as little litter as possible, while to tempt our waning appetite our faithful black friend would from time to time place another and, if possible, whiter comb before us. Memory brings back many a scene of this sort, with the horses quietly grazing near, and the everlasting forest surrounding us with its everchanging shadows and glorious sunshine. We believe that the English bee is now to be met with in most parts of the colony. In a few years it will have penetrated to its great unknown interior. When that time arrives the explorer may push out with confidence as to a supply of food, for no one need be hungry when the bee can be seen, humming among the grass and flowers.

There are some other insects which have come in with the white man by no means so welcome as the bee, nor is their presence to be so easily accounted for. Their presence rather appears to indicate a wonderful but as yet inscrutable law of nature, which looks more like a new creation than anything else. We allude to the various parasitic insects which prey on the different plants which have been introduced to the colony. The cabbage, cotton, tobacco, and sugar-cane, all are subject to the ravages of a peculiar insect or grub which was entirely unknown in the country before these various crops were grown. Sow a little tobacco seed and raise a few plants, and at once a little beetle of a colour corresponding to that of the leaf makes its appearance and begins its ravages on the tender leaves, necessitating constant supervision and watchfulness. These insects prey on the tobacco-plant in other countries, but how is it that they appear here at the other side of the globe as soon as the plant is grown? Do their eggs adhere to the seed? It does not appear very probable, but it may be the case. But if a tobacco-plant is carried from where the seed-bed is to a distance of some miles, as it grows up, there will be the little fly to prey on its leaves. The cotton-plant, too, has its particular parasite, which sometimes makes great havoc, destroying whole fields. The "borer" is the pest of sugar-growers all the world over, and at first Queensland planters were jubilant because of their apparent freedom from it. But, alas! it soon made its appearance here also, causing additional labour, and calling for precaution here as elsewhere. So also with the aphis, known as the " cabbage-louse," and that destructive grape blight, the *oidum tuckeri*. How do all these curses to the agriculturist find their way across the waste of waters to the antipodes?

The snakes of Queensland, although including many varieties, are by no means formidable. None of them will attack a human being unless inadvertently stepped on. The largest of them, the carpet-snake, is not venomous, although a bite from its huge mouth and triple row of teeth would be no slight matter. We never heard of an occurrence of this kind, and from the extreme sluggishness of the creature it is not very likely to occur. We have killed carpet-snakes measuring over twelve feet, and thicker than a man's arm. Their teeth are all bent inwards, so that when they bite any animal they can only swallow it, but not loose their hold otherwise. A friend of ours killed one in a torpid state having a whole paddy-melon in its stomach. This snake is a great thief and pays frequent visits to fowl-houses, when any orifice is left through which it can pass. We once killed one in the kitchen at night, which measured between eight and nine feet, that had just taken from under the hen a fine chick, which it had in its mouth when struck with the axe. It delights in common with some other snakes in crawling about the roofs and wall-plates of bush-houses. The wife of a labourer near us was lying ill in bed, when she was horror-struck at seeing one crawling along the wall-plate just over her bed. She called a neighbour who was within earshot, and who soon despatched the intruder. The brown snake often grows to a great size, like the carpet, and is sometimes mistaken for it. The tiger-snake, so called from its marks and colour, is also a large snake and said to be venomous, which others again deny. The same remark holds good of many smaller snakes, such as the diamond—a very beautifully-marked snake, the whip, and the green snake; one person will insist that each of these is venomous, and another as stoutly proclaim the contrary, which, to say the least, is pretty conclusive evidence that they are not very harmful. The general opinion is that the whip-snake is poisonous. This is a small snake usually from two feet six inches to four feet in length, and more common than most others. The most dreaded of all is the black snake, which is very venomous, being particularly deadly in the hotter months of summer. It is a thickish snake, usually about three to four feet in length, with a yellowish belly. It is often found in water-holes, and is sometimes come on very suddenly in such places. It cannot spring forward further than its own length, but care must be taken in pursuing it not to keep directly behind it, as it has the power of throwing itself backward a considerable distance and rising to a height of four or five feet in its leap. It is rarely that any one is bitten by a snake, and still more rarely that a life is lost through this cause.

There is another deadly reptile known as the death-adder. This is a creature with two short legs in front like a lizard, and a thick, heavy body about eighteen inches long, which tapers off very suddenly to a short tail, in which is a sting. The mouth is also furnished with poison-fangs, so that it has a double power of death at its command. It is a slow, sleepy creature, and, as if aware of its powers, never attempts to move out of the way of man or beast. If stung or bitten by this reptile, death follows very quickly unless immediate and strong antidotes are applied. The usual remedies for all snake-bites are tightly bandaging, cutting out and cauterizing the wound, and an outward and inward application of ammonia. In cases where this drug has been injected into a vein, the best results have been experienced.

There are various sorts of lizards besides this creature, which is a sort of connecting link between the lizard and snake tribes. · Some of the smaller lizards are very lively and interesting, and soon become tame. Others, like the jew or hooded lizard, are ugly enough. The jew lizard is almost startling in its ugliness, as it lies basking on a fallen tree or clinging to a growing one. It is, however, perfectly harmless. Of iguanas—in common parlance "granos"—there are many sorts, some of them as much as four feet in length and three or four inches broad on the back. The settler destroys these fleet gentlemen on account of their love for eggs; yet, as they bravely attack snakes and devour them when victorious, they are deserving of some consideration. A friend of ours once witnessed a pitched battle between an iguana and a black snake; whenever the former was bitten he ran to a little distance, apparently to eat some antidote, and then rushed to the attack again, following the snake until he had killed it. The iguana can run exceedingly fast either on the ground or up the smooth boll of a tree, and always endeavours to keep on the opposite side from his pursuer, as if aware of the existence of revolvers. The flesh of the iguana is white and tender, much resembling chicken, and if we could have forgotten its huge ugly mouth, well filled with sharp teeth, and its serrated back, we should have relished it much. The fat is much sought after for rheumatic affections and for oiling saddles, having peculiar emollient properties.

The iguana is a very courageous creature, and no mean antagonist for a dog; we have seen one keep a bull-dog at bay for some time. Very few other dogs will face one single-handed.

The alligator is not found south of the Fitzroy River. In that and all the northern streams it is always to be seen. They bask on the mud on the river banks about Yaamba, above Rockhampton, and when disturbed slide into the water, or roll over and over like a log of timber. They are to be found all lengths up to seventeen or eighteen feet, with thick hides that turn the best rifle bullets at any but the shortest range. They principally resort to fresh-water holes and lagoons, where they lie in wait for their prey, and often commit great depredations among sheep and cattle. When the valley of Lagoons was first taken up for sheep, it was noticed that every day when the flock went down to drink a sheep was missing. This went on for some time to the consternation of the shepherds, until at length a huge alligator was seen to poke his nose above the water and quickly pull down his woolly victim. A gentleman connected with the native police was once crossing the Burdekin River, with some troopers and spare horses, after a fresh. The crossing-place was consequently hardly to be discerned. One of the troopers, in endeavouring to guide the horses, got off the ford into deep water; the current sent him and his horse a little way down. The horse disappeared, leaving the man struggling in the water. He struck out for the shore, but in a moment the water was black around him with the ugly noses of alligators. One snap, and nothing remained but a red tinge on the water. The officer described the snapping of the alligators' mouths, who all at once made a dash for their prey, to be like the sound of so many huge castanets.

Not only will they attack human beings or cattle when at their mercy in the water, but they occasionally lie in wait among the long grass close to a cattle track, on the banks of the rivers or lagoons, to seize calves or colts when watering. They will here make nice cosy nests of the long reeds like a huge bird's nest, in which to await their prey. It is not often that they attack mankind on shore. At a station on the Burdekin we were told that an instance of this sort occurred. It was customary for the black gins to do the station-washing at the river bank under the shade of a big tree. One day one of the two gins so employed came rushing and screaming up to the station in a state of the most abject terror. As soon as she could be quieted she stated that while the other woman had been stooping down to lift a bucket of water from the river an alligator had pushed his nose above the water and snapped her up in his capacious jaws and drawn her into deep water. From that time no clothes were washed under the big tree.

A friend of ours had quite an adventure with an alligator during the big flood of 1870. He was engaged in the telegraphic department, and had the charge of a northern station and the line for a considerable distance, including that over the Burdekin River. The flood having stopped communication, it became necessary for him to set out to find and repair the damage. For some miles before he reached the river he found it almost or entirely submerged. With his tools strapped on his back he swam from pole to pole in those lower parts, walking on the higher portions. When a few miles from the river there was a long stretch altogether under water, which it was necessary to pass. It was what is called back-water, with no current. After proceeding for a mile or two, and being over a mile from the next dry land, he saw an alligator,

which had got out of the river or some lagoon, making
towards him. Some men would have lost their presence of
mind, but our hero was equal to the occasion. After
swimming so many miles of water in the public service
he was not to be put out of his way by the Saurian
monster. Where he then was the water was as high
as the wire where it drooped between the poles. Here
various logs and saplings had drifted and formed a barrier.
Among this *débris* was a large log. Ensconcing himself
behind this and selecting one of the longest and most
manageable saplings he could find, he awaited his enemy.
He had no sooner come to the opposite side of the log than
he received a smart "job" in the eye from his anticipated
victim, which made him sheer off. Taught a wholesome
lesson he did not for some time approach so close again,
our friend all the while hiding himself behind the big log.
He waited his chance, and every time the monster came
within reach he gave him another punch, accompanying
each blow with as terrific a noise as his lungs would
enable him to utter. When the alligator took a circuit
he quietly slipped round the other end of the log, always
carefully keeping himself as much as possible out of sight,
so as not to whet the brute's appetite too keenly. After
receiving a few punches in addition to the blow in his eye,
and being now and then assailed with short billets of drift-
wood, the alligator, perhaps growing frightened at his
unseen antagonist, and perhaps having a natural terror of
the human voice, turned tail and made off, leaving our
friend to continue his avocation, which he did after assuring
himself that his antagonist was gone for good and all.
He had been bailed up in this singular manner for over
two hours, and assured us he was very glad when the
water shoaled sufficiently to admit of his wading through

it. There are very few of these unpleasant neighbours to be found in the settled districts even of the north. In Southern Queensland, as we have said, they are entirely unknown.

CHAPTER XI.

THE subject which at the present time is most agitating public opinion in Queensland, as well as calling the attention of people at home to that colony, is the trade which has of late grown to such importance with the New Hebrides and other islands of the South Seas in the importation of Kanakas under an agreement for three years' work. At the late general election in 1871 seats were won and lost on this question, and it has been considered of sufficient importance to form the matter of parliamentary debates and despatches from the Colonial Secretary.

Before giving an account of the present state of this question it will be necessary to point out the causes which first gave rise to the introduction of Polynesians into the colony. These causes are various, and a thorough knowledge on this point cannot fail of being instructive in the future.

When Mr. Jordan was first engaged in procuring emigrants for Queensland, England was in the throes of the cotton famine, and as a consequence thousands of the idle operatives were anxious to proceed to the colony. The Immigration Act had not provided for the exportation of factory hands, but by one means or another some thousands of them were sent out in 1863 and 1864. This was effected part by stretching the Act a little to meet the exigency, and partly by independent funds raised for that purpose by a benevolent public at home and in the colony. Thus it resulted that thousands of these people, totally unacquainted with agricultural work, were thrown on this little community just as it was struggling into existence. Not only so, but of the other immigrants by far the larger portion were mechanics and tradespeople, the percentage of farm labourers in each ship being very small indeed.

We do not wish to object to a factory hand or artisan merely on the score that he knows nothing of field work; such men often make excellent colonists, and we know many such in Queensland; but there certainly was a grievous error in flooding the country at the very first with a class of labour unused to open-air occupations, to the exclusion of those agricultural labourers who were so greatly needed. When it is remembered that on the 31st December, 1862, the population of the whole colony was only 45,077, and that two years after, at the close of 1864, it had increased to 74,036, an increase of about sixty-five per cent., it will be at once seen that it was of the utmost importance that the new arrivals, who formed such a large percentage of the population, should be of a class able to develope the resources of the colony, to become in point of fact producers. Those 29,000 persons, even if mostly operatives and mechanics, might, for instance, have been absorbed among the 3,000,000 of Canadians, and would have been everywhere surrounded by farmers able to teach them their business, which they would easily have learnt. But in Queensland they came to form the bulk of the population, and had literally no one to teach them the farmer's art.

In short, the colony was flooded with the wrong class of

people. The population sprang from 38,198, in June, 1862, to 94,710, in June, 1866,—an increase probably unparalleled in the history of colonization. Seeing that these people had to make their living off the soil, at least one-half of them ought to have been agriculturists, while not more than a tithe of them were. It is true, many to secure free or assisted passages passed themselves on the Agent as farmers and gardeners who had never handled a spade or held a plough in their lives; but the evil lay more in the ideas entertained by Mr. Jordan than anywhere else. He thought, and was in the habit of telling his audiences, that the less a man knew of farming the better chance he had of becoming a successful farmer in Queensland. His reason for this belief was, that the climate and crops of the colony were so different from those at home, and all the conditions so varied, that a person with no preconceptions on the subject was likely to do better than a man with fixed ideas,—an argument which would have some force where the immigrant would have other settlers and labourers around him to put him in the way of working in his new home, but which entailed various weighty ills on Queensland.

It resulted that farmers had to employ labourers who knew nothing of the first elements of husbandry,—the same all the world over—and being in most instances as ignorant as their *employés*, a chaotic state of things ensued, and farming had to be evolved from the inner consciousness or dear-bought experience of the settlers. This state of affairs would have frightened an English farmer out of his wits, or, as it did some, home again; and would have been looked on by a Canadian or Yankee, well versed in the formation of farms from the primeval forest, with devout wonder.

Not only the entire absence of good farm-labourers, but other causes led to the employment of Polynesians. The workmen themselves, finding their services at a premium, and that they could command 40*l.* to 45*l.* per annum, with a ration that in those times cost about half as much more, gave themselves great airs, and acted as if they were their employers' superiors ; as in point of fact they were in one practical sense; they always made money, whilst he usually lost it, very few of them being able to earn the wages the masters were obliged to give. Having been unused to hard work, and knowing nothing of farming, a large proportion of them refused to work for farmers except on high weekly wages quite out of their power to pay. As a rule most farmers had their capital so nearly sunk in their land, that they needed to raise the money out of the land before they could pay for the labour.

The large employers experienced another difficulty. It was found that at the season when they required their workpeople the most, and when, inefficient as they were, their services were most required, many of these men would take advantage of this to walk off and leave them in the lurch. This sort of thing occurred so frequently that those engaged in cotton and sugar growing on a large scale had a certain amount of truth on their side when they said that one of their chief reasons for importing Kanakas was the uncertainty of white labour, which might leave them at any time, and that perhaps the picking or crushing season, than which nothing could be more disastrous. Then they had also the fear of a new gold-rush breaking out and enticing their men away by its golden visions. This is probably the greatest evil when it does occur, but there has as yet been but one instance of this kind in the colony, the Gympie rush, 1867-68.

There can be no question that these reasons—the incapacity of the labourers, their frequent insolence and overbearing manners, and the uncertainty of securing their services for any length of time—had much to do with the movement for the introduction of Polynesians.

So long ago as the year 1863 the writer pointed out to the Under-Colonial Secretary, Mr. Manning, the viciousness of the principle on which colonists were being introduced. Mr. Jordan drew his immigrants chiefly from the cities and large centres of population. Had he obtained only one-half as many country people he would have done far more to enhance the prosperity of his adopted country, and would, most likely, have entirely prevented the introduction of Polynesian labour. Men brought up on farms not only know how to do their work satisfactorily, but having a different set of ideas and other habits than townspeople, are less likely to act in any way detrimental to their master's interest. To use a homely colloquialism, they know what belongs to farming, and are therefore less hard to manage, and more likely to think and act in the interest of their employer. Having been always accustomed to open-air work, they are far more able to stand the climate of Queensland and do a good day's work in it than men brought up to work under a roof at home, although the latter certainly find no greater difficulty than they probably would in an English harvest-field.

We have thus given the reasons that operated in favour of the introduction of black labour to Queensland. There appear to be one or two scarcely legitimate reasons which weighed in its favour. There is a certain amount of pleasure experienced by every man in having around him as labourers a class of people over whom he can exert despotic authority. It is so much more pleasant to be

able to issue instructions to workpeople who never entertain the idea of any opposition to authority, than to men
who may have opinions of their own and desire to put
them in execution. White men in the colonies are proverbially independent, the Polynesian is equally docile,
and the master or overseer reigns monarch supreme.

Then there is the powerful argument of increased profits.
It was fully anticipated that by hiring men at 6l. per
annum, and a much lighter ration than the white man's,
a very material saving in wages would result; and if
the absurd statement of Mr. Trollope in a recent newspaper
article was correct, that a Kanaka could do as much work
in the cane-field as a white man, that anticipation would
have proved correct. But the Anglo-Saxon has not come
to that as yet.

Before proceeding further it may not be amiss to state
that a very stringent Master and Servants Act is in
existence in Queensland which, as far as possible, protects
the interests of both master and servant. Among other
provisions it provides under a penal clause that no master
shall discharge a servant without due and sufficient notice
or an equivalent in wages, that a regular written agreement, of which a form is annexed, shall be made between
them, and that every man shall receive a regular weekly
ration unless he boards in his employer's house, not a
very usual thing in the colonies, where the workmen
have usually separate huts or small slab houses, and have
to cook their own food. This ration consists of a diet
which would rejoice the heart of an old-country labourer.
It is as follows:—8lbs. of flour, 14lbs. of beef or mutton,
2lbs. of sugar, and ¼lb. of tea, salt, &c., weekly. This is
sometimes varied; we have known 10lbs. of flour given
and less meat, and on sheep stations it is usual not to

weigh out the meat, but to let each shepherd, or two when two stop in one hut, kill a sheep as they want it, so long as there is no undue waste. The Act also provides that no man can leave his master without the regular notice, but a bench of magistrates can cancel the agreement at any time if sufficient cause be shown on either side. This Act is very valuable to all parties, and usually works well. We have heard many complaints made that in the bush in the far interior this is not always the case. There, as a rule, every squatter or superintendent is either a magistrate himself or very friendly with his neighbour who is. We have often heard men complain that it happens that one neighbour will bring some man of his before his brother magistrates, and have him fined the amount of his wages, or in some other way assist the master, who in turn does the same friendly act for him. Shepherds when suffering from any injustice often find it prudent to bear the wrong rather than to attempt to right themselves before a bench composed solely of their masters' friends and neighbours.

Many stories are told in reference to this sort of thing which savour more of "out West" than of her Majesty's possessions and monarchical institutions. As a rule there is no respect in which one is more struck with the vast superiority of a monarchy over a republic than in the higher tone of the bench; but in the interior of Queensland some queer things occasionally happen, perhaps because we have run our constitution down so near the level of a republic. A friend of ours once saw a scene of this nature. In the town of Springsure a case was being heard, and a few persons besides the plaintiff and defendant were in the Court-house to hear the decision and pass away the time. One gentleman was sitting smoking, with legs astride on the table in front of the bench, busily engaged in chipping a notch in the table with his sheath-knife. Presently another gentleman lounges up to an open window, rests his arms on it, and, after surveying the situation leisurely for a minute, calmly takes his pipe out of his mouth, and addressing the bench, says, "I say ——, ain't you going to finish that —— case and come and have a drink?" The day was hot and the question suggestive, and it was agreed, as the "case" would last some little time longer, to adjourn from labour to refreshment, and resume the sitting in half an hour.

However badly the Master and Servants Act may be administered in some districts in the back country, where population is sparse, there can be only one question as to its benefits in the more populous districts. It is a measure of protection alike to master and man, and the Polynesian Labourers Act has been framed as nearly on its model as was found practicable. Under the former, a master unwilling or unable to pay his servants' wages may be either fined or imprisoned, and the same regulation exists in the other case, with the further proviso that in the case of hiring Polynesians the employer must give security for the due carrying out of his contract.

There has been in Queensland from the earliest period since the existence of free labourers, a powerful party who have objected to it, or rather who have endeavoured to supplant the free white by some other kind of labour. When squatting first began to be followed on the Darling Downs and other country west of Ipswich, which was in the year 1829, the only sort of labour available was that of the convicts. There was not much intercourse in those days between the camp, as Brisbane was then called, and the squatters of the interior, no one being allowed to enter the former without a pass signed by the commandant.

Most of the shepherds, stockmen, bullock-drivers, and bush carpenters employed on the runs at this time were convicts, officially known as " assigned servants." So numerous were these men, and so curiously is public opinion frequently governed by majorities, that in those days if there happened to be a " free man " on a station he was fain to hide the disgraceful fact in his bosom, that he had come out at his own expense, and not at that of the Crown. These men were assigned to the squatters for three years, who had no difficulty in obtaining as many as they required by simply finding them in a " dry-ration," that is beef and flour and tobacco, without any tea or sugar, and a very small amount of clothing. It is the universal testimony of old settlers, that most of these people were first-class workpeople, which may have arisen from the strict discipline they had gone through. It must be also remembered that many of them were sent out for offences that would now be punished with a month in gaol. But of course they were not all alike, some were very poor men, and others everything a master could desire. Neither were the masters all good. Some of them gave their assigned servants regular wages to a small amount, and returned them with good characters at the end of their term.

But many of the baser sort used to deal with their men in quite another fashion. It is said that if such a one had a valuable man, it was the custom, shortly before his term was expired, either to trump up a charge against him, or more generally to exasperate the man into saying or doing something improper, when he was hurried before a brother magistrate and reassigned for a fresh term, with probably the addition of three or four dozen lashes. When it is remembered that these people were re-transported felons from Sydney, it will be admitted their moral tone must have been very low, but official reports assure us that they were often very badly treated at the hands of their irresponsible masters, who could, whenever they saw fit, send a man or woman to the camp with a note requesting that bearer might receive so many dozen lashes, when the poor messenger would at once be placed on the triangles and have the thrashing duly administered.

There were many advantages connected with this class of labour. The men had for years been accustomed to open-air work, and were thoroughly acclimatized, besides having a good knowledge of colonial occupations; their labour cost a mere bagatelle, and it could be obtained in any quantity. It is not so much to be wondered at that masters who had become accustomed to having these people about them should have objected to their withdrawal and sighed for their return.

In 1842 the district of Moreton Bay was thrown open for free immigration, and those convicts still held in bondage were removed. From that time began an agitation on the part of the squatters for the return of convict labour. For many years this was the great political question of the district. As a rule, the townspeople, both of Brisbane and Ipswich, were opposed to convict labour, and the squatters were in its favour. Elections to the Sydney legislature turned on this question, until the gradual increase of an urban population left the squatters in a hopeless minority.

The next phase of the question was the attempt to introduce Chinamen into the colony of New South Wales, of which Queensland then formed a part. This the squatters desired as a cheap kind of labour, and the townspeople opposed. This question settled itself very easily. It was found that " John," after he had been long enough in the colony to learn the lay of the land, asked as much wages as another man, and would take no less. The cheap labour men had to look farther afield.

The next agitation was in favour of the introduction of Coolies, and a Bill was actually passed through Parliament to regulate the trade, but for some reasons, principally of a financial character, nothing of any importance was done in the way of their introduction.

We have already shown how the great influx of British immigrants caused the price of wages to fall, and there is little doubt that if that labour had only been of a better class, no further agitation would have taken place in favour of black labour. But unfortunately the large employers were not satisfied with the class of men imported. They began to look elsewhere for field-hands. When cotton-growing on a large scale first began to be thought of, Mr. Robert Towns of Sydney determined on establishing a plantation on the Logan River. The history of this gentleman, had we space to relate it, would be a romantic chapter in colonial life. He had long been engaged in the collection of sandal-wood, tortoise-shell, and *béche de mer*. His vessels were known in almost every part of the South Seas, and he had long been in the habit of employing Polynesians on board these vessels as sailors, boatmen, and divers. He now determined to introduce some of them to work on his cotton plantation. A shipment arrived, and were very quietly removed from the vessel in the Bay up to the plantation on the Logan River, without passing through the town, and after some time the people of Brisbane were favoured with a sight of some of these strangers driving the bullocks which drew the cotton crop into the town. A great deal of talk and some writing to the newspapers ensued, but nothing was as yet done in the matter.

About this time it began to be thought that sugar-cane could be grown to advantage. The experiments of Captain Hope pointed in that direction, and the practical success of Captain Whish made the fact patent to all. Mr. Raff and others determined to invest largely in this industry, and, with a view to this, brought pressure to bear on Government to make some regulations on the question of Polynesian labour. At first it was considered that the provisions of the Coolie Act would meet the case. But it was soon found that other restrictions were needed, and after considerable agitation the Polynesian Labourers Act was passed, which came into operation in 1868. It was not only the general public who agitated in favour of this measure as a protection to the islanders and a preventive against slavery, but the employers themselves, feeling the delicacy of their position, and that the eyes of people in all parts of the empire were turned to their proceedings, urged on the Government to pass a Bill which would place the trade on a solid and respectable basis.

This Act provided for the obtaining of labourers in the islands of the South Seas by captains, who were, if called upon to do so, to carry a Government agent with each vessel. Written agreements were to be made with those engaged, which were to be witnessed by a consul, missionary, or some other responsible person, who would be requested to sign a document stating that the natives came willingly, and understood the nature of the agreement. They were to be engaged for a period of three years, and were to receive 6*l*. per annum for their services, besides necessary food and clothing. Each Polynesian, on coming on board and signing the agreement, was to be furnished with a shirt and trousers and a pair of blankets in which to sleep. Ample provisions were to be supplied them on their passage, and each vessel had to be inspected before sailing, and licensed to carry a certain number of labourers. The captain and owner were each to give a bond of 500l. for the due fulfilment of the terms of the Act.

On their arrival the vessels were to be inspected by the Immigration Agent in Brisbane, or by some other officer, if in any other port. This officer was to satisfy himself that the natives had been properly recruited, that they knew the nature of their agreement, that those agreements were duly signed and witnessed in conformity with the Act, and that the passengers had been properly treated while on board. Then, and not till then, he was to admit of their landing and being passed over to their masters, who were to execute the agreements and other documents before him.

These latter agreements provided that the masters should properly house and feed the men, pay them 18l. in cash at the expiry of their term, part of which must, if the authorities so willed, be paid into the Savings' Bank at an earlier period, and that they should pay the cost of their return to their homes. The cost of their passage to the colony they had also to pay the importer. These rates varied, as the demand for Polynesians was greater or less, from 8l. down to 5l. An officer was also provided for, called an Inspector of Polynesians, whose duty it was to visit the plantations at intervals, and satisfy himself as to the treatment the men received.

These provisions appeared to be sufficiently stringent to prevent anything improper transpiring, and for a time the friends of white labour, although by no means satisfied, had no argument to adduce against the traffic. But they had other arguments, which although not so likely to arouse the sympathies of people at home as the more sensational ones arising from the developments of recent times, had yet great weight in the colony.

It was held that as Queensland was a British colony, it was the duty of those who composed its population, and to whom the Crown had granted a constitution, to legislate so as to benefit not only the 100,000 British subjects then in the colony, but with a view to the good of the whole empire. That there were tens of thousands of people at home who would be vastly benefited by coming out and having a share in its fine climate and rich soil. That the introduction of black labour would place an insuperable bar to the emigration of these people, as the British workman would strongly object to placing his labour on the level of that of a black, and that thus this traffic was debarring our own countrymen from settling in the colony, where their circumstances would be so vastly improved. It was also urged that as being a British colony, the laws adopted ought to tend to foster a white and British population, and not a black and foreign one which might in future generations equal, if not exceed, the former and by virtue of our liberal constitution, which allows of nearly every man having a vote, become the practical masters of the situation.

Another series of arguments was drawn from the existing state of things in the colony. It was pointed out that a large proportion of the working class had not only come to it from home on the representations of a paid agent, who had been sent to England to induce them to come out by offering them officially the advantages of constant labour and good wages, but that to make the case stronger, large numbers of them had been actually brought out at the expense of the colonial government, which had thus made itself doubly responsible for their well-being. It was asked how these people, many of them men with families, were to maintain themselves and families, and compete with a class of labourers who wore little or no clothes, and had no one to maintain but themselves. Where, it was asked, were the future employers of labour to come from, if the class from whose ranks masters naturally spring in a new colony, were to be continually kept in an impoverished condition by the presence of a servile population, who, at the expiry of their term of service left the colony, carrying with them the fruits of their labours? Had only the working class of Queensland been more able, more sober, and more obliging, the arguments in opposition to the Polynesian traffic would in all likelihood have prevailed.

The passing of the Polynesian Labourers Act at once opened the door for their introduction on a considerable scale. In 1868 six vessels, with 437 males and 2 females, arrived from the South Seas; in 1869 five ships, with 276 males and 2 females, arrived, and in 1870 nine ships, with 581 males and 14 females, making a total of 1294 males and 18 females. When it is remembered how poor the times were during much of this period it will at once be seen that so many men must have made a considerable alteration in the labour market of so small a population.

The Act had not long been in existence when it began to be seen that many enormities were growing out of it, tending to bring disgrace upon the colony and the English flag. It began to be said that instead of the men coming willingly, they were in the majority of cases purchased of their chiefs, who sent them aboard, not on as large a scale, but on somewhat the same principle as the kings of Africa deported their captives and subjects. It transpired that it was usual for the captain to come to terms with the chief, who sold him these men usually for a tomahawk and knife, with probably a handkerchief or some other piece of "trade" added, per head. The captains said this was only a present made to the friends of the man who wished to come; but the "present" was always arranged before the man was sent, and there was a regularity in the tariff which savoured more of barter than of compliment.

In the South Seas each chief is absolute master of the lives and actions of his subjects. Were one of them to refuse to obey his commands, if such an idea were to present itself to his mind, which is not very likely, his death would be the immediate and certain result. Hence if a chief sees fit to send any of his subjects away for three years or for life, they have to go or abide the consequences. In no case does a chief spare a large number of men at one time.

It was also found that the Act had been so loosely worded that it could be evaded in many ways. It had provided for the agreements being witnessed by some respectable person, who was to state that the man knew the nature of the agreement, and entered into it willingly. This clause was burlesqued in many instances, by the mate witnessing the agreements, which were prepared at their leisure by him and the captain on the way home, so as to be ready when they came to anchor. In some cases the captain was himself the owner or charterer of the vessel. Where this was not the case it was usual to pay him not only his monthly salary, but a bonus of so much per head for every Polynesian imported. Hence these men had always a direct pecuniary interest in the venture, besides that natural desire for equal success with his compeers which actuates every man.

At the early stages of the traffic there was much complaint on the part of the Polynesians that they had only engaged for twelve moons, whereas they were expected to work for thirty-nine. In some cases they refused to work after that time, and were brought before the magistrates in consequence. In one notable case several of these poor fellows, who evidently acted *bonâ fide*, were sent to Brisbane gaol by the Maryborough bench for refusing to continue longer at work, saying their time for which they had engaged was expired. To his honour it must be said that Mr. Kenball, the police magistrate, objected to the decision of his brother magistrates. An indignation meeting was held, in connexion with which some very disgraceful facts transpired, showing the lengths the black-labour men were prepared to go in bringing pressure to bear upon ministers and others to prevent an expression of public opinion. In this case the magistrates, who were nearly all of them interested directly in the traffic, relied on the written agreement which bound the men for three years, and which was duly signed, to prove that they fully understood its import. They had kept a correct account of their time, being educated Christian men, able to read and write, as most of them can who come from " missionary " islands, but of course had no knowledge of the English language at the time of their engagement. Yet it was urged that they must be bound by their agreement, as the Act provided for their understanding it.

Another case of a very glaring nature, tending to throw a deal of light on the operation of this clause of the Act. came before the notice of the public in 1871. In March of that year six Polynesians were consigned to a merchant of Maryborough from another in Brisbane, to be forwarded to a squatter for whom the former was agent. On the arrival of the steamer in Maryborough five of the islanders were passed over to the consignee, but from circumstances which had occurred on the passage from Brisbane he refused to have anything to do with the other. The man was brought to Maryborough chained and guarded, and was said to be in a most furious state. As the captain of the steamer could not induce the agent to take delivery of his passenger, and as he was unwilling to carry him on to Rockhampton, where the steamer went before her return, viâ Maryborough to Brisbane, he adopted the expedient of giving him in charge of the police, as being of unsound mind and for having attempted to destroy himself.

Thus charged, the Polynesian had to be brought before the police magistrate, and his case came on for hearing in the Maryborough Police Court. From the evidence given, and as stated by the police magistrate, it was evident that there had been in this case a direct contravention of the Polynesian Labourers Act. No one who saw the man could doubt that he had been kidnapped by the captain and crew of the " Spunkie," the vessel in which he reached the colony. Yet he had been examined, or rather the vessel had been, by the immigration officer in Brisbane, who had, in the terms of the Act, " satisfied himself that the islanders understood the terms of their agreements, and had come willingly." The other requisite documents for this man must also have been prepared and witnessed by some one. Here was a man who spoke a language which no one could understand, not even one of the many hundreds of Polynesians in Brisbane or Maryborough being found who could converse with him. It transpired that he had tried to drown himself, or escape by swimming, when on board the " Spunkie;" the captain admitted that no one understood him, and that he had been chained nearly all the passage. His account of the man was that, while passing the island of Ambrym, he came swimming off to him on a log of wood, and had expressed his willingness to come to Queensland. It was very pertinently asked how he had expressed this willingness if unable to converse with any one on board, and why it became necessary to chain up a man who was so anxious to visit Queensland, that he actually came off to the vessel on a log.

This case, when published in the press, convinced many persons of what they had long suspected, that direct kidnapping was sometimes resorted to, as well as the more respectable method of purchasing the men at so much "trade" per head. It was certain that one man had been brought to the country who knew nothing about any agreement, and evinced the utmost dislike to his present position. If this man could be kidnapped, and, after being imported, could be passed from person to person against his will, why might not many similar cases have occurred in which the victims were probably men of less determination, and had therefore made less strenuous efforts to escape from their bondage? A very strong public opinion developed itself, yet the black-labour men, as they are called, had influence enough with Government to cause the matter to be hushed up. The islander was placed on some neighbouring plantation, and nothing more was heard of the matter. This "Spunkie" had already a very notorious character as a recruiting ship. She had once or twice been chased and fired on by the French cruisers, but she was so fast a sailer that she had each time got clear off.

Other revelations were made about this time which tended to bring the traffic into greater disrepute. A sailor on board the "Jason" made a proven statement revealing gross breaches of the Act: and a long letter from the Rev. J. Paton, a Presbyterian missionary at Amina, in the

New Hebrides, to Dr. Steele, of Sydney, also appeared, giving a long and circumstantial account of the misdeeds of the recruiting vessels, and the evils arising from the traffic. Yet the authorities made no move. At length what the people of Queensland could not effect was done by the Colonial Secretary. A circular from him obliged the Queensland Government to put into force that clause of the Act providing for the sending a Government agent in each vessel. Up to this time this had been a dead letter; but now, under an executive minute, agents were to be sent out in each vessel, in order to see that the Act was properly carried out. Three or four vessels were despatched, with each of which an agent was connected. It was, doubtless, in a large measure owing to the action taken by certain philanthropic persons in England, in particular those connected with the Aborigines' Protection Society, that the Imperial Government was induced to interfere in this matter. So strong is the black-labour party in the colony —the premier himself being a large employer of Polynesians on his station, and the Minister of Works a shareholder in a sugar company where they are employed [1]—that the people of Queensland had long come to the conclusion expressed in the Rev. Mr. Paton's letter, where he says that "unless the British Government puts a complete stop to this trade, and disperses the ruffians engaged in it . . . we have given up all hope of redress from the colonies. . . . They are all too deeply involved and interested in this trade now to stop it entirely, and their half-measures have only facilitated and increased the evil."

[1] As before stated, this government is now out of office, and with the advent of the other party to power, in no small measure accelerated by their strongly pronounced opinions on this question, a much better state of things has resulted.

Two vessels, only partially filled with Polynesians, returned from their first trip, in which they carried a Government agent. Both these gentlemen, whose name in each case happened to be Watson, gave a damaging report, and as a gentleman had been killed who had gone out in one of these vessels while in-shore trading for men, and it was reported that the natives of all the islands were becoming dangerous in consequence of the irritation caused by the recruiting vessels, public opinion became more set against the trade than it had even been before. But the worst blow was about to be struck. The notorious " Jason" had sailed from Maryborough on her first trip with a Government agent on board, on the 6th April, 1871, and from the circumstances connected with this ship public attention was specially directed to her.

These circumstances were as follows :—The " Jason" was the property of a firm the principal of which was a particular friend of the Member for the town, who was also a Cabinet Minister, and by many supposed to have an interest in her. She had, as already stated, drawn considerable public attention on herself, so that the " Jason " and her captain were more frequently before the public than any other vessel in the trade. The gentleman who went in her as agent was a man moving in the highest society in the colony, an old squatter and sugar-grower, having for some years owned a plantation on the Mary which he had recently sold, and on which he had employed Polynesian labour very largely. He was also a magistrate of the colony, in which capacity, as in every other, he commanded the respect and esteem of his fellow-colonists. All who knew him looked on him as an upright, truthful gentleman, who would not be swerved from the path of duty, and who was therefore certain to bring back a truthful report on this much-vexed question. He was not a person of the class who would usually solicit such an appointment, in which the salary was very paltry; but having a son whom he was anxious to establish in business either as a cotton or sugar grower, he wished to visit the islands with a view to sending him down there to settle, if circumstances should be favourable. Thus his appointment met with universal satisfaction. On the one hand, the black-labour men knew him to be one of their own class, and prepossessed in favour of their views; while the general public had confidence in his integrity and truthfulness, and in his expressed determination to bring back a full and impartial report.

As we have said, the "Jason" sailed from Maryborough on April 6th, and nothing was heard of her until July 13th, when it was reported in Maryborough that she was again in the Bay. At first a vague rumour, which seemed too ghastly to be true, spread through the town, that the agent had been maltreated and brought back mad. But soon more particulars became known, and the people of Maryborough and the colony generally grew sick with horror, as they learnt the dreadful tragedy which had been enacted and the sufferings this gentleman had undergone. On the arrival of the "Jason" at the river heads, the Presbyterian clergyman, who was a son-in-law of the unfortunate Government agent, and who had been informed of his being unwell, went down the river and boarded the "Jason," in company with the family doctor. They found him in a most abject and lamentable condition, reduced so low that he could give no signs of recognition, being quite insensible. The doctor asserted that he was nearly dead from exhaustion,—starvation in fact,—and that it would have been impossible for him to have retained life over another day.

A little weak brandy and water was administered, which slightly revived him. The account given by the captain was that he had gone mad, and he had been obliged to confine him in the hold with the islanders, where he had been kept in chains. He admitted that for four days he had had nothing to eat, stating that he would not eat it if offered to him. There was, however, no difficulty whatever in administering the brandy and water, the sick man only apparently suffering from exhaustion. On arrival opposite the residence of his son-in-law, which is on the bank of the river, he was taken ashore in a boat. While being landed he gave the first evidence of returning consciousness. In the house a little food was administered, and he was washed and cleaned, having before been in the most wretched condition. It was found that while he had been chained up in the hold, the rats had actually commenced to gnaw away his feet. From the time of reaching home he evinced no signs of madness, and his restoration was continuous, though very slow.

As may be supposed, on these facts becoming known, a perfect storm of indignation arose. The public and that portion of the press not in the hands of the black-labour men called loudly on the Government to cause an investigation to be made into the case. It happened that just then the Minister of Works was in Maryborough, and the agent when well enough to ride out had seen him and expressed his intention of demanding an investigation when sufficiently recovered. The Minister of Works at once took the unprecedented course of himself appointing three gentlemen, one of whom, although the mayor of the town, was not even a magistrate, to form a board of inquiry into the matter. Their only appointment was a letter from this gentleman, which, of course, gave them no power to take legal evidence on oath or to command the presence of witnesses. The whole affair was what it was doubtless intended to be, a mere burlesque on an investigation, and simply intended to quash further proceedings. Nothing more absurd in the shape of an inquiry could well be conceived.

The friends of the traffic thought that thus the agitation would be crushed. But they were mistaken. On recovering health the agent caused proceedings to be taken against the captain, whose name was Coath, a native of West Cornwall, which ended in his being sentenced to five years' penal servitude. This occurred after the author had left the colony. Subsequently the ministry remitted the remaining portion of Coath's sentence, and he was set at liberty. By a recent mail news has been received that this man has been killed by the natives of one of the South Sea Islands, where he had gone as captain of a vessel in the Polynesian labour trade, having been struck with a poisoned arrow.

The effect of these revelations was to make the black labour more and more unpopular. Public opinion became thoroughly aroused, and even the employers had to admit that if Kanakas could not be obtained in a more honourable way, they would have to do without them. From this time the trade fell into disrepute, and although some hundreds of Polynesians are still brought yearly to Queensland, as many or more return to the islands, having completed their terms of service, and the trade has become comparatively far less than formerly. Her Majesty's cruisers are also very active in the South Seas, in order to prevent this recruiting from developing into a slave-trade, of which at one time there was great fear. Add to this the wonderful tide of prosperity that has of late set in, which has caused labour of all sorts to be abundant and

x

wages high, and the consequently largely increased white immigration, and it may be seen that there are sufficient reasons for believing that the danger which once seemed imminent, of Queensland becoming a country of white employers and black labourers, has happily passed away.

There never has been a time when labour was more plentiful or commanded higher wages than at present. As the wonderful, almost fabulous, resources of this colony become more largely developed by the application of more capital and the presence of a larger population, the accumulation of wealth goes on at an ever-increasing ratio. Hence, although wages are higher, the employer's profits are also larger, and as the employing class is regularly and constantly being increased by the labourer of this year becoming the employer of next year, there is a constant and increasing demand for labourers of all sorts. Thus, while it is true that there never was a time when such inducements were held out to the moderate capitalist as at present, it is also true that the colony never offered a more promising home to the mere worker, with nothing but a pair of strong arms and a knowledge and will to use them. For either of those classes no part of the world offers so many opportunities of obtaining a competency or an independency as does Queensland at this present time. Wages are certainly very high, but thanks to the excellence of the land laws, the liberality of the government, the richness of the soil, and the beauty and salubrity of the climate, there are equal chances of success for those who pay as for those who earn wages. And it must always be borne in mind that one great advantage offered to the labourer in Queensland is, that not only can he or she earn very large wages, but, under the provisions of the Land and Homestead Acts, can so lay out the money when earned as to reap as much or more profit from the investments thus made as from the labour performed. It may safely be calculated that money judiciously laid out in land will return from twenty to twenty-five per cent., and in many cases far more, merely from the constant and continuous rise in the value of land, as the population increases in numbers and wealth.

From Pugh's Almanack for 1875, we quote the following rates of wages current in Southern Queensland. In the northern parts rates are usually higher.

Masons, plasterers, blacksmiths, and wheelwrights, 10s. to 12s.; bricklayers, 10s.; carpenters, 12s. to 14s. per diem, without rations.

Farm labourers, 35l. to 50l. per annum, with board and lodging.

Shepherds, 35l. to 40l.; stockmen, 40l. to 50l.; but keepers, 35l.; generally-useful men on stations, 40l. to 50l. per annum, with rations. Sheep-washers, 5s. to 7s. per diem; shearers, 17s. 6d. to 25s. per 100 sheep, with rations; quarry-men, 8s. to 10s.; general labourers, 5s. to 7s. per diem; seamen, 4l. to 6l. per month.

Married couples, 35l. to 60l.; men cooks, 40l. to 70l.; grooms, 40l. to 50l.; gardeners, 50l. per annum, with rations.

Female cooks, 26l. to 40l.; laundresses, 26l. to 35l.; general servants, 20l. to 35l.; housemaids, 20l. to 26l.; nursemaids, 15l. to 20l.; farmhouse servants, 20l. to 30l.; dairywomen, 25l. to 30l., with board and lodging.

As a rule, all new arrivals have to be content for the first year with the lowest quotation, their services never being so valuable as those of more experienced persons.

CHAPTER XII

No work on Queensland would be complete without some account of the aboriginal blacks, or "blackfellows" as they are invariably called. Having passed two or three years in a part of the country into which few whites had at that time penetrated, the writer had an opportunity of studying the natives in their primitive simplicity.

The first thing that occurred to us on seeing the Queensland blacks, was the misrepresentations usually indulged in, in reference to their physical development. Instead of dwarfed beings, with huge heads and shrivelled shanks, incapable of much exertion, we saw a fine race of men, among whom are as finely-formed and well-developed specimens of the race as are to be found elsewhere. When seen in his primitive condition, before ardent spirits have deteriorated him, the native has usually a dignity of gesture, a firmness of tread, a litheness and gracefulness of motion, that we look for in vain among our own labouring classes, and that we usually connect with the idea of a gentleman. Among the Newsa tribes there were several who measured over five feet ten inches, while few or none were absolutely short men. The two tribes who lived on the Newsa waters were, when we first knew them, some hundreds in number. About two years after the Gympie diggings broke out, the king told me there were not twenty warriors left, so great is the havoc made among them by liquor, of which on the diggings they obtain an unlimited quantity in payment for stripping bark, chopping wood, &c.

Their strength is very considerable, although, perhaps, they have not the endurance of white men. We have seen a blackfellow carry a 200 lbs. bag of flour on his head a distance of two miles, only resting once on the way. They can also walk long distances without tiring, while the power of muscle and dexterity they exhibit in climbing the enormous gum-trees, iron-barks, and blackbutts, is something unique and wonderful, and is, perhaps, unequalled by any other race of men. Could a tall gum of 120 to 130 feet to the first branch, and of a diameter at that height of perhaps three feet six inches to four feet be transplanted into the Zoological Gardens in the Regent's Park, and a Queensland blackfellow be imported, and daily climb its side either with or without the aid of a vine, half London would go to see the sight, and think it well worth the time and cost. Many an excellent meal have we made from the pure delicious honeycomb which has been fetched in this way by a kind blackfellow from one of the huge giants of the forest. The usual way of climbing a tree is to procure a vine of sufficient strength, from the scrub, which is either passed around the tree and held by both hands and jerked up simultaneously with the movement of the feet, the top of the tree being thus gained by a series of jumps; or it is tied around the tree, leaving sufficient room to admit the person of the climber, who, tomahawk in hand, cuts notches for his feet as he jerks himself up. In the former case, he often holds the vine with his left hand and right great toe, while chopping with his other hand, securing his tomahawk in the hollow between his shoulder and head when he again begins to climb. A person unused to the sight would expect to

see the poor fellow slip his hold or lose his balance, and fall
from his giddy height; but such a thing occurs rarely, if
ever.   Blacks have told us a traditional story of a vine once
breaking and killing a man, but it was always a story they
had only heard of.

They also often excel as axe-men and bullock-drivers,
and all coast blacks are capital hands at an oar.   We have
known many instances of a black, who had no family con-
nexions to coax him away, working for a year continuously
as a sawyer or feller.   A timber-getter on the Commera
once pointed out a blackfellow to us as the most efficient
hand he had, being able to do more work and better than
himself or any of his men.   We saw him in Brisbane in
company with his master, in the dress and having the
bearing of a sensible and civilized working-man.   A friend
of ours had a black who worked as mate with a white man
in felling, cross-cutting, and squaring 70,000 feet of cedar,
and also in cutting the scrub roads to it.   He thought himself well remunerated by having his rations and tobacco
while working, and a suit of clothes, 100 lbs. of flour, and
1*l.* in cash on leaving.   The writer has found them invaluable
in rafting, boating, working timber, and cattle, and has a
thorough conviction that, if systematically treated, they
could be induced to work regularly, and become very valuable indeed.   At any rate, one thing is certain, it is not from
any lack of strong muscles and a well-knit frame that the
Queensland black has not been civilized and christianized.

But it may be argued, although this race is athletic
and powerful enough physically, they entirely lack
that mental calibre requisite to appreciate the truths
of Christianity, or the habits of civilization.   There are
few races so quick in their perceptive faculties, while
their reasoning powers, too, are by no means despicable.

It is true their very primitive style of life precludes the necessity of much forecast, nor is it conducive to the development of habits of thought. Their utter carelessness for the morrow so long as to day's wants are supplied, has, in our opinion, given rise to a deal of misconception as to their mental ability. But when we consider the excellent climate with which they are blessed, and the little pains necessary to obtain their food, it will probably be admitted that they have very little cause in their natural state to worry their brains or tax their minds.

Their oratorical powers are very considerable; we have often listened with pleasure to speech after speech uttered with an ease, fluency, and intonation, coupled with a graceful gesture, that bespoke the orator. One chief we remember in particular, whose bearing and deportment marked him as a complete master of oratory, while all who looked on him recognized one of nature's gentlemen, though in a black skin and with little clothing. Indeed, as a rule, a black divests himself of his garments before either speaking or acting in a corrobboree.

Perhaps the principal indication of the possession of an inventive faculty in the Australian black is to be found in the bomerang, than which there are few more curious instruments; and its use argues considerable skill.

To see a black carrying through the street two or three of these flat, crooked pieces of wood, would convey to the uninitiated no idea of their peculiar powers; you see only a piece of very hard wood, worked to a particular curve, about fifteen or sixteen inches long by two broad, and varying from three-quarters to a quarter of an inch in thickness; being always thinner at the edges than in the middle. But see him throw it : first, it skims along the ground, then rises to a considerable height to sink again, and again to rise ; now, when you think it must stop in its rapid and erratic course, and fall to the ground, you see it, urged by some occult power, suddenly cease its onward flight, and, turning towards the thrower, sometimes circuitously, sometimes directly, and sometimes in a course similar to its outward flight, come swiftly back, and strike the ground with great force almost at his feet.

Besides the bomerang the black has the spear, nullah-nullah, or small club, the hatchet, knife, and shield. The spear is of a peculiar wood, hardened by the action of fire, as is also the nullah. The hatchet and knife were, before the arrival of the white, always of stone, ground to a sharp edge. The hatchet was used in procuring food, while the knife was principally a weapon of warfare.

The sight of two tribes of blacks on a grand field day in actual combat is a curious and interesting scene. Before the battle commences, all the females are obliged to retire to some distance, with the camp equipages and baggage. Then the chiefs lead out their men to the scene of action; if on the coast, the beach is generally the scene of strife, and the non-combatants look on from the sand-banks above; if in the bush, a place clear of undergrowth is used. Usually the action of the day begins by a sarcastic and abusive harangue on the part of the hostile chiefs. They tell each other that they are men with little legs, and hearts like women; they accuse them of having used the black art to compass the death of some one who has recently died in their own tribe. A battle often takes place over an occurrence of this sort, they having a belief in a sort of mesmerism by which an enemy steals away a man's soul while he is asleep, and by taking it into the bush and working a spell on him, causes a fatal sickness to follow. A number of remarks are vociferated in the hearing of all, very similar in style to the vilification of two pot-house champions, and replied to in a similar strain. Then every man singles out his opponent, and hurls first his bomerangs, afterwards his spears. It is a rule among the blacks that as soon as a death occurs the fighting ceases, and each party withdraws to its camp, the side to which the dead man belongs being conquered. But many battles occur in which no death happens.

The spears and bomerangs being gone, the waddies or nullahs come into use, some being thrown, others used as clubs. This weapon is generally laid horizontally on the head, and each warrior invites his antagonist to give the first blow. When the waddies are all expended, if one side or the other has not succumbed sooner, the knives are brought into play. And here we must notice another very humane and singular provision. Although these men meet in deadly strife when close quarters are come to, and the knife is taken, no man is allowed to strike or cut his antagonist in any vital part. The only places on which it is admissible to operate are the arms, shoulders, buttocks, and thighs. No stabbing is ever resorted to under any circumstances. In fact, it is now a mere question of strength, dexterity, and courage, and as soon as one intimates he is beaten the other leaves him. The gashes given in these hand-to-hand combats are sometimes most frightful; it is not at all unusual to see a black with his arm laid open to the bone in a gash of several inches long. Their flesh heals with the greatest rapidity. A black will be so cut up in a fight as to be unable to reach his camp unassisted, with his limbs nearly covered with wounds of the most ghastly description; yet in a few days he will be quite recovered, with only his scars to show, and which, warrior-like, are pointed out with feelings of pride. The gins and old men apply various sorts of leaves, and frequently ashes and dirt, to staunch the wounds, and we suppose their primitive habits and wholesome food have no small part in the healing process.

It not unfrequently happens that while the battle is raging between the warriors, the gins become too excited to be mere spectators; seizing their yam-sticks, they fall on each other with cries, shrieks, howls, and gesticulations truly barbarous. This yam-stick is a sort of heavy spear, and is used in digging yams in scrubs. It is of very hard wood, and is no mean weapon when dexterously handled. We have seen a gin challenge a smart stockman to a trial of skill with her favourite weapon, which is as constantly in her hand as the waddy in her husband's. Holding it in both hands, she will act either on the offensive or defensive with equal adroitness. After a while, however, women-like, they get tired of the yam-sticks, and, throwing them down, rush pell-mell at each other's hair. We believe it is in consequence of this weakness of the sex for getting their hands in each other's hair that they always cut their hair short. The gins in the bush wear their hair much shorter than the men, and as many of them have the most beautiful curly hair imaginable, this is much to be regretted. It must not be supposed that any great amount of enmity or ill-feeling exists between the various tribes which thus engage in wars. It would seem that these gatherings are as much in the nature of feasts as fights; for it is very usual for a day or two to elapse before the battle, after they are all met in the appointed place, which time is spent in learning and practising new corrobborees. These corrob-borees are another evidence of the intellectual capacity of the blacks. It is not an uncommon thing for a poetical blackfellow to get up a new one and set it to music. There is generally a great deal of repetition in these songs; in

fact the chorus is the principal part. We have had some
of them interpreted to us by blacks, and have found, mixed
up with much that is vulgar, not to say obscene, some very
poetical ideas and sentiments. It would seem as if the
corrobboree was only a sort of opera, the acting being done
by the men and young women, while the older ladies form
the orchestra, and all take part in the singing. The noise
an old gin will make by slapping her hollow hand on the
inside of the thigh is something like that of a small drum.
The paint and pipe-clay in which the men are decorated for
these occasions is usually designed to give the effect of a
skeleton, all the ribs, &c., being carefully marked. Seen
by the glare of the fire—for their performances are always
at night—one could almost imagine he saw a bevy of
spectres dancing around him, were it not for the noise
produced. We have never been able to ascertain why this
style of ornamentation is practised, but as they also paint
themselves with pipe-clay in a similar manner on the
death of a friend, as a sign of mourning, we have an idea
that the white marks are considered the most hideous and
unnatural. Listened to at a sufficient distance to tone
down the din of the instrumental music—generally produced
by knocking waddies together, and the other means already
alluded to—the corrobboree may not be so high an artistic
production as an Italian opera, but it is not without its
peculiar beauties. Sometimes these corrobborees are learnt
at these gatherings of the tribes; more frequently a
member of a particular tribe will make a visit of considerable duration with a distant tribe for the purpose of learning theirs and imparting those of his own people. In this
case, on his return, night after night will be spent in
practice until perfection is attained. Then about the full
moon a grand performance takes place in full costume, and

the greater portion of the night is spent before they retire to
rest. In short, the corrobboree is to the blackfellow what
the theatrical and operatic performances are to the European,
and being nearly the only amusement he has, is looked
upon as a matter of the first importance.

From the corrobboree of the blackfellow to the various
indications of his religious belief is a natural transition.
We say indications, for we have never been able to arrive
at the conclusion that we fully understood all their belief as
to a Deity and the future state. But in our intercourse
with them, conversation often reverted to this subject,
and the information obtained has thrown some light upon
the subject.

It is to a great extent believed that the blackfellow has
no knowledge of an hereafter, or of any superior being.
There is, however, a great amount of error mixed up with
this opinion. It is true his idea of the Godhead is exceedingly ill-defined and fragmentary, but in common with
other races of men he fully realizes the immortality of the
soul and the future existence in another state of being.

We had journeyed down one of the many fine rivers
of the Queensland coast; night came on, and we camped on
the river bank. After the fire had been made and the
evening meal consumed, fresh fuel was heaped on the fire;
then, rolled in our blankets, we lay looking up to the
Southern Cross, marking the hours of the night like
a huge dial, and those wonderful and mysterious Magellan
Clouds, which look like holes broken in the firmament.
Drawing Tommy's attention to the shining orbs above
us, the swift-flowing river at our side, the ocean whose
evening song broke ever on our ears with a low, mournful
cadence, the trees overhead, with their tenantry of birds,
and the tall mountains away to the west, where the early

ow,
we asked him, did all these things come to be? He held a
short conversation with his wife, who lay beyond him,
either to refresh his memory or to consult her as to the
propriety of giving any information, and then, turning to
us, said, that many, many long years ago, the whole of the
world, with everything in it, as well as the sun, moon, and
stars, had all been made by Bedall, who he believed was
the same to the black as God to the white. He did not,
however, think that he was identical with God, as he
thought that Bedall only made the blackfellow and his
country. He was like a huge turtle, and made all these
things as he floated about on the surface of the big waters.
His dimensions, as Tommy gave them, were at least two
miles across his back, by a proportionate length; he could
not indeed give his exact size, which might be double
what he had stated. Bedall had made the land of this
country by brooding on the mud, which he caused to
become land. He had gone away over the ocean so long
ago that our informant could give no idea of the lapse of
time, and never took any further heed of the country or its
inhabitants. Where he was gone he had created a large
number of young, but these had none of them attained to
anything like the magnitude of their parent; nor could
we learn that he knew anything of these offspring of
Bedall's. The whole account had about it the vague-
ness of an old story which had not been recalled to
mind for many years. There was connected with this
traditionary First Cause no idea of a superintending and
protecting Godhead. It was "too many years ago" since

he had heard very old people talk of Bedall, and he had forgotten particulars.

Beyond this we never obtained any information as to the Creator. The devil is a more familiar being, bearing some comparison to the vampire of the northern nations, or the Obi of the negro race, and is, like the latter, some powerful and physically-developed being, having power to work evil but not to do good.

If, however, the blacks' notion of a Supreme Being is rather difficult to understand, there need be no doubt whatever as to their belief in the immortality of the soul. Every one is familiar with their belief that they will after death "jump up whitefellow." It has generally been thought that this idea must have originated since the advent of the European. But we are by no means of this opinion. When Morrell, who was for nineteen years among the blacks in the north of Queensland, first appeared among them as a shipwrecked sailor, he was at once claimed by one of the gins, who had recently lost a son, as her boy returned to life. At this time the tribe had never before seen and probably had never heard of the white man. The same thing occurred to Davis, who was for many years with the blacks in the Wide Bay District, by whom he was recognized as the son of their king restored to life. These people at that time had no knowledge of the whites, and it therefore appears that their belief as to their children coming to life white must be looked for in another direction. Perhaps the reason may arise from the facts connected with their mode of disposing of their dead.

As is pretty well known, they make it a point of duty, when any of the tribe die, to eat the bodies of the departed relative. As the flesh is considered too great a treat for all to share, or more probably for some religious reason, none but the old men are allowed to partake, or in default of enough of these, the old gins and the more accomplished warriors. When this ceremony has to be performed the body is carried to a convenient place and laid on the ground. Then a small fire is lit all round the corpse at a distance of from one to two feet. By exposing all parts of the body to a moderate heat all the cuticle becomes removable, and is carefully scraped off, when the body presents a dull whitish colour. When the flesh has all been removed the bones are carefully gathered and placed in a dilly-bag, which is carried about for thirteen moons by one of the female relatives in all the journeyings of the tribe, after which they are rolled in bark and either placed in a tree or on a sheet of bark elevated on forked sticks five or six feet from the ground. Now, as all the elders are acquainted with this process and have seen their relatives, so to speak, turning white, one can fancy that it does not require a great stretch of imagination to look upon the white stranger as the risen son.

The belief in the existence of disembodied spirits is universal, and is one great reason why blacks will never willingly leave their camps after dark. The following curious story was related to the author by an old and well-known colonist who lived near him. Being on a visit to his place, the name of a certain blackfellow was mentioned whom we had been accustomed to see about the house, when we were informed he was dead, and that too under very remarkable circumstances. He had been sent to a neighbouring station, a distance of twelve miles, on an errand which necessitated his seeing the superintendent. Unfortunately that gentleman was out on the run, and did not return until nearly nightfall, when, finding an answer would be expected, he sent

the very unwilling black away on his return journey
just at sunset. The road was very wet, and riding consequently tedious; so it was not until his master had
retired to rest that the messenger returned. He was
awakened by his knocking, and arose and let him into
the house, when he was surprised, not to say horrified,
at seeing his countenance, instead of being of its usual
black shiny colour, presenting a pale ash colour, painful to
look on, while the rolling of his eyes and the incoherence
of his speech showed the poor fellow to be in mortal terror.
On being asked what was the matter with him, he said
that he had been sent away home at sunset, against his
own will; that his horse had been unable to travel most of
the way faster than a walk, and that after dark, when near
a creek about half-way home, he had seen the spirit
of a certain black who had recently died in a neighbouring tribe at Mooloolah, and that he was himself doomed
to die within forty-eight hours. We really forget whether
he had received this information from the ghost or whether
it was his own deduction; but he was positive as to what
he had seen and who it was, although, as is the invariable
rule among his race, he would not mention the dead man's
name. He found great fault with the superintendent for
sending him home so late, and seemed to lay his death,
which he took for granted, at his door. His master
endeavoured to laugh him out of the idea, but with no
success, and was fain to allow him to sleep by the kitchen
fire that night, as he was evidently afraid again to move
out of the house. The next day he sickened, and the
following day died, although up to the time of taking this
ill-starred journey he had been in perfect health. What
proved that there was nothing opposed to the belief of the
members of his tribe in this affair was the fact that they

all believed that his death was occasioned in the way stated.

Another instance in which the belief in the appearance of the dead had a powerful effect on the conduct of a black-fellow is that of the surrender of Tommy Skyring, one of the murderers of the ill-fated Stevens, the botanist, who was treacherously murdered in the year 1866, some few miles below Mooloolah, by Skyring and two other blacks. Skyring subsequently gave himself up and wished to be hung, giving as his reason that although he shifted his camp daily, and sometimes oftener, the murdered man always came and looked over his shoulder, so that he could neither eat nor sleep. This man also died soon after reaching Brisbane gaol, perfectly emaciated.

There are other very peculiar beliefs amongst the blacks in reference to the dead. One is that all thunder-storms, tornadoes, &c., are caused by the departed blacks. It is supposed that the last man who has died in the district thus influences the weather; hence, when a heavy storm is imminent, the principal men in the tribe or camp, instead of retiring under shelter, advance to a short distance from their gunyas, and commence a series of the most piercing shrieks and stentorian calls. They are understood to be addressing the departed spirit, and by expostulations, entreaties, and threats, are endeavouring to induce him to stop the storm, or, at any rate, to take it in some other direction.

We were once camped in a little valley on the coast range, on an occasion of this kind. About dusk, it became evident that a storm was approaching. The fires were made, and the supper cooked as quickly as possible, extra stakes were driven for pins for the tent and fly, or outer covering. We were none too soon; before we had had time

Y

to do more than make these brief preparations, and cut a small trench round the tent, to prevent the inflow of water, the storm came down on us in sublime fury. Its approach was like the march of a thousand locomotive engines, howling, and shrieking, and hissing. The giants of the forest bent and groaned with the fearful pressure put on them; here and there a huge limb broke off, and fell with a noise like thunder to the ground; while smaller branches, twigs, and leaves filled the air, and appeared to act as an advanced guard to the storm-king. The thunder—which had gradually been coming nearer and nearer, until from sounding like a distant cannonading it seemed as if we were on the very edge of a pitched battle—now broke immediately over-head, with a terrible crash and rattle that completely drowned all other noises, and seemed to shake the foundations of the hills. Peal followed peal in such rapid succession as to appear almost like one continuous roar. Such was the fearful noise of the thunder, that a large limb of a gum-tree fell to the ground near us, from a great height, without the noise of its fall being heard. It was as if the crack of doom was come. The black clouds had brought the densest night in a few minutes; but the glare of the never-ceasing lightning lit up the whole forest. Streams of the electric fluid ran down the sides of the tall trees and along the ground, or in massive sheets flashed through the openings, giving a most unearthly glare to the whole scene. It was well we had taken the precaution of double pegging our tent. Huddled up inside it, three white men and two or three blacks,—too frightened to remain in their bark camp,—had all we could do to hold down the sides to prevent the wind from lifting it clean away. The tent-poles bent as if they would break, and amid the universal din it was impossible to converse in any other way than by signs with the aid of the lightning. And now the rain poured down in apparently one solid sheet, which beat through the tent and fly as if they had been gauze, and filled the inside with a fine rain like a Scotch mist. It was one of the severest thunder-storms ever known in the colony, and, as we subsequently learnt, did much damage in some places.

During all this time, Tommy, with spear in one hand and nullah in the other, was standing about half-a-dozen yards in front of the tent, shrieking and hallooing in a way that seemed almost supernatural. In the very height of the din of the storm, his sharp, shrill shriek could be heard uniting with the noise of the elements, while he took every occasion of the least lull in the thunder to call out at the top of his voice to his imaginary hearer. Not being conversant with their belief on the question, we asked his gin to tell him to come in, but she refused. On our going out to expostulate with him, he could only find time to tell us to go in and leave him, and then commenced his ravings again. At first we were inclined to think he was simply amusing himself by trying his voice against the storm; but his pertinacity at last caused us to fear that the terrible character of the hurricane had upset his mind, and that he was gone " cranky."

However, after the rain had set in steadily, the tempest somewhat lulled; he at length entered the tent, and threw himself down completely exhausted. A cup of tea and his supper soon recovered him, and he then condescended to inform us why he had been hallooing and carrying on so strangely. He said it was a black who had recently died, and whom he knew very well, who had raised this storm. Of course he would not mention his name, for under no circumstances will a blackfellow name a deceased person of their race; nay, if there are any others of the same name, as not unfrequently occurs, they change it for another, so that the name may by no means pass their lips. From what we could gather he had an idea that if he could raise his voice above the storm he should succeed in quelling it, and he was very proud of the assumed fact that he had done so. The storm-maker had been standing some way over across a creek, and Tommy had heard his voice in the storm,—to say truth, it needed little imagination to hear many voices in that terrible weather. We asked him what good all his hallooing had done, and told him it was the Great Father of all who made the storm, as well as every-thing else, and that He could watch over us as well then as when the sky was clear. He replied, that might be all very true, so far as white men were concerned, but it was very different with black men. The black men when dead grew angry at times, and hence they made these storms. In the present instance, he had been highly successful in his struggle with his ghostly opponent, as the storm had divided in two, a little way up from us, and one part was gone on the one side and the other on the other. Had it not been for his opposition, the whole strength of the blast would have swept over where we were, and tent, men, and all would have been blown away. Being in the tent as we were, we could not hear the storm so well as he could; but if we had stood with him we should have heard it divide and pass on each side. There was no use in arguing with him; he and every black there evidently believed all he said, and put down our incredulity to the fact of our ignorance, not being black, and therefore unable to under-stand their affairs. It was curious, and confirmed Tommy in his belief, but we afterwards found that the storm had been much fiercer elsewhere; many houses having been blown down, and in some places nearly half the forest uprooted.

We remember on another occasion being in a whale-boat on the coast. As we drew near Double Island Point the wind shifted round nearly ahead, and a very heavy sea began to run. It became a question whether we could weather the headland or no, and having to keep very close to the wind, a little water was shipped over the bows. There were a few blacks with us, most of whom had been sick and lying in the bottom of the boat all day ; but the sight of the huge waves, the dashing of the spray, and the danger which they readily perceived of our not being able to clear the point, put them in a terrible fright, and one and all began invoking the spirit of the wind or sea in much the same way as Tommy did on the other occasion. The child-like pleasure and glee they evinced when we finally weathered the last projecting rock and ran down before the wind was something worth seeing. They are indeed much like children, quickly frightened and easily pleased.

Some of their customs are of a nature that evince their barbarism in its most degraded form. Among these latter may be classed the treatment their infants receive. Among the blackfellows it is very usual to destroy the female children, especially if the poor little things are puny or troublesome ; when this is done, sometimes they are eaten by the elders, and sometimes disposed of in other ways. On one occasion the wife of a blackfellow, engaged for a fortnight, gave birth to a daughter. We all adjourned to have a look at the new arrival. It was a queer sight to look on ; the poor little thing, without the semblance of a covering, was lying in its mother's lap in the full glare of the sun ; it was a very light colour,

which evidently did not meet the approbation of the parent,
as she was in the act of plastering its poor little head with
a composition of grease and charcoal, with which she afterwards anointed its body. It was a fine female child, and
looked quite flourishing before it was greased. Tastes differ,
and we told the gin she had spoiled the baby's looks, but
she assured us it was " collanger," or very good, in its coat
of paint. We afterwards saw it peacefully sleeping in a
nice soft bed, which had been prepared by rubbing up a
lot of the soft bark of the tea-tree, until it was just like a
little nest made of tissue paper, which this bark much
resembles. The child grew and flourished while its parents
stopped at the camp. When he was paid off they left, and
we did not see them again for a few months. On inquiring
after the baby, to which, by-the-bye, we had stood god-
father, so far as giving it a name was concerned, we were
told it was dead. The black said " that piccaninny no
good—baal budgeree fellow, too much cry," and that's all
we could get out of him, but his gin told us he had knocked
it on the head with his nullah-nullah, because it was cross ;
it was always crying, and was not a boy. From motives
of delicacy, we refrained to question her as to the disposal
of the body, not wishing to follow the subject any further.

In those portions of the colony where there is great
intercourse between the two races, a very considerable
number of half-castes are born. As far as our observation
has gone, by far the largest proportion of these poor unfor-
tunates are girls. We have heard it asserted by many
bushmen of experience, and we have seen enough to fully
warrant the assertion, that nearly all these female half-castes
are eaten sooner or later. It is a horrible statement to
make, and revolting as well as humiliating, but more than
one instance of the kind has come under our personal obser-

vation, so far as being told by a tribe, when we have missed
a certain child, that such had been its fate.   It is probably
the only description of cannibalism pure and simple that is
perpetrated among the South Queensland blacks, there being
circumstances connected with the eating of their dead
which perhaps remove that habit out of the region of
mere cannibalism.   Their own pure-bred children are most
likely killed more for the sake of being rid of them than for
anything else; but in the case of half-castes, this will not
account for the killing and eating of fine little girls of four
or five years of age.   Singular to say, their adopted fathers
—who subsequently marry their mothers—are usually very
proud of the superior beauty of their wife's offspring.
We knew one man, now dead, who had a sweet little girl
of this sort, which we frequently attempted to purchase
from him for the purpose of placing her in a family who
had offered to take her; but we were always unable to
induce him either by the offer of blankets, tobacco, or flour,
or of all combined, to part with the child, which he really
seemed to believe was his own.   But when the diggers' rum
had killed her protector, we subsequently learnt that one
very wet time, when food could only be got with difficulty,
the poor little offspring of some so-called Christian was
knocked on the head by an old greybeard, and roasted on
the camp-fire and eaten.

Among the customs of our blacks, perhaps the most
curious and mysterious is that of kipper making. So fruitless have been all our attempts at learning the mysteries
of this operation, that nearly all we can say of it is, that
when lads are passing from boyhood they are in a formal
and solemn gathering of one or more tribes initiated into
the state of kippers.   There is something in the secrecy
which hangs over this affair that reminds one of the ancient

Eleusinian mysteries; like them, the ceremonies connected with kipper making are carried on at night, and apparently the same secrecy is observed in reference to the rites. In some places "kipper rings" may be seen, where these mysteries are performed and the initiations take place. Those we have seen are on somewhat elevated ground, and are always on the apex of the hill or crest of the ridge. There is about them something which reminds one of the Druidical circles on Stonehenge and Dartmoor, and other places. The ring consists, as its name imports, of a circle, which, in the only case where we actually measured, was fifteen paces in diameter. The centre is higher than the outside, which is hollowed about a foot or eighteen inches below the natural level of the ground, and this ring or way is sometimes walled up on the outer side with stone work. Leading away from this ring is a similar path or roadway, something like a shallow drain, also excavated slightly below the level of the ground. This continues down the hill for about forty yards. We have never noticed two of these paths, but others have assured us that they have seen them with two,—one on each side of the ring. The encroachments of the white man have driven the black-fellow from the localities where the kipper rings that we have seen are situated, and we believe that kippers are often "made" now where no ring is in existence. But from the appearance of the neighbouring soil, we have little doubt that as other nations in ancient times sacrificed in their "high places" in warm latitudes, and worshipped in rings in the northern ones, so this despised race has been in the habit of conducting one of their observances in set places, bearing a certain similitude to both. At present, we think a tribe will initiate the kippers in any place where they have sufficient privacy, without heeding the formation of a permanent ring, for we have a notion that the ring is requisite.

All boys are made kippers as a matter of course, at or before their arriving at puberty. There is something in this kipperhood of a masonic nature some have thought, and if, as Dr. Lang informs us, Leichhardt met with natives in the interior who exchanged masonic signs with him, they were probably given when initiated into this state. There is also something about kipperhood which reminds one of the knights-errant and their novitiate, as well as of the restrictions of a like character put on the *mystæ* in the Eleusinian mysteries already alluded to. A kipper must eat only certain food, and must conform himself to certain usages. He passes from the freedom of boyhood into a state of abstinence and denial to a certain extent. There are several articles of food of which he may only partake in case of absolute want, and then only by permission of his chief. He must by no means eat of human flesh; he must sleep in a certain part of the camp—at the opposite end from that occupied by the unmarried girls; he is under certain laws of service to the warriors; in short, he has to undergo a period of abstinence, self-denial, chastity, and obedience, from which he cannot pass before he has proved himself to be fitted to enter the ranks of the warriors.

Nothing has surprised us more in making investigations into the habits of our aboriginals than the discovery of a degree of chastity and virtue which are quite at variance with all our preconceived notions on the subject. We speak not, it must be remembered, of those blacks who have mixed up with and been demoralized by the white man, but of those who have resided remote from the evil influence of the lowest class of white men. We have found among them a code of morals as strict as is to be found elsewhere; and

although their standard of modesty is very different from
ours, yet in their own way, and according to their own
standard, many coast tribes, at any rate, are by no means
inferior to their white supplanters in this respect. One
instance of this is to be seen in the treatment of kippers.
They are by no means allowed to associate freely with the
young girls, and are always under the surveillance of the
seniors. If a kipper, who has grown into manhood, wishes
to be ranked as a warrior, he is put through a series of
ordeals to test his strength of nerve and powers of endurance. Many of these tests are applied, and if the
neophyte shrinks or gives any indication of cowardice he
must continue in his kipperhood still longer. Many of
these tests are more like what might have been expected to
prevail among North American Indians than the natives of
the sunny south. They consist of cutting with knives,
hitting with nullah-nullahs, tearing the hair, burning the
flesh, fighting with warriors, and, wonderful to relate,
delivering orations. If, in addition to this, the kipper
have the good fortune to kill or seriously wound an enemy,
or even an opponent of his own tribe, his claims to manu-
mission from the novitiate are at once recognized, and he is
duly admitted among the warriors of his tribe.

When the young man has been admitted to the ranks of
the warriors, his next ambition is to have a wife. But
before the chief allows him to take this step, he must have
proved incontestably that he is able to hold his own in
battle. One or two successful fights must be passed through,
and then he is at full liberty to marry. There is connected
with the marriage of the blacks—at least, of some of them—
a most singular and unprecedented law, which either applies
to every member of the tribe, or only to such as marry
wives from a distance. They are not allowed to cohabit

with their newly-wedded wife for three moons. Such
was the way in which, Tommy informed us, his marriage was conducted, but for how far this custom extends
we are unable to say. We have never understood that any
particular festivities or observances of any sort attend a
wedding. Sometimes a young man marries a member of
his own tribe, in others he visits a neighbouring one, either
stealing his wife, or obtaining her as Isaac did Rebekah—
on account of the ties of consanguinity and certain presents
made.

Probably this question may be governed by the state of
things in his native tribe; for it may, and often does, occur
that there are several marriageable females in the tribe, and
yet none from whom he may select. This arises from the fact
that every tribe is divided into two parts or orders, from
the other of which alone are young men allowed to marry.
There does not seem to be any particular rule for the placing
of various parties in these classes, at any rate we have never
learnt it; but each child, of either sex, at its birth is at
once named as a member of one or the other, and is known
as belonging to that particular moiety all through life. A
white man, to whom they are attached, is generally nominated to one of these divisions, as well as being renamed
with an appropriate name and admitted to the tribe. The
writer was much astonished on one occasion on learning
that he had been honoured with these tokens of regard,
being told that in future he was a brother of the chief, who
had given him a long name, denoting a habit of moving
quickly about.

It is never usual, it appears, for the young man to make
the first advances to a young woman of his own tribe. The
gin has the acknowledged right of showing her partiality
for a particular person. It is done in this way:—When-

ever the young man who may have charmed her affections
comes into her presence she looks steadily at him, and when
she catches his eye she looks on the ground; this silent
courtship, or language of the eyes, continues all the time
he sits at the camp, and, perhaps, for two or three occasions. "That Mary not look too much first time," said
Jacky; "by-and-by that fellow look too much, every time
that blackboy sit down." It then always happens that
the love-sick gin falls in the young man's way in the daytime, when "that fellow look out 'possum or sugar-bag,"
and gives him an opportunity of declaring himself. If,
however, he is tardy on this point, some other gin, usually
a married one, is deputed to bring the matter to a satisfactory conclusion. We could not learn that the poor fellow
had any right to refuse, unless he had been looking out
" Mary belonging to another country."

The mode pursued when a young man gets a wife from
a distance is very different from this romantic way of
mating. He either proceeds by treaty, in which case his
father and mother and several friends accompany him; or,
in the case of a forced abduction, he usually goes by himself, or accompanied by one friend. They lurk about the
camp in which the dusky Dulcinea resides, until he can
follow her on one of those expeditions daily made by the
women after roots or other edibles; then at a convenient
moment she is seized and carried off. In these cases it is
not at all unusual for the young Lochinvar, instead of
placing his bride on a fleet horse to elude the pursuit of
relatives, to stun her at the outset with a blow from a
nullah-nullah, to prevent her screaming, and so occasioning
too sudden an alarm. Of course, as rapid a retreat as possible is beaten, and very frequently the tribe thus ravished
of one of its chief beauties declares war on the other, and

a pitched battle ensues. We once heard of an instance in which a young warrior waylaid a member of another tribe, and killed him for the purpose of securing his gin. As to the number of wives possessed by a blackfellow, we can only say that we can remember but two or three instances of a black who had more than one wife, and we never have heard of more than two belonging to one man.

When one of the tribe is sick he is said to have a "mudlo." "Mudlo" is a stone, and their belief is that death is caused by some hostile black placing a stone in that portion of the body which is affected. We have seen blacks with mudlos in their heads, some in their stomachs or breasts, and some in the legs. They will tell you with the greatest composure whether the mudlo will be got out, or whether the patient will "go bong;" and we have many times been surprised by the accuracy with which they can prognosticate the result of any ailment. They have medicine-men who practise with herbs, rubbing, and exorcisings. The cunning fellows, when they have a curable patient, announce by-and-by the extraction of the mudlo, which fact is hailed with shouts of joy by all hands. We have been shown stones which were said to have been thus extracted. They were always small smooth pebbles, somewhat larger than a pigeon's egg. Queensland blacks are by no means open to the charge laid against the bushmen of South Africa, to whom we have heard some people liken them, of neglecting the sick and the aged. So far from this, they show a large amount of attention to both. The aged of both sexes either travel with the tribe, in which case every assistance is given them in the construction of their camp, obtaining wood, water, and food, &c., or they are located in some sheltered, secluded nook, and waited on by some of the younger women.

We once came across a camp of this sort on the coast, nestled in among high, grass-covered sand-banks, and contiguous to a couple of native wells. A small grove of the beautiful casuarina, whose pendant fronds drooped like those of the weeping willow, almost to the ground, and of the native bread-fruit grew near, affording a luxurious shelter from the rays of the sun, where the cooling sea-breezes ever wafted a refreshing breeze, which sang in joyous cadence in the branches overhead. Here were living about half-a-dozen very old women and a couple of aged patriarchs, with heads and beards whiter than the sand, and bowed down with the weight of age. They were of a generation which knew not the white man or his tongue, further than the single word "pi-um" or pipe, used as a request for tobacco, of which they knew the use. We never saw people who, to all appearance, were older than some of these. One old lady was nothing but a mass of wrinkles, which nothing but the reverence due to age saved from being ludicrous. Bent nearly double and almost blind, we thought life must be a burden, until we saw a roasted bream handed her as she lay basking in the midday sun, when the full set of teeth were brought into play with a vigour which evinced a good appetite. The most pleasing feature at this infirmary was the evident respect and affection evinced by the men who accompanied us, as well as the younger women, to these old people; and perhaps one may be pardoned for drawing a comparison between these people, passing the evening of their lives in the lovely Queensland climate, with the grand old ocean before them, with its never-ceasing song and exhilarating breezes, the snug bark camps with their soft beds of dry sand, the shady grove ever cool and melodious, and the full supply of honey, shell and other fish supplied them by kind hands, with the lot of thousands of the old and infirm in our own civilized and wealthy country.

It is no unusual thing to see the youngest children among the blacks with pipes in their mouths. We have seen a baby at the breast, as soon as it had had sufficient nutriment, pluck the pipe from its mother's mouth, and commence very demurely to puff away in the most ortho-dox fashion. The mothers suckle their children for a much longer period than with us. As a rule the number of children in each family is small. We have known only one family of more than two or three.

As with their children so with their sick, great kind-ness is shown. If a man or woman fall sick, all the tribe come and condole with them; every attention is paid, kind words and sympathizing sighs are uttered, in a way that teaches the observer how much of kindness and love there is in the race. A pleasing instance of the affectionate character of the blackfellow came under our notice but a few days since. A blackfellow dressed as a stockman, with Crimean shirt, moleskin trousers, and boots, was coming up the street in the rear of a white stockman, when he was espied by a group of blacks. One of these latter ran across the street to the black, and calling him by his name, said, " Your brother been dead, your brother been dead, me come up," at the same time shaking hands with him and giving him a kiss. The poor fellow was evidently affected by the news, and stood stock-still for half a minute without speaking, while the other who had brought the fatal news stood by him patting him on the shoulder as one might a child. Then turning round, the poor fellow walked over to the wall, and, bowing down his head on his arms, gave way to silent grief.

Although the blackfellow has made no improvement in

house-building since the advent of the white man, his hut, or " mi-mi," is eminently suited to his style of life, the means at his disposal, and the tools he possesses. On the coast line their camps are almost invariably made of the " whichcru " or tea-tree bark, which, for a purpose of that nature, could scarcely be excelled in any part of the world. In fact, nature would appear to have pointed it out especially for the domestic uses of the aboriginal ; it is everywhere to be obtained within a reasonable distance ; it is easy to procure even with the ancient stone hatchet, it is flexible, soft, and warm, and from its lightness a large quantity can be carried in a bundle. With the assistance of a few flexible twigs and small branches stuck into the ground and interlaced at the top, a mi-mi can be put up in the space of half an hour, capable of containing four or five persons, perfectly waterproof, and by no means an uncomfortable place in which to pass a night.

We have often, while travelling with the faithful Tommy, seen the approach of one of those heavy thunder-storms so common in these latitudes in the summer season.   Taking warning by the distant thunder and the heavy banks of clouds rising in the horizon, we have camped for the night and prepared for the storm ; a few twigs, as already stated, are placed on three sides of a circle ; driven well into the ground, they are then bent over at the top, and fastened with a little bark so as to form a roof ; then a few sheets of bark are placed on the top and sides, and secured either with a branch or two, or a long vine from a neighbouring scrub. More sheets of bark are then laid to receive the blankets, and by the time the first big drops or hailstones fall, as harbingers of the coming deluge, everything is snug and comfortable, barring that luxury of the bushman, the quart pot of tea, and even that can be had if by

good luck a hollow tree is near in which to make a fire and
defy the rain.

The usual settled camps of the blacks are made in the
way we have here described with the additional size needed
for a family. In the winter season very extensive camps
are built, being as it were two or three let into one, and
large enough for a family, with a fire in the centre. The
entrances of these camps are always to leeward, and should
the wind shift, the whole tribe will be seen busily employed
in moving their houses round to suit the weather. As a
rule, the locality pitched on for a camp, if at all of a
permanent character, is generally a place of considerable
shelter and often of great beauty. The black has a dwelling which suits his tastes and habits, is easily constructed
at a minimum of outlay in labour—always a consideration
with him—and to which he is naturally attached by association and early recollections. They have an idea that there
are three classes of gentlemen in Queensland—blacks,
kangaroos, and hogs. "Whitefellow yacker (work),
bullock yacker, yarraman (horse) yacker, baal gentleman;
blackfellow no yacker, walk about, kangaroo walk about,
pig-pig walk about, that fellow gentleman."

Another very interesting feature in the blackfellow's
character is his great love for his dogs, which is at least
equal to that evinced towards his own race. We have
already noticed the custom prevalent of crying at the
death of relatives. The same thing is done on the loss of a
canine member of the fraternity; in fact it struck us that
greater sorrow was felt at the loss of a mangy cur than at
that of a human being. We remember on one occasion a
dog, which rejoiced in the name of Black Sailor, had been
lost in the bush. It appeared that Tommy and his wife
had been across the river in a canoe on a bee-hunting expe-

dition; when they returned the dog was overlooked, and it was not until some time after they had reached their camp that the absence of Black Sailor was noticed. Then the river was recrossed just at dusk, but the dog could not be found. During that night there was no singing and mirth in the camp, all were dull and listless. The next morning early all hands crossed the river, and the day was spent in a fruitless search for the dog. At nightfall, standing in the garden, we saw them all returning tired and sorrowful to their camp, the women crying and the men dejected. They had come to the conclusion that the wild dogs had eaten their friend, as not a vestige of him could be found. That night there was the usual crying for the dead, with the lacerations and tearing of the hair commonly practised for a near relative. On expostulating with them for this foolish practice, Tommy said, "That very good dog, that always eat up everything, plenty that eat gidla and English bee, and possum and kangaroo. That very good dog belonging to sleep along blanket, that very much like to sleep in blanket; very good dog, Black Sailor. Baal that sleep along bush, that too much look out belonging to me." The whole evening was spent in howlings and cries, and the next day all hands were again looking for him in the daytime and crying at night. The following morning we heard a great shout in the bush behind the house, and which was taken up at the camp, and directly the whole tribe were in a state of the wildest excitement. Running out to learn the reason of this great outcry, we were told that Black Sailor was come home. The scene of joy and congratulation could not have been exceeded if a long-lost relative had turned up, and we all looked on with astonishment at seeing so much strong feeling exhibited over a mangy dog. We say mangy advisedly, for all their

dogs have the mange. After that time Black Sailor, who
had before been valued for his willingness to "eat everything," and to sleep in the blankets, was looked upon as an
embodiment of intelligence equal to that of any other
person in the camp.

Not the least interesting sight in connexion with the
black's daily life, is to see them making a start when about
to perform one of their usual migrations from one camp and
hunting-ground to another. Having no beasts of burden,
all their goods have to be carried by themselves. It is
true their domestic utensils are limited to a billy or two
and a few dilly-bags. The men carry nothing but their
weapons, and perhaps a billy in which to put any honey
found on the road. These start first, marching off in single
file; then come the youngsters and kippers, each with a
tomahawk and a few nullahs; then come the younger
women and children, and finally closing up the long
straggling procession are the old women, loaded almost
to the ground with possum rugs and blankets, old clothes,
a number of dilly-bags filled to overflowing, and probably
a litter of puppies poking their noses out at the top. The
younger married women will usually have a child either
in a pouch behind, or else astride their shoulders;
but the ratio of puppies to piccaninnies will usually be
five to one. On the march the men hunt for bandicoots,
kangaroo rats, birds, bees, and grubs, and as they roam
to some distance from the track at times, they seldom
fail to provide sufficient food for the next night's wants
before reaching the camping-ground. No stoppage is
made for a mid-day meal, as they scarcely ever start
till the morning is well advanced, and camp early in
the afternoon. Like all other races who live by the
chase, they scarcely ever stop many days in one camp,

as were they to do so their sources of supply would become exhausted.

As the lands in the settled districts become more and more occupied the blacks become more confined in their movements, and their natural supplies gradually diminish. They constantly decrease in numbers as the white man advances, and it cannot be long before in the more populous parts of Queensland, as in the older colonies, the aboriginal race will be confined almost entirely to the interior.

Any notice of the blackfellows would be incomplete that said nothing as to their treatment by the whites. Here one would willingly draw a veil over the sad picture. But truth compels us to say that all the treachery and murder has not been on the side of the blacks, little as they value human life, or can be trusted at one's back in the solitary bush. The black police, although a most useful force, being composed of members of distant tribes, is always, as far as the native portion is concerned, more ready to shed blood than to make prisoners. No question is more difficult to solve than how to secure the pioneer squatters and at the same time act kindly to the native tribes, whose ideas in every respect are so different from those of the white man. There is a strong desire on the part of the Government and the great bulk of the people to exhibit a Christian deportment to the blackfellow, while at the same time protecting the march of civilization, although constantly recurring events almost lead one to believe that their co-existence is impossible. As a rule, at the present day the natives are not ill-treated; on the contrary, they are often too much petted, and thus take liberties and commit depredations. But this was not always the case. In the earlier years of settlement, before the era of separation, when the whites were very few and the native tribes were in a great measure intact, there were deeds so black and diabolical committed as one almost shrinks from recounting. While some squatters acted as Christian gentlemen, others, goaded to acts of reprisal and, as they perhaps put it, in self-preservation for themselves and property, surrounded by swarms of natives, committed acts which were simply scandalous. For instance, on a run in the Moreton Bay District, a squatter found his cattle constantly speared and often killed by the natives, whom from the nature of the surrounding country it was very difficult to follow, even had he had a sufficient force to make it prudent to do so, or did he know what to do with them if caught. From time to time some of them were shot when caught on the run, but still the evil was unabated.

At length altering his procedure, the squatter established friendly relations with the blacks, and finally gave them a 200 lb. bag of flour, in which he had mixed a quantity of arsenic or strychnine. Elated at their good fortune and the hospitality of the squatter, the poor creatures soon divided the flour, and one and all making cakes of their portions ate them without any suspicion. A dreadful scene followed. Some accounts say forty, others twice that number, soon lay dead in their camp. Some few escaped death; but nearly all the children of the tribe died, with many of the adults, while the remainder were so frightened that they fled from their native district and joined other tribes. For many years, on offering a present of flour to any blackfellow, one was met with the inquiry, " Mackenzie sit down ?"—the name by which poison became universally known among them for many miles. The man who thus acted was never called in question for his conduct, the real facts being perhaps known to no one but himself or through the reports of the blacks, who can give no evidence.

We remember an old squatter, one of the first men who drove sheep into what is now Queensland, who often recounted some of his deeds in this line to us. He evidently looked on the killing of a blackfellow as a meritorious act, and thought no more of shooting one than he would of shooting a kangaroo. It would perhaps have fared hardly with any man who had taken any steps to bring him to book, had he fallen in his way in the bush, for he was one of the most powerful men we ever saw. His theory was that blacks stole sheep, speared cattle, and waylaid white men when they had an opportunity, and that therefore it was as necessary to destroy them as it was native dogs or vermin; and he put his views into practice in a matter of fact way. On one occasion while we were residing near him, he saw two black boys near his house who lived some four miles distant, and who he suspected meant to catch one of his horses and ride home. He ordered them off, and seeing they did not go far determined to watch them. Soon he saw them catch one of his horses, and both mount and ride off. Running in for his loaded rifle he followed them for nearly a mile, until getting within shot he fired and killed one, when the other with the agility of a deer sprang from the horse and ran for the scrub close by, into which he soon disappeared. He related this incident, some time after, much in the same way one would speak of firing at a brace of partridges. One other story of his relating to a period many years previous we may recount. He was at this time sheep manager on a large and important station, one of the first in Queensland. Two blacks had committed some depredation, and he determined to punish them. One day when in the store-room he mixed a small quantity of strychnine and sugar, and making it into two little lots passed it over the counter to the two blacks who happened to be present; being what is called station blacks, as designating those who reside on the station premises, in contradistinction from bush blacks. Calling them by name he said, "Here, you eatem sugar," and gave first one and then the other his portion, which the poor fellows took and ate unsuspiciously. He then told them to go and fetch up the horses, and have a drink at the waterhole on their way. By-and-by he went out to have a look round, and near the waterhole lay one of the blacks, who, on seeing him approaching, cried out, "Here, Missa ——, you see em me. Cabona (very much) me directly buck-jump!" referring to the convulsions caused by the poison, and which he called buck-jumping. Soon another paroxysm came on in which he died. Our informant added, that somehow the other black got over it, having been very sick, and taking the hint left the neighbourhood.

We once incurred considerable odium on account of protecting the blacks in our neighbourhood from the superintendent of a neighbouring run, who wished to shoot certain members of the tribe, who he averred had killed a bullock on his run. There is, of course, as severe a penalty for the murder of a black as of a white man, but in isolated districts it would often be well-nigh impossible to adduce satisfactory evidence. But these are now, we believe, very exceptional cases.

It would be satisfactory if it could be said that effective means have been employed to civilize and christianize these poor savages. One or two attempts in this direction have been made, but each has proved a failure, principally perhaps because the efforts have been not enough directed to improving their temporal condition, and giving them a settled home and occupation. Among these failures was the establishment of the aboriginal mission of Frazer's Island by the Rev. Mr. Fuller. This gentleman was in many ways well fitted for the work, but he fell into the radical error of establishing himself on an island that does not contain a rod of good soil, but is one vast sandbank. He threw away a large amount of time and labour in testing the capacities of this island for cultivation. Had he gone to some equally isolated spot which contained some agricultural soil and grazing-land, there is reason to think his scheme would have been successful. His pupils, men, women, and children, made great strides in the arts of reading, singing, &c.; but from not being able to employ them in some useful and remunerative work, he was unable to retain them with him, and so all his efforts led to no practical results. We once paid a visit to his mission, and were pleased to find many of both sexes able to read tolerably in the Bible, and sing some hymns very nicely. Recently a gentleman has established a sort of industrial school and farm near Mackay, with a view of teaching the natives the useful arts of life as well as spiritual truths. Government think so well of this scheme, that lately a vote of 500l. for the support of the enterprise was made. One thing appears certain, if something is not done for their social elevation as well as spiritual enlightenment speedily, the blacks of the Queensland seaboard will soon be among the extinct races of mankind.

CHAPTER XIII.

THAT Queensland has of late entered on an era of great prosperity there can be no doubt. The difference between the position of Queensland in 1871, when the larger part of these pages was written, and at the present time is most striking. He would have been a very sanguine man who at that time would have predicted that such a wonderful expansion as has actually occurred in almost every one of her industries, in her population, revenue, and wealth, would have been witnessed in four years. Queensland is fast taking her place as one of the foremost of our colonies, and will, in all probability, before many years, be more populous and wealthy than either of the other colonies. The fact that Queensland has so large a number of navigable rivers and ports—and already no less than thirty rivers navigable for greater or less distances have been discovered —must give her eventually a vast superiority over the other Australian colonies, all of which are incomparably inferior to her in this respect.

Nor is the possession of all these navigable rivers and harbours the only advantage on its seaboard possessed by Queensland. Her coast is studded with numerous islands of all sizes, which, with the abundance of fish teeming in her waters, the advantageous position of the colony for commanding the trade of India, China, Japan, the Archi-

pelago, as well as that of the new colony of Fiji and all the
wealth of the South Seas, mark her out as the future home
of an imperial race—a new Britain in the Southern
Hemisphere.

Allusion has been already made to the beneficial changes
which have taken place in the politics of Queensland.
After many weary struggles, the party of progress, who
desire to see the lands of the colony occupied and cultivated,
have obtained a large majority in the Legislature; and in
the nature of things it appears certain, that as the settlement increases, this party must increase in strength and
influence. Thus there is a guarantee that every facility will
be given to emigrants and others for settling on the lands,
and that no return will be made to a retrograde policy.
Indeed, it may be hoped that those who were most opposed
to a measure of this sort, will, by degrees, learn to alter
their opinions as the blessings of industry and cultivation
become more widespread. The last session of the Legislature
has made a very important mark on the Land Laws of
Queensland. By an Act just passed, every person of the
age of eighteen years who has resided one year in the
colony, or three years if brought out free, may select a
farm of from 40 to 640 acres under the Homestead clauses
of the Land Act—thus doubling the extent of this class of
selections. It is true there has been also passed a law for
abolishing Land Orders—a most unfortunate and unwise
measure—yet the fact of a farm one mile square being
obtainable in fee simple by the nominal payment of sixpence per acre for five years cannot fail to attract a very
desirable class of settlers. There is no part of the world
where land can be now had so cheaply as in Queensland,
which may fairly claim the title of the Queen of Colonies
for the cheapness of her land, the richness of her soil, and

the great variety of crops which can be produced, being
equalled in this respect by no other English-speaking
country. What may be her future as an agricultural
country it is impossible to say; that she will speedily
attain a very high position in this respect no one can doubt.

It will perhaps be interesting to quote here from a writer
in Queensland itself as to the present condition of the
colony. The author of the article on the " Progress of the
Colony " in *Pugh's Almanack* for 1875 says,—

" In a fair retrospect of the last twelve months it cannot be said
that there has been any serious drawback which could mar the satisfaction which must be felt at the rapid, but, at the same time, steady
strides the country is making towards the first place in the Australasian
group. The most determined pessimist will admit that there is
nothing in our state of progression which can possibly lead to the
belief that our present prosperous state is ephemeral, or that we are
likely to feel a check by the collapse of any one or two of our largest
industries. The growth of our general prosperity is not of that feverish
character so often engendered by the rapid development of one extensive industry, as was the case with the first discovery of gold in
Australia. Although, no doubt, our gold-fields have undergone an
immense extension, our present healthy condition cannot be said to be
derived from that source alone. It would be hard, indeed, to say
which of our now numerous industries should be credited with contri-
buting the largest share towards our present prosperity, which may
rather be attributed to the gradual development of the almost exhaust-
less resources of the colony. So great is its producing power, that the
most sanguine would scarcely imagine half the results which will
probably be seen before many years have gone over our heads. To
speak of the present only, it is quite certain that at no period of her
existence as a colony (not excepting the good times—times of feverish
excitement and speculation) has Queensland ever shown such signs of
wellbeing as at the present moment. Never has labour been better
paid or been in greater demand than now. As things are at present,
and as they seem likely to remain, the worst-paid labourers may
become small capitalists; and that they do so to a great extent is
evident from the large quantity of land which is daily taken up by the
working-class. The days of speculation and company-manufacturing

seem to have passed away—it is to be hoped for ever. Larger capitalists, too, in the other colonies, are becoming alive to the prosperous future which awaits us, and are beginning to invest largely—a clear evidence of belief in the permanency of our condition."

It is a very characteristic fact that the same writer complains that immigrants do not arrive in sufficient numbers and that there is a great dearth of labour, a fact that speaks well for the colony when we recollect that nearly 7000 immigrants reached its shores in 1874. Were double or even three times as many to arrive, there is every reason to believe they would all be easily absorbed and find lucrative occupation.

The population, which on the 1st of September, 1871, was 120,076, had by the close of 1874 reached 163,517. The revenue shows a similar expansion, and in 1873 amounted to 1,120,031l., which was 189,170l. more than the expenditure, a very marked contrast to the state of affairs a few years since, when the expenditure always exceeded the revenue, and the Treasurer had always to deal with a large floating and unfunded debt. A glance at the statistical tables, published in the work quoted above, reveals the fact that in every department of industry there is a constant and surprising expansion. The same remark may be made of the social institutions of the colony. Whether it be the Freemasons, Odd Fellows, Temperance, or Religious Societies, all have the same history—a continuous formation of new branches and a large annual increase of membership.

There are thirty-three newspapers published in the colony, many of which are quite equal to English newspapers in the style and tone of their leading articles and the accuracy of their reports, while all have that elevated tone which, as a rule, characterizes Australian newspapers.

In one important item Queensland papers far excel nearly all English papers—they are printed on far better paper, and usually in a superior manner. In most towns of any importance Schools of Art and Public Libraries exist. In Brisbane a very respectable Museum is being formed, so far as specimens and articles are concerned; and in the last session of Parliament the question of building a Museum was taken into consideration, and will, without doubt, lead before long to the erection of a suitable structure. An Education Act has also just been passed, from which great things are expected, and by means of which every child in the community will be entitled to receive an education perfectly free of expense.

In social matters also a great improvement is taking place. A marked diminution in crime and the gradual formation of a high tone of morals indicate that in Queensland our race is not at any rate deteriorating in consequence of the greater degree of wealth enjoyed by the majority of the people.

In public life also there is much to be proud of. Having a constitutional Government and a franchise which is practically within the reach of all, it is pleasant to record that there is but little of that roughness in politics which unfortunately characterizes too many of the communities of America. There is a desire on all hands to elevate the tone of political life, and it is by no means detrimental to the career of a public man for him to be a gentleman; none other has much chance with the constituencies. Among the public men of the colony are some who have evinced considerable statesmanship and capacity for government; and, although in all young communities like this there must for a time be a scarcity of first-class men, there appears reason to hope that Queensland will not suffer so much in this respect in the future as in the past. A measure has lately been before Parliament which, when it becomes law, will undoubtedly add to the intellectual wealth of the Legislature. We allude to the Bill for the Payment of Members, which had the support of the Ministers and passed through the Assembly to be practically thrown out in the Council. The same reasons which could be urged against a measure of this sort in England weigh in the other scale in a new community, where so few men of education are to be found sufficiently wealthy to devote their time to public affairs. That this measure will before long be carried into effect there can be no doubt, and that it will tend to the improvement of the Legislative Assembly is equally certain.

The Legislative Council, being a nominee chamber, is composed very largely of men of large means and more or less leisure. A few of its members are Government officials, but the larger number are men of independent circumstances. It is to be hoped that should the present enlightened Colonial Secretary remain long in office he will inaugurate, what would be a most conservative as well as popular measure, the creation of a Colonial Nobility. For many years it has been the wise policy of the Imperial Government to reward the services of eminent colonists with knighthoods and baronetcies, and this policy has had the most happy effect both in Canada and Australia. But a larger and more permanent measure than this is urgently called for. One of the most difficult problems in all our colonies has always been the question as to the constitution of an Upper House. It is admitted universally that our English House of Lords is, without exception, the best Upper House possessed by any nation enjoying parliamentary institutions. There appears to be no reason why this excellence should not be enjoyed by the various colonies, by the creation from time to time of colonial titles of nobility conferred on the same principle as in the mother country. Nothing can be conceived more calculated to knit into one homogeneous whole the various dependencies of the empire and its imperial parent, and nothing would tend more easily to settle in a natural way the question of the construction of a second chamber. In all our colonies there are gentlemen, who, by their education, abilities, influence, wealth and public services, are eminently fitted to be the recipients of such an honour.

We could point out many gentlemen in Queensland, who, if they were thus honoured, would grace their titles, and whose elevation would be hailed with universal satisfaction. Such titles would of course only confer nobility in the colony where granted, and while being another link in the strong chain binding the colony to the parent nation, and a powerful and now lacking incentive to noble and worthy deeds, would also in a very great degree tend to abolish the curse of absenteeism, from which Victoria suffers so severely, and from which Queensland cannot hope entirely to escape; although her superior climate will tell in her favour in this as in other respects. The writer has often thought that it only needs such an inducement as the hope of thus attaining to the highest social status to make Queensland not only the Queen of Colonies but eventually, as one of the chief dependencies of the British Empire, the Queen of Nations. With her unrivalled climate, never too cold in winter, and the cool and refreshing sea-breeze tempering the heat in summer; her marvellous and inexhaustible mineral and metalliferous resources, including gold, silver, copper, tin, lead, iron, coals, and marble; her endless downs and prairies where cattle and sheep can be depastured at the minimum outlay of labour;

her rich and far-spreading agricultural lands, capable of producing nearly every known crop and fruit, watered and intersected by innumerable rivers and streams; her free institutions and liberal laws; her numerous and flourishing ports and towns; her geographical position, enabling her to command the richest commerce of the world;—she only needs to be settled and populated by as many millions as she now has tens of thousands of enterprising and industrious inhabitants to become one of the greatest, as she now is in natural resources one of the richest, countries of the civilized world.   That her future must be grand and magnificent no one acquainted with her can doubt.   Quite as much as Palestine she answers to the Mosaic description of " a good land, a land of brooks of water, . . . a land of wheat, and barley, and vines, and fig-trees and pomegranates; a land of oil olive, and honey; a land wherein thou shalt eat bread without scarceness, and thou shalt not lack any good thing in it; a land whose stones are iron, and out of whose hills thou mayst dig brass." What wonder if many thousands of Englishmen yearly repeat the words of Caleb, and say, " Let us go up at once and possess it; for we are well able."

In conclusion, we would again refer all who may contemplate emigration to Queensland to the Agent-General for the colony, R. Daintree, Esq., 32, Charing Cross, whose urbanity and wide range of information eminently fit him for his position, and who will be found ever ready to afford information on all matters of interest to emigrants.   In him and his able Secretary, T. Hamilton, Esq., another old colonist, the colony possesses two representatives quite competent to furnish all those details so useful to the emigrant, but which hardly come within the scope of this volume.

GILBERT AND RIVINGTON, PRINTERS. ST. JOHN'S SQUARE, LONDON.

www.ingramcontent.com/pod-product-compliance
Lightning Source LLC
Chambersburg PA
CBHW021108270326
41929CB00009B/777